Praise for
CREATIVE TOGETHER

●　●　●　●　●

"Steven Kowalski has unpacked and elucidated a fascinating and thorough exploration of perspectives and practices on the subtleties of how we really get things done and how we could potentially do that better. This is a must-read for anyone curious about elegant productivity."

DAVID ALLEN, author of *Getting Things Done: The Art of Stress-Free Productivity*

"Steven Kowalski shares a deeply insightful and step-by-step approach for anyone driving change and transformation inside large organizations. Learn how to become a beacon for unlocking enterprise value while staying true to the story in your heart, and that what you see and know is truly possible."

MICHAEL MARGOLIS, CEO of Storied

"*Creative Together* by Steven Kowalski lays a good foundation for developing your own creativity and that of the organizations you lead. I especially value the lesson that creativity is inherent in all, and that it requires a walk together into the unknown."

BOB ANDERSON, founder of Leadership Circle

"If you've ever doubted your own creativity or longed to have the creative juice you see in others, then this book will be a life-changer. Steven Kowalski will absolutely show you how to rethink the view that you're either creative or you're not, and you'll come away rethinking your own potential for creativity."

DR. BEVERLY KAYE, co-author of *Love 'Em or Lose 'Em: Getting Good People to Stay*

"In this remarkable book, Steven Kowalski takes us on an adventure, showing us what it means to bring your whole, creative self into new ways of working together. This is required reading for all seeking to heal the fragmentation in our society at this moment in time."

JOSEPH JAWORSKI, best-selling author of *Synchronicity: The Inner Path of Leadership*

"Steven Kowalski has written a refreshingly creative book about creativity! Engaging, insightful, and most of all practical, *Creative Together* will ignite the creative potential in all of us. A perfect book for times like these!"

GARY PISANO, professor and senior associate dean of Harvard Business School

"In *Creative Together*, Steven Kowalski shows how we can tap into our creative potential to navigate the realities of working around obstacles to develop solid innovations that are fresh and always evolving. This is a deeply realistic book, one that shows us how we can bring our best—and the best of others—into the world."

MICHAEL RAY, author of *The Highest Goal*

"In this immensely practical guide, Steven Kowalski shows you how to amp up your organization's performance by harnessing the power of collaborative innovation. *Creative Together* offers essential advice for any organization that hopes to stay relevant in today's hyper-connected economy."

GARY HAMEL, co-author of *Humanocracy*

"In *Creative Together*, Steven Kowalski brings together a unique combination of personal experience, formal training, and rigor that brings to life the power of implementing a structured and easy-to-follow road map for building the creative self. It is a must-read for every organization hoping to build resilience and future readiness through innovation."

PETER WILTON, professor of marketing at Berkeley Haas School of Business

"Steven Kowalski has captured a core truth of our complex, uncertain world: when teams work together to pioneer new solutions for our greatest challenges, we have to get creative together. And, as Steven reminds us, this journey to greater team effectiveness starts within."

MIKE ROBBINS, author of *We're All in This Together*

"In *Creative Together*, Steven Kowalski has captured the essence of his methodical approach for developing next-level leaders who meet critical business challenges while also developing the creative capabilities of both individuals and teams."

CARLA BORAGNO, former senior vice president of Global Engineering, Genentech

"Beautifully written and jam-packed with wisdom, practical models, inquiries, and exercises, *Creative Together* is essential reading for any leader who wants amplify their impact. Steven Kowalski illuminates the truth behind our own genius and how to strip away the obstacles, habits, and beliefs so we can tap into our inherent superpowers and co-create."

JACKIE MCGRATH, executive coach

"*Creative Together* by Steven Kowalski is like a beacon of light that shines on the very misunderstood competencies of creativity and innovation, and the difference between the two. If you want to truly unlock your potential as a leader, I recommend this book... What a great gift to the world to help navigate during these uncertain times."

CHAD LUXENBURG, chief executive officer of scitrain, ltd.

"Steven Kowalski's insights on mindsets that are disrupting our creativity are worth exploring... he leads you toward a deeper understanding of the potential you have been gifted."

JUSTIN TOMLINSON, co-author of *Live with Intent*

"*Creative Together* provides an important navigation and guidance framework for those seeking more meaningful work and to discover our greatest creative gifts. With tremendous insight, Steven Kowalski weaves together research, storytelling, and experience so we can all learn how to meet the increasingly challenging requirement of being 'co-creative' in our ever-accelerating world."

PETER MISCOVICH, managing director at Strategy & Innovation, JLL

"We're all experiencing a new and challenging world at work. It is no longer sufficient for the lone wolf leader to address the critical issues before us. Steven Kowalski offers an effective road map for collaborative leadership that creates opportunities and activates creativity and innovation in our workplaces and communities."

CRAIG AND PATRICIA NEAL, co-founders of the Center for Purposeful Leadership

"Steven Kowalski brings forward conscious creativity as a way to navigate life in general—and work life in particular—through innovation, resilience, and resourcefulness. Go on a journey of discovery and adventure as you explore what it takes to be creative and let go of mindsets that may be keeping you from the realization of yourself as a conscious creator. A must-read for anyone wanting to rewrite their story and step into their future now!"

RON HULNICK, president of the University of Santa Monica

PAGE TWO

CREATIVE
TOGETHER

Sparking Innovation
in the New
World of Work

STEVEN KOWALSKI

Cataloguing in publication information is
available from Library and Archives Canada.

ISBN 978-1-77458-162-9 (paperback)
ISBN 978-1-77458-163-6 (ebook)

Permissions (Adventure One, Chapter 3)

Steps of Indigenous visioning path from
Gregory Cajete, *Look to the Mountain:
An Ecology of Indigenous Education*
(Kivaki Press, 1994).
Used with the author's permission.

Excerpt from "Lost" from
Traveling Light: Collected and New Poems.
Copyright 1999 by David Wagoner.
Used with permission of the University of Illinois Press.

Page Two
pagetwo.com
Edited by James Harbeck
Copyedited by Tilman Lewis
Cover design by Jeff Winocur
Interior design by Taysia Louie
Interior illustrations by Meng Tian
Indexed by Donald Howes

stevenkowalski.com

This book is dedicated to you—and to all our colleagues, partners, and allies around the world proactively engaged in transformation, seeking to dance in the intersection of purpose, possibility, and constraint, and committed to creating our future, together.

Contents

• • • • •

INTRODUCTION

• • • • •

MAGINE FOR a moment that your life is happening in a theater. You're up on stage where the action is taking place. Rows of seats stretch back toward the lobby. Further away from the stage, there's a mezzanine and a balcony with more seats.

Where is your creativity?

Is it up on stage with you, front and center, contributing to your work and to the unfolding story of your life? Is it waiting in the wings for a cue to make an entrance? Or is it watching from the first row, reacting to what's happening but not involved? Maybe it's sitting way up in the balcony in the dark—and has been for a long time.

What if it's out in the lobby, just waiting for the show to end?

Where is your creativity? *It's in the theater somewhere.* But now more than ever, you need it right up on stage with you and the people up there with you.

You need your creativity to rebound and adapt to what comes your way and to proactively invent new possibilities that disrupt the status quo. You need it to uncover opportunity, find the humor in what's happening, and rise out of the ashes of tragedy when it strikes. You need it to work around obstacles in your path. And you need it to create together with others—to spark innovation in a world that's changing faster than any one of us can keep up with.

In our work and at our workplaces, we're all chasing after innovation—the generation of new value. But we're focused on the wrong thing.

1

Innovation is actually an outcome, the result of one of the most power-ful and sustainable forces available to us. Creativity is the spark driving innovative results. If you want innovation, you must activate creativity.

So this book is not about innovation. It's about creativity. Your cre-ativity. It's about reclaiming your creativity so that you can co-create more effectively with others. Why? So that you can invent new futures for yourself and for the companies, organizations, and causes whose mission you share.

Our world is changing quickly, right before our eyes. In the new world of work that is emerging, going it alone doesn't cut it any longer. We have to *get creative together*. In fact, co-creating is fast becoming the best way to generate new value that is scalable and sustainable. And it's the only way we'll move past the familiar routines of exe-cution and across the threshold into the unknown. Discovery and invention is the new world of work.

The problem is, we're not particularly good at creating together or venturing into the unknown. To start, most of us are working and living our lives in an old story of what creativity is and how it works. When we show up to create together, we bring our old story and all the limiting beliefs, habits, and patterns that come along with it. And typically, we're not big fans of the unknown. When it shows up in our life, we tend to greet it with dread instead of passion. We avoid it and plan to prevent it.

To spark innovation—and bring the full power of our own creativ-ity into the process of co-creation—we must each embark on a journey of discovery and adventure. That's the promise of what lies ahead in this book. First you will rewrite the story of who you are as a creator. Then you will learn to adventure together with others—bringing your whole, creative self into new ways of working together.

The good news is you are at the center of everything happening in your life. You're producing, directing, and starring in the comedy and drama that's playing out. Up on stage, in the bright lights, and at the heart of the action is precisely where you need "conscious creativity." That's when you're proactively engaging creativity, paying attention to the choices you're making, taking accountability, and learning from your choices. That's where you have the greatest power to shape what's happening now—and what happens next.

Unfortunately, if you're like most of us, you're not sure where your creativity is. But—surprise! *It hasn't left the stage.* This incredibly powerful force is still right there with you, and always has been. So, what's getting in the way of using it more intentionally?

The biggest threat to conscious creativity is what I call CDD— Creativity Disruption Disorder. CDD is not a medical condition or a function of biology gone awry. It's a disorder of our mindset; it comes from believing an old story about what creativity is and who we are as creators. CDD disables access to your potential to transform circumstances and change your world. It's the reason that right now, it might seem like your creativity is checked out in the lobby or stuck up in the balcony. CDD even tricks you into thinking you're out on that stage all alone. It depletes your strength, resolve, and motivation. And it's insidious; you're likely walking around afflicted and wholly unaware that it is curable.

The old story at the root of CDD says that creativity is something elitist—a kind of unique "giftedness." It tells us that a few of us are gifted and the rest of us are not. Or it confuses creativity with a special talent, like in the arts. But creativity is not an ability, as most of us believe. *It's a potential that every one of us has been gifted.*

This is the first and most important key to unlock conscious creativity: you are GIFTED—and far more creative than you think you are. Embracing the new story frees you to reclaim your potential and develop creative accountability that is trusted and unshakable. Then you can participate, with all your gifts, in the process of co-creation as a living example of the new story.

You will encounter discovery and adventure on the journey ahead, and tests and challenges as well. To guide and support you along the path, this book includes three adventures that explore, stage by stage, how to activate your creative potential and use it to create together:

- **Adventure One** starts the inner work required to overcome CDD. By exploring your relationship with your creativity and challenging the old story, you develop a strong inner core. This is the foundation for a fuller expression of creativity in your work and life. It is essential as the first step on your path toward more effective co-creation. You will learn to greet the unknown with passion, ignite your creative potential, and flex your Superpowers to navigate the tests that show up on creative quests.

- **Adventure Two** is where you realize the benefits of your inner work. Here, you take your gift out in the world to co-create more effectively within social systems. This requires you to let go of the illusion that you can create alone. That's the second key to this book: *your gift of creativity must be shared*. True strength, especially amid upheaval and uncertainty, comes from creating together. You will learn to thrive in co-creation, experiment in the Swamp, and dare to dream big as you bring conscious creativity to collective pursuits.

- **Adventure Three** is your springboard to living the principles of conscious co-creation every day and building a lifelong practice of proactive creative accountability.

Together, these adventures guide you through the GIFTED methodology:

- **G**reet the unknown with passion.
- **I**gnite your creative potential.
- **F**lex your Superpowers.
- **T**hrive in co-creation.
- **E**xperiment in the Swamp.
- **D**are to dream big.

There are people who are already embracing the new story and using this methodology to invent, innovate, and transform their work and life. You'll learn from their stories, drawn from all walks of life and combined into composite case studies of professionals just like you. Lily, a biostatistician by training, faced the loss of her job in a company restructuring and needed to reshape her skills. Mark, a public school teacher, wanted to reinvent the way science was taught in his school district but had to deal with old habits that got in the way. Andrew realized he hated his job but didn't know where to go or what to do. And Regina, a senior leader in her firm, was stymied by traditional governance structures and needed to chart a new course.

Like them, you will learn to work (and play) with your creativity—to spark innovation in collective pursuits. Once you claim your potential, there's no turning back. By participating in your life with conscious creativity, you will transform the landscape of your future. You will become anew—with a deep faith in your resilience and resourcefulness, and a future full of possibility.

Consider your passage through these pages as your own hero's journey toward a more fulfilling and proactive expression of your creativity. At the end of each chapter, take time to pause and reflect on the questions posed along the way. Powerful questions are at the root of any meaningful quest. They are crucial to bring more clarity and awareness to the choices you make. Through these questions, and the ideas and practices we'll explore, you will recognize more quickly when circumstances around you call for conscious co-creation. When you hear that call, I invite you to courageously answer it—to step, despite the risks, across the threshold into the unknown together.

Are you ready to connect more deeply with your creativity and to truly own it as your life unfolds? Do you want to learn how to create more effectively with others—to innovate together in the new world of work? Think about the challenges and opportunities in front of you right now. What about the ones around the corner and further down the road? What would be different if you knew your creativity was right up on stage with you, actively there every day?

Let's see what we discover in the adventures ahead.

ADVENTURE ONE

CLAIMING YOUR GIFT

"Anyone can count the seeds
in an apple. No one can count
the apples in a seed."

ANONYMOUS

PROLOGUE

• • • • •

I T WAS a foggy June in Laguna Beach back in 1999 when I closed my consulting practice, sold my car, packed up all my belongings, and gave the keys back to my landlord. My partner and I exchanged a tearful goodbye at the airport. Though painful, we decided to let go rather than try to make things work long-distance. As I boarded the plane, I didn't know when or if I would return—or how long I might be gone. I took a leap of faith.

This wasn't the first time I had left the familiar for an adventure into the new and unknown. We'd moved around a lot when I was a kid and I got used to saying goodbye and then hello, leaving one world to join another. But this journey was different. I was crossing an ocean to work with a team at one of the top five global consulting firms on an exciting project called Creative Leadership.

This felt bigger than anything I had ever done—and scarier, because I really didn't know what was ahead. At the same time, I knew it was the right thing to do. I grew up exploring my creativity as an artist, and I loved designing and making things. I became fascinated with creativity—what motivates us to create and how it works—so I studied creativity in college and in my graduate programs. In my boutique consulting business, my work focused primarily on leadership development. Because creativity and leadership had been my focus for so many years, I was certain this opportunity was the perfect way for me to combine the two into something new.

The first few months were tough. I learned that another team had been working on this project before I arrived and had exploded in conflict and disarray. Each week was chaotic and not much was planned. I had to invent my way every day and I spent a lot of time feeling lost—as if I were in a deep, dark forest.

It reminded me of one of my favorite plays, *Into the Woods*, by Stephen Sondheim, an American musician and lyricist. This masterwork combines familiar fairy-tale stories into a tangled web of choices and decisions—illuminating the consequences when we set out on journeys of discovery to fulfill our wishes, hopes, and dreams. At one point in the play, we find a baker and his wife together, deep in the woods. Like me as I moved to Europe, they have left the safety of home and their familiar routines and ventured into the unknown—despite the risks. In the song "It Takes Two" (accessible on YouTube), they share the changes they see blossoming in each other: a new sense of courage and confidence, generosity, and decisiveness. And they wonder together whether their transformation would have been possible if they had stayed at home.

I hoped that somehow I, too, would blossom and change through my experiences and by being so far out of the familiar. But something about venturing into these woods—navigating the complexities and dynamics of the team and the consulting firm—was different and harder than I expected. Why was it so difficult to bring my creativity into the company and into the work? This didn't make any sense. After all, the project was named Creative Leadership. We were the experts who should have known how to activate and enhance these two powerful forces.

Like the team before us, our team eventually failed. For two grueling years we met—week after week and month after month—and tried unsuccessfully to create products and services the firm could sell to clients. We argued about everything. Each of us had a different picture of what we should be doing and why. We talked about creativity and innovation, but we didn't practice anything close to what I would now call conscious creativity. In the end, we spent over a million Swiss francs and produced absolutely nothing.

Discovering Your Creative Potential

• • • • •

FEW YEARS before I closed my business and moved to Europe, I was deep into research for my doctoral dissertation at UCLA. I had already been in the program five years by then, and working while attending university full-time was taking its toll. After years of rushing to work in the morning, to the UCLA campus in the afternoon, and home by late evening, I was exhausted and frankly scared about whether I had any energy left to work on my dissertation. But I felt a deep sense of urgency to finish what I had started.

My dissertation focused on what teachers believed about creativity and how they expressed their creativity within the confines of a highly bureaucratic school system. I spent hours in the university library, combing through articles and books to help explain what creativity is and how it arises. I knew one thing for sure: the toxic idea that *only some of us* are creative really pissed me off. So I was looking for answers to help me understand how, collectively, we came to believe something that simply was not true. Where did these definitions come from? How do they shape what we believe about our own potential? And how, in turn, do our beliefs shape how we express creativity day to day?

It's hard to believe now, but back then, you had to find resources in the library using card catalogs and microfiche. That meant hours in dark rooms and in the stacks searching for books, printing articles, and underlining hard copies. What I discovered was astonishing. The roots of our collective understanding of creativity came largely from articles in journals on giftedness and from psychological treatises that described creativity in highly elitist terms. According to these publications, creative people were gifted and special—different from the rest of us (who, by comparison, were not creative). With some exceptions, these themes permeate the literature even to this day.

The pervasiveness of these theories took me by surprise. I had discovered the origins of an old, elitist story that didn't align with my experience or what I was learning in my coursework. In the field of education, we were exploring emerging theories about how people learn through a sense of agency, participation, and apprenticeship. We were talking about awakening everyone's potential—and the need to democratize knowledge and educational opportunity to do so. And we were exploring how dominant theories of learning advantaged some at the expense of others. But in the research and literature on creativity, the story was completely different. The idea that some were advantaged while others were disadvantaged was written into the very definition of creativity. The contrast between these two conversations was striking. I became even more frustrated and deeply convinced that we were all missing something about creativity.

The New Story of Your Creativity

● ● ●

My quest to answer this riddle took an unexpected turn when I came across a relatively obscure article by Carl Weinberg, one of my professors at UCLA. In the article,[1] Carl proposed that creativity is a *potential*—not a quality or ability of a person. According to him, we all—as human beings—are conceived with the potential to participate in creative activity. The potential is there, within us all throughout our lives. And this is an important key: while our potential to create is always there, the conditions that give rise to its activation come and go. Our potential doesn't change, but the conditions do—along with our conscious awareness of what's happening.

What a revelation! This was the missing piece I had been searching for—the answer to my quest for an understanding of creativity that didn't separate people into haves and have-nots. Suddenly I was able to understand the difference between an ability and a potential. Abilities are qualities of people—like talents, skills, or proficiencies—that exist before, during, and after they are exercised. Maybe I have mathematical ability, athletic ability, the ability to speak multiple languages, or the ability to draw insights out of complex data. Because abilities are qualities that people have, they can be tested. You can improve through learning and practice, but ultimately, with an ability, some people are just going to be better than others no matter what.

A human potential, on the other hand, is not a fixed quality or characteristic that someone has, but instead it exists as a possibility—until it is brought into existence. As a potential, creativity only exists *as it is happening.* Creativity is there when it's activated and then it subsides. This helps explain why no valid test has been successfully developed for creativity: the very process of examining and testing creativity extinguishes the conditions for its occurrence.

"If I create, I create. If I do not create, I do not create," Carl Weinberg said. "Doing so doesn't make me more or less creative—or anyone else more or less creative. The occurrence is simply an instance where I participated in creative action." How freeing! You are highly creative because you have the potential to engage your creativity when conditions for its emergence and enactment appear. It's there whenever you—and the circumstances of your life—call it forward.

If you're walking around with an ability-based definition of creativity, you are disadvantaging yourself. That's because your beliefs about creativity—and about yourself as a creative person (or not)—have consequences. But before you can change how you create in your work and life, you will need to do some inner work. You need to change your mind about what creativity is. Here's my offer: *creativity is your natural potential to invent new solutions to the challenges and opportunities you face or design for yourself.*

Notice the word *potential* and absence of any reference to *ability*. Now notice the word *solutions*. I'm talking about solutions in the broadest sense—all the way from a response you might have to stress, to the invention of a new technology or an innovation that opens new markets for existing products and services. Solutions need not be tangible. Also notice that creativity arises in response to both external and internal forces. The purpose that activates your creative potential can come from outer challenges and opportunities as much as from your inner drives, struggles, dreams, and desired aims.

This is the new story about creativity—a new way of seeing yourself. Creativity is not about some people being "gifted" and others not; it's about an amazing potential that we have *all* been gifted. What is special or unique? You are. What ends up being unique is what you bring to creativity; why you care to create and how you uniquely express it in the circumstances of your work and life.

No one else shares exactly the same combination of motivations, talents, and skills and the same collection of experiences in the form of tests, obstacles, and opportunities that you have encountered. No one else shares the same perspective on the world, arising from what you've learned in your life. All these factors—and more—add up to give shape, color, and texture to how you apply this very ordinary, very extraordinary gift in your life.

Instead of wondering, "Am I creative?" or even—as most of us do—asserting that you aren't *that* creative, you can develop a profound faith in your creativity. With that faith come deeper questions, such as these:

- How is my creativity being called forward in my life?

- What meaningful motivations and pursuits are activating it?

- What external circumstances might activate my creativity today?

- In which contexts do I leverage my creativity more effectively, and where do I struggle to bring it forward? What's getting in the way?

- What if I gave myself permission to fail and learn?

- How can I reframe this situation as an opportunity to create something new?

- What are the lessons for me here?

The importance of this distinction between an ability-based view and a potential-based view of creativity has amplified over the years since my doctoral work. I've watched and worked with people and seen them struggle to access their creativity in response to challenges they face. Now I'm more motivated than ever to help people shift their perspective.

In my coaching and workshops, I've asked hundreds of people, "How creative are you?" My aim is to test their implicit definition of creativity and help them unpack the implications of that definition on their work and in their life. To answer the question, I have people choose a spot along an imaginary line—a continuum where the left end is "not creative at all" and the right end is "highly creative." People line up, laughing nervously or making jokes about each other.

Where would *you* stand on the line?

When everyone is lined up, I ask them to consider the shape of the result. Without fail, people form a classic bell curve—a few on each end and most in the middle. This simple activity reveals our deeply held collective belief that creativity is an ability that different people have in different doses. Despite a general acknowledgment that all people are creative, most of us still believe that some people are simply more creative, others are less creative, and most of us are somewhere in the middle. We compare ourselves to each other and place ourselves somewhere on the spectrum of "creative ability."

When I ask people why they chose the spot they chose, the detail in their answers may vary, but the same categories show up time after time:

- "I don't think of myself as creative because I'm not good in the arts."

- "What I do every day—my work—it's not creative. It's routine."

- "I'm creative in my personal life, but not at work... so I put myself in the middle."

- "Sometimes I'm creative, but not as much as Lavanya" (or John, or someone they know in line, or children in their lives).

- "Steve Jobs was capital-C Creative, and I'm no Steve Jobs, but I do some creative things in my job."

- "I'm up on the 'highly creative' end because I'm doing things in my work that are outside of the box."

- "I'm creative because I'm always coming up with lots of ideas."

Do any of these responses sound like what you might say? Are you stuck in a narrow, ability-based definition of creativity? This matters—because creativity is the spark driving innovative results. It's your most valuable resource when you face complexity, step into uncharted territory, seek new value, and solve seemingly unsolvable problems. Anything that limits your potential to create also limits your success on journeys of discovery and invention that require crossing the threshold into the unknown. Creativity is critical as you navigate the depths of your "woods" and pull yourself out of the pits you'll find yourself in. It's one of your most important gifts.

Your Creative Potential

• • •

Over the years I have sought to understand exactly what's different between the view of creativity as an ability or as a potential. And I've watched how my creativity, and the creativity of others, shows up day in and day out. I've learned that viewing creativity as a potential—instead of an ability—transforms who I believe I am as a creator and how I show up in the world. This in turn translates into how successfully creativity shows up (or not) in action, in my world and in my endeavors. When you understand creativity as a potential, important shifts take place.

Shift One: Purpose becomes more critical

In this first shift, I'm not talking about purpose in the sense of your Life Purpose—I'm referring to the *reason why* (the purpose) your creativity might show up *in any given moment*. The conditions arise because a purpose sets you on a quest toward something new. It's that simple and that important. The more personally meaningful and relevant that purpose is to you, the stronger your motivation will be for creativity to come forward and the longer it will remain active. Weak purposes generate weak conditions—not "less" creative potential. Weak purposes impact the durability of creativity; it's more likely to retreat when met with stronger, more urgent demands of execution or obligation. But it's vital to remember that nothing changes about *you*; you are not more or less creative with a strong or weak purpose. Your purposes—and their importance to you—shape and guide what's needed in any specific instance of creative expression. We'll learn more about this in chapter 2.

Shift Two: Let go of comparison and judgment

We've been brought up to identify creativity and creative people through comparison. "Creative people stand out in a crowd," I've heard many say. We use words like *original, unconventional*, and even *dazzling* to describe creative people. We think they have more ideas than others. "They think outside of the box" (the box that everyone else is supposedly in). We label people "creative" because the products they generate are evaluated as special and different from the norm. Or we confuse success with creativity—suggesting that when some solutions are more successful than others, it means some people are more creative than others.

This is simply not true. You no longer need to separate yourself from other people by comparing. Creativity doesn't make you any more special or less special than anyone else. Why call some people "creative" anymore, when doing so suggests that you or others are *not*—or not as much? Creativity is simply either activated in response to a meaningful purpose, or not activated because the conditions don't require the energy expended in creative action. What a weight off your shoulders to set down the false labels, pride and/or shame, expectations, disappointment, and judgment. You can simply get genuinely curious about yourself, and you can generously honor and explore the ways your unique life experiences bring different perspectives that shape your creative participation.

Shift Three: Gain greater access by choosing to activate creativity more often

Holding a potential-based definition of creativity doesn't mean that everyone has equal awareness of and access to their creative potential. The more you engage with creativity consciously, the more you gain access to its power. A colleague recently said, "When I don't consciously use my creativity for a while, and then I need it, it's like going into a dimly lit room. The lights are low and it's hard to see. But when I activate it more often, and pay attention, more light goes on in the room and I can see more."

Very few of us pay close attention to what awakens creativity within us—our inner challenges, struggles, dreams, and desired aims—and the part we play in how creativity arises and occurs. We can even stop seeing the evidence right in front of us that we are, in fact, creating. It appears to go dark. A friend once shared with me that he had just retired; he had been a lawyer for over thirty years. In his retirement, he had started painting again—something that he had loved but had no time for as a partner in his law firm. He said, almost with tears in his eyes, "Now I get to be creative. It's still in there. I didn't kill it."

First, he *couldn't* kill it. Creative potential can't atrophy over time. But access to that potential had become blocked by his beliefs, assumptions, and biases and the decisions he made about himself as a creator. That made it harder for him to understand how he could express creativity through the practice of law. Second, how sad that his definition of creativity was so narrow that he couldn't see how it was showing up in his life and in his work on any given day. He believed that creativity was an ability that showed up through the arts when he painted. Because the work of practicing law didn't fit into that definition, he'd let his awareness and connection to his creativity go dormant.

Over time, most of us simply get out of practice. Access gets clogged and CDD sets in. We narrow our definitions of what creativity is and where it shows up. We shy away from adventures filled with wonder and discovery. Most destructive of all, we stop believing in this most powerful, most sustainable gift. Instead, choose to activate creativity toward pursuits and circumstances that call for it. Change the shape of your life so there are more spaces for creativity to emerge. If you want more creativity in your life, choose to explore the purposes you hold dear and make different choices. Finally, choose to actively and consciously change the beliefs and behaviors associated with an ability-based approach.

Shift Four: Give up elitism and gain connection

In an ability-based approach, creativity is doled out in different measures to different people. We are not all equal. But if creativity is a potential that everyone has been gifted without the need to compare, you can relax in the joy that comes from sharing this common human experience. No separation required. No elitism required. This will become even more critical in Adventure Two, when we explore the second key to this book: you cannot create alone—your gift of creativity must be shared.

While letting go of elitism might be hard for some people whose identity is grounded in being special or different as "a Creative," when you give up elitism, you gain connection. You live and breathe inclusion, generosity, fairness, and respect. You help contribute to a world of opportunity where your creativity is needed, along with everyone else's. I encourage you to enjoy this newfound equality. Be open and share what you bring. Connect with others out of your genuine curiosity for who you are, who they are, and what you each bring to your creative expression.

Shift Five: Give up victimhood and gain responsibility

In his evaluation of my final project for the class, one of my professors at Brown University wrote, "In dreams begin responsibility." He referenced this famous quote from a 1916 book of poems by William Butler

Yeats. Back then, I truly had no idea what he could be trying to tell me. Now, many years later, I believe I am finally beginning to understand that as we awaken to the power of our creativity, we must take accountability for what happens in our lives in a different way. Once we understand that creativity is a potential, we can't "uncrack the egg."

When you view creativity as an ability, you have an easy out when it doesn't show up. If I believe I'm just not that creative, I don't expect it of myself. Either I have creativity or I don't. There's no reason to try to change things, to think differently about my circumstances, or to work too hard to improve them. "You can't expect more of me than I'm capable of," said one of my clients on the "not creative at all" end of the lineup.

When you view creativity as a potential, on the other hand, there is no easy out—and no excuse for missing all the ways you are creating on any given day. Accountability becomes a critical factor in how you actively engage:

- You ensure you have meaningful and compelling purposes to drive your creativity.

- You believe you can shape the future when you set yourself to it.

- You set up the optimal conditions for creativity to emerge and to be sustained.

- You trust yourself to step across the threshold into the unknown.

- You meet the tests you'll face with courage and vulnerability.

- You find allies and collaborators to support you and work toward shared purpose.

- You stop now and then to recognize progress, celebrate success, recharge, and rejuvenate.

- You cherish the diversity of ways people activate their creativity and the uniqueness each one of us brings to our creative contribution.

I invite you to try on the idea of creativity as a potential. Test it out and see what shifts for you. Push yourself to clarify the purpose—the reasons why something new and different from the status quo is required today. Check to see how meaningful these purposes are. Try letting go of comparison and elitism and see if that promotes connection and inclusion. Let go of the idea that you got whatever measure of creativity you got, and watch how this promotes ownership, proactivity, engagement, and activism. Pay attention to your environment and how it catalyzes or inhibits the occurrence of creativity. Free yourself to dream, to hope, to imagine—and take responsibility to turn those dreams, aims, and desires into solutions that enrich your life and the lives of others.

Applying Creativity to Different Kinds of Challenges

In the new story of your creativity, and with a deeper understanding of what it really is (and is not), you can explore four arenas where creativity gets activated. While there are no firm boundaries between them, it can be useful to consider these arenas as distinct types of challenges and opportunities.

Arena One: Rebounding

In this first arena, your creativity shows up as resilience in the face of unpredictability, complexity, disruption, failures, and unforeseen accidents. When you rebound, creativity gets activated as you design responses to absorb, heal, and even strengthen from these kinds of disruptions. Here, creativity can arise in response to painful events like a divorce or periods of high stress at work, and when there is a loss of things as they had been. It helps you work through the anger, pain, and loss and find new ways to connect with people and shift priorities. Consciously bringing creativity to the challenge of rebounding is vital to living in our increasingly complex and volatile world. Now more than ever, you'll need all of your gifts to help strengthen resilience in the face of disruption.

Arena Two: Adapting

In this next arena, your creativity shows up when you generate new value in the face of changing conditions. These changes can arise from disruption, as well from the emergence of new opportunities and advancements. As the pace of change and technological progress quickens, adapting with "agility" has become popular in the business world. Adaptability shows up when you need to reconfigure things, accelerate progress, open up access, and gain greater flexibility. Your circumstances may call for adaptability as you navigate evolving conditions at work at the same time as uncertainties in your personal life. Whatever your circumstances, when you adapt you activate your creativity to seize new opportunities, turn on a dime to incorporate new approaches, flexibly reframe and resize your "shape" to gain advantage, and evolve your capabilities.

Arena Three: Inventing

Inventing is what many people think of most naturally when they think of creativity. When you invent, you come up with new ideas. Turning your ideas into approaches, solutions, products, and services that add new value is the classic definition of innovation. Inventing can happen on several different levels. Improving things, the most basic level of inventing, has become a standard expectation for most people at work. In living your daily life, you might see any number of opportunities to help make things better, easier, faster, less stressful, or more efficient. Your creativity is at work when you spot these opportunities for efficiencies and advances and take action to improve outcomes and performance.

Other times, inventing means generating new and novel approaches, new products and services that create markets, new processes that bypass existing ones, and new technologies that generate value. Depending on your work and the kind of culture and system you are in, your inventions—whether improvements or fundamentally new approaches—may be welcomed or perhaps met with resistance. They will put pressure on the system. When the system resists, your creativity might take a turn away from your primary focus to work around the resistance. This can be incredibly frustrating. Most people want more from their creativity than to work around resistance: we want to invent proactively, with freedom and with intention.

Arena Four: Disrupting

Disrupting is possibly the most revolutionary application of creativity. It's also the riskiest—personally and professionally. Those who are successful are often heralded (inappropriately so, within a potential-based definition of creativity) as "creative with a capital C." Think of Steve Jobs introducing the iPod or the iPhone, and how Apple transformed the ways we live and work with mobility, speed, and access. Think of how Southwest Airlines famously disrupted the airline industry with a new model for low-cost, no-frills, quick-turnaround travel. We raise these instances up as beacons of innovation. And they are, because of the value generated. But examples of successful disruptions are few and far between because disruption fundamentally changes current models and provides a value proposition that overtakes previous models and approaches. Aiming for disruption can be tricky because of the strength of forces supporting the status quo. When you invent, you'll encounter your share of organizational sludge. But when you disrupt, the resistance is amplified exponentially.

YOU MAY find that you are applying your creativity in any number of these four arenas. Each one calls for a different investment of energy, commitment, and perseverance. But remember: nothing about your creativity changes depending on where or when you apply it. In the old story of creativity as an ability, you might be tempted to assign a value judgment to these arenas. But in the new story, you are freed of comparison and judgment. Your primary concern is how you can bring your creativity forward more fully and more consciously, to realize your own aims and desires, to benefit the people, communities, and causes you care about, and to progress goals, projects, and efforts at work.

ASK YOURSELF...

Now, at the end of this chapter, take time to pause and reflect on the following questions.

The New Story of Your Creativity

- What would it mean for you—in your life and work—if you had unlimited access to your creativity?

- What would you gain? What might you have to let go of?

Your Creative Potential

- What circumstances are calling for your creativity (e.g., get a new job, navigate a divorce, solve a scientific or engineering problem)?

- What would be different if you brought more "creative accountability" to these situations?

- What unique talents, skills, and perspectives—drawn from your life experiences—augment your creative potential?

Applying Creativity to Different Kinds of Challenges

- How are the conditions around you catalyzing or inhibiting your creative expression?

- Which kinds of challenges (rebounding, adapting, inventing, or disrupting) are capturing your creative energy?

- How might a potential-based view of creativity change the way you approach problems, pain, and struggle?

2

Activating Creativity

· · · · ·

AFTER OUR Creative Leadership project was disbanded and I returned home from Europe, I often wondered what had led to our team's demise. Could it have been prevented? What was my role in our failure? After all, I had already discovered this remarkable new story of creativity as a potential. Though I didn't fully understand the implications of the new definition, maybe this new story could have saved the day—if only I had known how to integrate it. I chastised myself for a long time, thinking I should have known better and done better. But I couldn't save the ship from sinking.

In the years since, I've come to a deeper understanding of what brings creativity forward—the specific conditions that awaken it. What I've discovered has helped me understand the dynamic forces that were in play on our project and how they contributed to what happened. I've learned that each of us has ultimate accountability to change our conditions in order to give rise to creative expression— if that is what we desire. We are the ones making decisions about whether to bring our creativity forward and how to bring it forward.

These decisions and choices are made at the intersection of three powerful forces: purpose, possibility, and constraint.

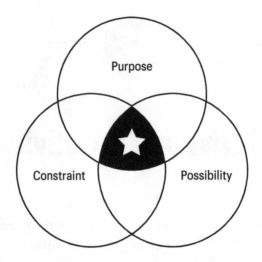

Purpose

• • •

Looking back, it's clear that the most challenging force undermining our Creative Leadership project was a misalignment of purpose. I had my own purpose—my reasons for venturing far from home and joining the team. Others on the team had different purposes for participating. The consulting firm had yet another different purpose—and Josef, the expert that the firm had hired to lead the team, had still another purpose of his own. None of these purposes overlapped in any meaningful, shared way, where we could all come together and create together. This misalignment generated conflict, including disagreements about what success looked like, how to make decisions, and what kind of progress got recognized and rewarded.

Purpose, it turns out, is the most powerful force that gives rise to conditions that call for creativity. Hope and aspiration, pain and struggle, dreams and passion, fear and regret, gratitude and forgiveness—these are the seeds that give birth to purpose and initiate a creative quest. A compelling and meaningful purpose that you care about can overcome all the challenges, fatigue, stress, and biases that you might have brought into the room.

Purpose generates gravitational pull. It gets things going. It activates creativity because the status quo is not good enough. When purpose is missing, or when there is a conflict between different purposes, creativity tends to stay out of sight.

The strength of your purpose has a powerful impact on whether you choose to create or decide not to bother. In times of unknowingness (and of risks, mistakes, danger, attack, and vulnerability), courage and perseverance are found in the strength and power of a meaningful purpose. Now I can see that the firm's purpose for investing in our Creative Leadership project—making money by deploying consultants on client projects—was not meaningful to me. Neither was the purpose held by Josef, our team leader. He hoped to train a few experts in his own image. In the absence of shared purpose, we defaulted to action—the completion of tasks. And action, when devoid of purpose, becomes routine and lacking in what's needed to activate creative potential.

Organize around purpose, not action. Three components amplify the power of purpose to move energy, activate creativity, and fuel discovery.

Component One: Mission

Mission is at the heart of purpose. It describes where you are headed and why it's important—your "vision of breakthrough." Consider the power of a mission like "A world free of cancer" or "A man on the moon in ten years." These are grand visions, framed as a breakthrough, that have mobilized the creativity and contributions of tens of thousands of people. When we set them into motion, we don't even know if these kinds of missions are attainable, and we don't know how we will get there. But we are called to believe and we want to support them. Whether the mission is far-reaching or shorter-term, with smaller doses of unknowing, what matters is that it is meaningful: the mission is inspiring, it includes some measure of unknowing, and it generates commitment.

Mission serves a critical function: it draws you in and keeps you engaged through the dark times. It becomes your compass out on the open ocean, in the darkest Swamps, and even when you think you are lost. It inspires you to see beyond obstacles and keep your eye on your desired outcome. Many people stop short of drawing on the full power of mission: they frame their vision only in terms of arrival at a particular destination (like the achievement of a goal). But the gravitational pull intensifies when you also take the next step: to detail the benefits you anticipate once you've arrived. Now you can also tell the story of *why* it's important to get where you're headed.

Component Two: Focus

Focus strengthens and concentrates purpose. I once asked a senior leader, "What's the most important thing we can do to help draw out creativity?" She said, without skipping a beat, "Focus that creativity." That's because directing your creative potential—with intention—to critical priorities and challenges increases the likelihood that creativity will yield innovative results. Focus generates power, like the narrowing channel of a riverbed (or the nozzle of a hose) increases the force of the water moving through it. We become laser-focused: listening and watching for clues about our mission, making connections, and piecing together fragments of ideas even when we're not paying conscious attention. Focus helps us stay on course—or at least not wander too far off as we experience tests and challenges along the way.

That doesn't mean you won't get lost or that you shouldn't explore your curiosity. We all need some measure of play that is unstructured, unfocused, and free. You can make valuable discoveries during these times of free play. But when you're working toward a meaningful mission that involves crossing into the unknown, it's important that you focus in on that challenge and direct creativity toward the drivers you want to impact and the places you want to experiment and learn. Be specific about the challenges and opportunities where creativity will have the greatest impact. And while you're focusing, remember to hold that focus loosely and be ready to adjust given what emerges. Set the focus and let creativity get to work.

Component Three: Aim

Aim improves results. When you aim, you set your intention for how much change from the status quo is needed to achieve your purpose. Think about a sport like golf, baseball, or tennis, where your intention and aim greatly influence the trajectory of your shot. The same is true when your purpose calls for innovative outcomes. You can aim closer to where you are now—with less change from the way things are—or you can aim for transformative changes, big dreams, and urgent imperatives. These different aims will give rise to completely different kinds of hero's journeys, with different levels of risk, different amounts of unknowingness, different probabilities for success, and potentially different levels of transformation.

Have you ever heard someone say, "I need to completely change my life"? Maybe that's true, but often, the pain and struggle they are experiencing is in one part of their life. Maybe their manager is giving them hell. Or they're struggling with relationship challenges. Or they're overwhelmed, juggling too many competing priorities. Too often, people miscalculate how much change from the status quo is really needed to achieve their purpose. Why? We're wired to think that bigger is better. It's sexier to aim for disruption and blue-sky solutions than to ask for just a small-step change from what currently exists. But aiming for bigger changes comes at a cost. And in many cases, smaller, simpler approaches can help realize your purpose. Hone your skill of accurately assessing where to aim—given your mission, pressures, and how much "unknowingness" is inherent in your journey.

Possibility

● ● ●

Possibility is the second of three powerful forces in the intersection. Can you remember a time when possibility played a prominent role in your day-to-day experience? I can. In college, my gang and I used to say we were students at MSU—the school of Making Stuff Up. We would come up with possibility after possibility like we were pulling rabbits out of a hat. It was magical. Back then, we were free to invent and experiment in a learning context without real consequences or the need to defend our inventions. We were creating to satisfy our own purposes; we didn't need to prove anything or even necessarily generate value—except for our own learning.

This certainly wasn't the case on our project in Europe. When I arrived, it seemed as if the whole world of possibility was open to us. But it didn't take long to realize that our team leader, Josef, had a very definite idea of what we were supposed to be doing—and the right way to go about it. In fact, he was downright tyrannical. There was no room to deviate from his plan, which was slow, structured, precise, and methodical. At the same time, the firm was investing hundreds of thousands of Swiss francs in our efforts—and each of the country partners had allocated consultants full-time to the project. We were under enormous pressure to show progress, meet deadlines, and produce tangible evidence of new value.

I believe this was the second core reason for our failure. We simply had no space, no permission, and no degree of freedom to play with possibilities. I felt as if I was stuck in a pressure cooker and the crush of obligations, imposed rules, and structures sucked out any chance for creativity. There was no tolerance for questioning our approach or asking for more time to play with different options and explore different paths.

It takes courage, self-awareness, and a unique company culture like Pixar has (more on this in chapter 3) to encourage and support exploration of possibilities. Imagine telling your boss that you "made it up" when they ask how you arrived at your conclusions and recommendations. Even though making it up might involve deep expertise, intuition, wisdom gained throughout all your experience, and an understanding of relevant data, it doesn't carry the same weight as drawing on what has been tried and tested.

Possibility is essential when you are called to take a leap of faith into a world you haven't been to. Whether you gather possibilities from around you (through best practices or benchmarking) or invent new, unique possibilities in a class by themselves, the focus is on what *might be*, not what *is*. How far you choose to venture into the unknown depends on the nature of the challenge or opportunity and the aim you have set. The further you venture into the unknown, the more possibility thinking you will need.

Imagination is at the root of possibility thinking. We humans have a unique capability that allows us to envision something that doesn't yet exist as if it were real, and then make it real. We can see, hear, taste, smell, and even touch things in our imagination. Here are some attributes to keep in mind:

- Imagination is open-ended, pictorial, and metaphorical. It isn't governed by the laws of reality or by the constraints around us.

- Imagination generates tension between reality and what we can envision. That tension pulls us toward the future. Think about Jane Jetson, talking with her friends via video conference back in 1962 when the animated show *The Jetsons* first aired. Back then, a video conference would have been impossible. But here we are, years later, using video conference technology every day. The tension generated by our imaginings, combined with a meaningful purpose, propels us forward in the creative process.

- What we can imagine, we eventually can make real. In your imagination, you can invent and refine solutions, work out potential bugs, evaluate viability, and visualize new value. The key to turning imagination into reality is to allow this tension to remain unresolved—without "satisficing":[2] shutting down imagination prematurely by being satisfied with the first solution that will suffice.

Bringing more imagination into your personal and work life means asking "What if... ?" and "How might I... ?" more often, in large and small ways throughout your day. For those of you oriented toward possibility, this will seem obvious—although you may know the sting of being shut down earlier than you might have hoped. For those of you who are more oriented to rules, guardrails, and feasibility, this will likely require conscious practice. Where do you land on the spectrum? How comfortable are you with engaging in possibility thinking?

What beliefs have formed about how the world around you responds to the generation of possibilities? For most of us, the systems we work and live within do not reward everyday engagement in possibility. Over time you may learn to constrain possibility itself.

Some people live in worlds dominated by scarcity thinking—where possibilities don't even show up on the radar. But don't be afraid to let yourself go. You *need* to make stuff up. At almost every meeting I facilitate, when we're capturing our objectives for the time together, eventually someone says, "We should have fun!" What they're seeking is to step away from the constraints, rules, and realities of our everyday experience—to engage in adventure with each other. Enjoy the enthusiasm you generate when you carve out spaces to play with possibilities, seek out opportunities, and ask questions that engender divergent thinking. These activities are critical to your creative expression and to your well-being.

There are, however, some aspects to watch out for with possibility thinking. For one thing, you can have too many possibilities. Every possibility generates a choice and requires some investment of energy; you must choose between options and ideas and choose to play with them, discard them, set them aside for later, or develop them further. In *The Paradox of Choice*,[3] Barry Schwartz suggests that 85 varieties of crackers, 285 varieties of cookies, and 275 varieties of breakfast cereal might be too many. That's because an increase in options forces an increase in effort to make a decision, which in turn leads to delay or the diminishing of enjoyment with our decisions. When generating possibilities, you must be able to say, "Good enough—it's fit for my purpose," and get to work testing possibilities against real-world constraints.

And as much fun as it might be, it is also possible to spend too much time in possibility. Most of us have the opposite problem—we don't spend enough time in possibility and discovery. But there comes a point when questions that yield divergence must give way to questions that encourage convergence. To realize your purposes, especially if new value is required, you must act: make something to test, set up an experiment, or develop a prototype. Again, possibility must interact with reality.

I invite you to engage in an abundance of possibilities. Enjoy the process of seeking (for answers, possibilities, options, solutions) without knowing. Learn to play in the spaces between seeking answers and making things. Take time to test what you have made through prototyping and experimenting. These spaces bear gifts that come when generous and abundant possibility interacts with the constraints of reality.

Constraint

· · ·

The final force in play in the intersection is constraint. No action on earth is free of constraints and boundaries. Constraints act as partners to possibility in a dynamic, reciprocal interchange. Constraints shape the landscape of discovery—just as the limits of our imagination do—and they form guardrails, limit the flow of action, influence sequencing, and impact time horizons that shape possibility. Right now, as I am writing, the word processing software I am using is both enabling and constraining my creative process.

Some years ago, I was asked to develop a new approach for working flexibly as part of a strategic initiative inside a tech company. Back then, before COVID-19 threw us willy-nilly into flexible working, a lot of companies in Silicon Valley were experimenting to help ease the crush of increasingly difficult commutes and rising housing prices. The topic was—as it still is—complicated. When I set out, I had no idea about the myriad employment laws and regulations, policy challenges, and restrictions I was about to encounter. And because I prefer not to be surprised by constraints, my first stop was the legal department.

Why? The legal department is one of my best allies in clarifying constraints and determining what is non-negotiable, what can be negotiated, where there is play in the system, and which obstacles can be worked around. Working with the legal department helped me understand how important it is to accurately assess the level of fixedness of a given constraint and the risk of messing with it.

Some constraints are truly non-negotiable for all the right reasons.
There are constraints you just don't want to mess with. An example in
the pharmaceutical industry is "patient safety." This is a foundational
constraint that—for the right reasons—*must* guide decisions and
actions in that industry. A non-negotiable constraint in the world of
social media might be "data security." These are external constraints
that are easy to understand and identify. It may be harder to identify
what your "inner non-negotiables" are—those boundaries that operate in your inner life for all the right reasons.

When you violate non-negotiables, you risk the trust that's required
for viability, vitality, and success; you risk losing the freedom to operate, and you may risk losing deeply held values. It takes care and
attention to navigate non-negotiable constraints. You must be able to
tease out all the secondary and tertiary constraints that have accumulated around the core—so you can be clear about what must remain
unchanged. Find what is truly non-negotiable in your life and work
and protect these constraints. They are often at the heart of your core
values—and they are clues to who you are and who you are becoming.

Some constraints are non-negotiable *for now*. Many constraints are
firm now but can be changed over time. Think of a law that is in effect,
that you would not want to violate, but that could be changed through
advocacy and activism. Think of contracts, trade agreements, policies, standard operating procedures, and tax codes. Think of cultural
norms that have outlived their service to an organization's mission
or, because of changing conditions or circumstances, have become a
drag on the system.

Navigating firm (but potentially changeable) constraints requires
skill to frame the higher purpose—and to use this higher purpose
to dislodge long-held norms, policies, and laws. Rather than being
stopped by "the way things are today," you dig for root causes to understand why these constraints exist and the purposes they once served.
What is the opportunity now? What has changed since this constraint
developed that could disrupt it or dislodge it—and maybe even
solve the problem it once solved, but in a way that suits your new or

emerging purpose? From this place of understanding, you can decide which constraints you want to eliminate, which you want to influence or evolve, and which might be best left alone (at least for now).

Other constraints are negotiable. Most constraints can be influenced in directions that enable your desired aims. A lot depends on who is invested in them, who is protecting them from evolution, and how conscious you are about your own beliefs about them. Many constraints can be overcome with a new perspective, new technology, or a new customer insight. But if your commitment is weak, any doubt you have about the success of the endeavor is likely to give you pause. As psychologist Rollo May has said, commitment and perseverance to a creative quest "is healthiest when it is not *without* doubt, but *in spite of* doubt."[4]

Navigating negotiable constraints requires curiosity, the assumption of good intent, patience, proactivity, and a healthy dose of possibility thinking. Because you're surrounded by these kinds of constraints, it's important to know when and where to challenge them. Do you tend to over-challenge these kinds of constraints just because they seem wrong? Or do you pick and choose more carefully based on your desired aims? Many of us aren't engaged enough to even expend the effort. It all depends on what you're committed to and how much effort it takes to challenge and change the status quo.

Don't get me wrong. It's not that I love constraints—especially the ones that arise out of senseless bureaucracy, blind rule-following, or controlling management. I love *knowing* about the constraints that intersect with what I am working to create. Try thinking of constraints as boulders in a mighty river. Water flows over them and around them. And sometimes, when the current is strong enough, the river can dislodge a boulder that's sat unmoved for many years. Whether you're facing policies, cultural norms, socioeconomic realities, contract terms, or even seemingly unchangeable core values, don't let them catch you off guard. Anticipate them and figure out how to work around them. Sleuth them out and don't let them override your purpose.

There are people who are more oriented to constraint than to possibility. But keep in mind that this has nothing to do with your creative potential. Being constraint-oriented does not mean that you're somehow less creative than others who play in the world of possibilities. This is a common misconception. I know many dedicated people across companies and industries whose primary orientation is toward the mitigation of constraints and risk. Sadly, they are more likely to place themselves on the "not creative at all" end of the lineup when I ask how creative they are. But remember, creativity is a potential, not an ability. Being constraint-oriented simply shapes the landscape of where ideas arise and how you pursue and implement them.

A keen awareness of constraint yields a kind of realism that is incredibly valuable along a journey of discovery and invention. To innovate, you must be able to assess risk, viability, and feasibility—to know what to change and what not to mess with, and to understand the dynamics that are impacting the achievement of your purpose. Possibility-oriented folks might drive constraint-oriented people mad with their enthusiasm for wild ideas. Constraint-oriented folks might dampen the enthusiasm of possibility-oriented people with their skepticism and attention to the rules. But when these two orientations are brought together (with self-awareness and a shared purpose), the effect is powerful. The dynamic interplay can arise from within the same person—someone who has a balance of both—or from having a diversity of approaches on a team.

Dancing in the Center of the Intersection

● ● ●

The activation of your creative potential starts within you. You are at the center of the intersection—with all that you bring to this moment from what has come before you arrived. Nothing happens until a purpose that is meaningful comes into focus. Once that purpose exists, your creativity engages and you start seeking for solutions. And this is really important: it doesn't matter which comes next—either possibility or constraint. Both are critical to creating. While each of us typically leads with one or the other, the trick is to not let one reign too long without involving the other. Eventually we must have both possibility and constraint to complete the intersection and bring power to creativity.

- **If you are possibility-oriented,** when you start seeking you are most likely to look for solutions that offer new rewards and open up opportunity. You'll look for what doesn't already exist. You'll have less of an initial awareness of obstacles, risks, and constraints. But fantastical possibilities do not necessarily produce solutions of value. The trick to dancing in the center of the intersection is to mine the depths of imagination for a wide range of alternatives and then pull out what can be shaped into real options. Test possibilities early. Apply a dose of reality to your possibilities even as you let imagination soar.

- **If you are constraint-oriented,** when you start seeking you are most likely to look for solutions that mitigate risk and relieve pressure from rules and obstacles. You'll likely look for workarounds and ways to bend or modify what already exists. You'll have less of an initial inclination to explore what seem like fantasy solutions. But only painting with the colors you have in hand can limit the vibrancy of your solutions. Without possibility, you're likely to forget to ask "What else?" or "Who else?" or "What if... ?" The trick to dancing in the center of the intersection is to get a clear understanding of what is non-negotiable and what is negotiable, and then apply imagination to gather new colors—to play with different options for changing what you can. Let your imagination soar without losing your solid footing in reality.

WHEN YOU dance in the center of the intersection of purpose, possibility, and constraint, you generate tension that sparks movement, strength, and power. Let that tension exist. Don't try to alleviate it too soon. Give it space and room to breathe. Actively participate in the unresolvedness of that tension—even as you set your intention to resolve it. Watch out for pressures arising from both within you and outside of you that might urge you to cut the tension and ambiguity short. Allow yourself to play in the spaces between seeking for answers, choosing avenues to explore, and inventing solutions to test in relation to your purpose. Learn to leverage this tension to drive creative energy forward.

ASK YOURSELF...

Now, at the end of this chapter, take time to pause and reflect on the following questions.

Purpose

- Think about something you are working on. What is your mission—your story about the anticipated outcome(s) and benefit(s)? How meaningful is that mission to you?

- What helps focus your creative energy for optimal power (e.g., partner with others, test out an assumption, break an unwieldy goal into smaller chunks)?

- How far are you aiming from the status quo? What costs (energy, time, resources) are you likely to incur?

Possibility

- Which current situations and circumstances would benefit from more possibility thinking?

- What happens to possibility thinking when you are in stressful situations or under urgent time pressures?

Constraint

- Who can you tap for an early assessment of the constraints you're likely to face on a current project?

- Which constraints are truly non-negotiable? Which might be movable?

Dancing in the Intersection

- Are you more possibility-oriented or constraint-oriented by nature? How does this show up in your day-to-day life?

- How does your orientation shape your perspective and the kinds of ideas you typically have?

- Imagine a problem or challenge you are currently facing. If you stand at the center of the intersection of purpose, possibility, and constraint and just listen, what do you hear?

3

Greeting the Unknown

· · · · ·

A WHILE BACK, I saw a bumper sticker on the back of a beat-up, dark-green truck that said, "Help! I'm making mistakes faster than I can learn from them." The man driving the pickup must have thought I was strange as I pulled up beside him and craned my neck to see who was at the wheel. Ever since that day, I haven't been able to get his call for help out of my mind. It spoke to a truth I know many people are facing: the world is changing rapidly around us.

At first, I wanted to shout out, "Hey buddy, it's not like we're going to slow down so you can catch up or catch a break." I decided not to. But I also didn't want to suggest what I hear so often now: "You have to learn to rebound, pivot, and adapt." Have you heard this too? The problem is, rebounding and adapting are primarily reactive approaches. In a way, you're back on your heels—responding to and making the best of whatever comes your way. And when change comes fast and furious, reacting and adapting won't be good enough.

In fact, mistakes and failure are on the rise when people rely on traditional approaches, work inside familiar boundaries, and try to adapt from within the current paradigm. Especially when you want to change the status quo in the face of vexing challenges. In the new world of work, success will depend on getting better at leaving the safety and comfort of what is known. To face the challenges ahead, you will need to venture into the unknown—with your creativity—to invent and disrupt.

I don't know about you, but I'm not a big fan of the unknown. When it shows up in my life, I more often greet it with dread than with passion. I avoid it and do everything I can to prevent it. I'll hang on to certainty and cling to the familiar long after it serves me. Given that, it might seem foolish to invite the unknown into my life when I don't have to. But that's exactly what each of us must do if we are going to activate conscious creativity and use it to spark innovation.

On the other hand, maybe you want to think outside of the box, but whenever you've tried, you've felt like you're swimming against a tide of constraints that thwarts your efforts. That's because the bureaucratic and hierarchical systems that rule the world of work can suck the wind out of our creativity and keep us stuck in the familiar. Over time, we stop taking risks. We get out of practice. We become afraid of the unknown.

Bureaucracy does deliver valued outcomes: certainty, replication, scalability, and predictability. And collectively, we've become experts at execution—at getting things done and implemented according to plan. It's what gets rewarded. We chunk and divide our work into tasks that are repeatable and can be performed as routines. We know how to frame a goal, sell it, plan to execute on that goal, and deliver. We can calculate the return on investment, predict risk and mitigate for that risk, allocate resources, and define accountabilities. Years of executing day in and day out have built well-worn pathways that are hard to break out of—even when you *must* break out of them.

The skills of execution alone won't carry you through the kinds of personal and professional transformation that so many of us are facing. And they don't often yield innovative results. But it's tricky to venture into the unknown. None of us can know how things will work out. You can't force your plan. And when outcomes are so ambiguous that you can't see past the first few steps, there are no guarantees. You must become as skilled at embarking on adventures of exploration and discovery as you've become at execution.

Three Truths About the Unknown

• • •

Over the course of my life, I've learned that in every moment, there are three co-existing truths about the unknown. Together, these truths generate dynamic tension—an energetic field where infinite possibility sparks with your creativity, courage, and vulnerable receptivity to bring forward what wants to emerge. What is at the center of all this possibility? You are. *It starts within you.*

Truth One: There are multiple possibilities ahead of you

Several years ago, I was invited to join a group of human resources (HR) professionals to preview a new technology for managing employee performance. This kind of invitation is common in the San Francisco Bay Area, and I'd already attended way too many presentations like this one. I was reluctant to go. But to entice us, the organizers held the event at famed Pixar Studios. In exchange for reviewing the presentation and providing feedback, we were promised a tour. I was intrigued by Pixar and how the team works together to craft iconic stories, so I decided to go.

The minute I walked into the building, I knew I had stepped into a different world. Life-sized statues of famous characters from movies were everywhere. There were open spaces filled with people and conversation. There were quiet spaces where people worked head-down or in small groups. The place was filled with light, color, art, and artifacts. It was alive in a way that surprised and excited me—and I knew in a heartbeat why it was so important that I'd decided to go. What I learned that day was a revelation.

Our guide took us to a hallway, lined with artifacts from the process of making the animated movie *Up*. (If you haven't seen *Up*, I encourage you to watch it.) He explained how the team had worked to develop the character of Carl Fredricksen, the old man and central figure of the movie. In the early stages of their exploration, they hadn't decided yet that Carl would be a balloon salesman. I was astonished at the investment of time and the level of detail that was evident as artists and storywriters sketched out what Carl would look like and how he would behave if he were in one profession or another. How would Carl age if he worked as a bank teller, for instance, instead of a balloon salesman? How would his character evolve in relation to his circumstances? How might he navigate frustration, the day-to-day routine, regret at the loss of shared dreams, and longing for the love of his life? How might his creativity and courage show up differently on the journey he takes?

I was deeply reminded that day of Truth One: on any creative quest into the unknown, there are multiple possibilities ahead of you. Like the limitless possibilities of how Carl's life might unfold, the forces shaping our multiple, possible futures are in play in a multifaceted, interdependent, and unpredictable dance. Our life experiences shape us and we, reciprocally, shape the circumstances that we find ourselves in. Outcomes are uncertain, and we all contribute to what ends up happening.

Truth Two: We have agency, but we are not in control

In *Up* there was not much Carl could do to stop the chain of events that led to his adventure. It's likely he would have preferred to grow old with his wife, Ellie, by his side. Instead, she got sick and passed away before they could share the adventure they had always dreamed of. Carl may have wanted the routines of his life to continue uninterrupted by the march of progress. He surely would have preferred that the construction threatening his house, his memories, and his whole way of life would stop. Like Carl, each of us lives in the space between what we hope for and what is actually happening around us. Our opportunity is to become more active participants in the dance that unfolds—to bring our creativity forward to meet the landscape that greets us.

This is the essence of Truth Two: we can shape what happens, but we are not in control of the outcomes. Even though our choices sculpt what unfolds in our lives, there are forces at play we cannot change. Sometimes the dance between our dreams and reality will be playful and sometimes it will be painful. That's the way that it is. But sitting idly by on the sidelines with our wants, hopes, and desires and expecting things to magically change isn't the answer.

Despite our lack of control over some circumstances, we still need to act, make decisions, and shape the opportunities and constraints that come our way. We need to understand and take accountability for how our own biases, filters, assumptions, and preferences might obscure our view. We need to explore how the stories we tell about ourselves shape how we participate when opportunities arise. And we need to activate and apply our imagination and creativity, and inspire the imagination and creativity in others, to sculpt emerging futures in ways that support our purposes.

Truth Three: The outcomes we imagine are reaching back to help us realize them

It can be frightening to realize we are not in control. We might imagine we're insignificant and at the mercy of the winds of change. But contrast this with Truth Three. Think about it for a minute. Our imagined futures are *coming toward us*. In fact, the outcomes we desire want us as much as we want them. There are clues all around. "What you seek is seeking you," said Rumi, the Sufi mystic and poet. There is a magnetism drawing us forward that we cannot explain. From this perspective, we understand that we are not alone in the dance. We belong to something bigger than ourselves. We don't have to move into the futures we imagine by force, by willpower, or by our efforts alone. Networks of support, guidance, love, and forgiveness are not only available to us—they are reaching out to us as we open up with vulnerability and courage. There is grace, serendipity, and empathy to receive along the way.

TOGETHER, THESE three truths generate creative electricity when you are at the intersection of purpose, possibility, and constraint. The future in your sights—the one you are creating, working for, influencing, and sculpting—might be big and far-reaching or it might be closer to home. Maybe you're building or running your own business. That could be happening at the same time as you're raising a family. You might be focused on advancing new technologies, developing a new standard of care or customer service, or inventing improvements to work processes that simplify things and generate efficiencies.

You might be rebounding from a difficult divorce at the same time as you've been asked to reimagine your business's operating model. You might be working on challenges like disrupting impacts of climate change or finding a cure for cancer. Or you might be taking on a new role with a bold vision for how to up-level your team's contribution to the organization.

Whatever your focus, by imagining a future that's different than today—for yourself and for others—you are engaged in a journey that is uniquely and intimately grounded in what it means to be human. For tens of thousands of years, we have asked how things might be better or different, sought out new answers to these questions, left the safety of our current circumstances, and persevered to see our ideas to fruition. The good news is that you were born with the potential to discover, to explore, and to create.

The Dynamics of Discovery

● ● ●

If you understand the dynamics of discovery—including the phases you're likely to pass through—you can better lead yourself through the unknown. You'll know when to answer the call and set out despite the dangers. You'll have greater faith and confidence, knowing you will be changed and transformed but not yet knowing how. And over time, as you become a student of discovery, you'll get better at greeting the unknown with passion instead of dread. The key is to practice conscious creativity—something I failed to do as I embarked on one of my most consequential journeys of discovery.

After our Creative Leadership project collapsed, I returned to the States and reopened my consulting practice—this time focused on creativity and innovation in business. As is often the case, we can learn more from failures than we do from successes. I hoped to bring these lessons to help my clients draw out people's creativity and apply it to the challenges and opportunities of achieving their company's mission. But something kept nagging at me—unresolved questions that I couldn't answer. What makes it so hard to bring creativity into the process of discovery, especially when we're working together with others?

It turns out our colossal failure in Europe wasn't just a fluke, though it may have been an extreme case. So many of us find it difficult to "be creative" as an employee inside a company or institution. Over the years I've talked with hundreds of people working in large and small companies, in complex health systems, in government agencies, and in educational institutions. I've learned just how common this struggle is—to bring creativity into the workplace and direct it to our work. And I've seen firsthand how much we all want and need the opportunity to express creatively—to go on adventures of discovery, invention, and even disruption. We're naturally curious, inquisitive, and imaginative. We want to tinker with things, poke around and explore unknown places, experiment, and learn.

It's clear we all need creative play for well-being, happiness, engagement, and meaning making, among other benefits. What's fascinating is that now more than ever, the companies we work for *also* need our creativity. VUCA (volatile, uncertain, complex, and ambiguous) has become a commonplace acronym to describe the whitewater conditions in which businesses now operate. Standard approaches are failing faster than ever. The business world is abuzz with the "agility imperative" as businesses work to get leaner, faster, and more flexible. In a 2019 report on global trends, LinkedIn reported, "creativity is the most in-demand soft skill in short supply."[5] A recent McKinsey study predicts, "as automation transforms the skills companies need, demand for creativity will rise sharply by 2030."[6]

But *discovery is hard work*. Like the baker and his wife in *Into the Woods*, like me getting on a plane to London back in 1999, like Carl Fredricksen when his house strained to tear free of its foundation and lifted off the ground in *Up*, and like you embarking on your own journeys of discovery, none of us can know what is in store. We can't know whether we'll make it, if we'll be safe, or how the journey will change us. These unknowns can be terrifying—and they can easily stop you from venturing forward. What happens if you get lost? What if you want to go in a different direction than the people you're with? How can you choose a direction when you don't know where it will lead?

Over the years, through both failures and successes, I've uncovered three critical insights that help to better navigate the dynamics of discovery.

Insight One: Learn from others who blazed the trail

One challenge of journeys of discovery is that they require you to cross the threshold into the unknown. We can't know the unexpected places that we will find along the way, just as we can't know whether we'll ever reach our intended destination. And because none of us has the exact same journey, someone else's map won't help.

But you can learn from others who have gone before, blazed the trail, and returned to report on the phases or kinds of experiences you're likely to encounter on a path of discovery. Use their wisdom as a guide to strengthen your footing and help you choose whether to charge forward, stand still, change direction, retrace your steps, listen inside or seek the advice of others, stick to your plan, or scout for a new perspective.

The wisdom of two particular pathways stands the test of time. These two have shaped how I work with individuals and groups to navigate the unknown, unleash creative potential, and transform the status quo.

The first is Joseph Campbell's hero's journey. In his book *The Hero with a Thousand Faces*,[7] Campbell captures the essence of scores of stories from across geographies and civilizations about the kind of transformation that occurs whenever we risk stepping across the threshold of the unknown. According to Campbell, the hero's journey begins with innocence—the time before the hero begins to know and learn what awaits them. They hear a "call" awakening them and urging entrance into a series of individual and shared tests that drive transformation. At first, the hero might refuse this call. But at some point, when they choose to answer, they will cross past the point of no return and embark into the unknown. Along the way, the hero meets new allies in the form of guides, wise sages, partners, and collaborators. Some are willing, but others might be reluctant to answer the call or have different motives. At any moment, the hero and their allies might find themselves in what Campbell calls the "pit"—that place where the unknowingness seems insurmountable and dangerous. The hero cannot know how long they'll be in the pit, but what pulls them out is the strength of the call and the process of collaborating and strategizing with allies.

The pit—or as I often refer to it, the Swamp—can be a place where ideas are born and a vision of breakthrough comes into focus. This vision, and the promise of the benefits that await, generates commitment to experiment and test different ideas and pathways. Fighting for that vision without knowing how things will turn out builds strength and courage. It engenders the kind of learning and self-awareness that arises when we persevere, accept what is true, and stand up for our values and principles. The hero is transformed through this process and returns to share the wisdom and fruits of the process in celebration with their community.

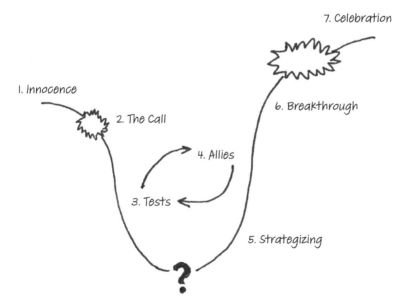

7. Celebration

1. Innocence

2. The Call

6. Breakthrough

4. Allies

3. Tests

5. Strategizing

?

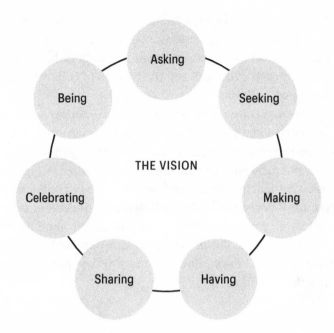

The second is an Indigenous "visioning" path. Here, we turn to the wisdom shared by Gregory Cajete, Tewa author and professor from Santa Clara Pueblo, New Mexico. Cajete articulates elements of Indigenous Cultural Knowledge to help educators synthesize Tribal traditions with Western traditions. In his book *Look to the Mountain*,[8] he describes a seven-step path of visioning that combines learning, creativity, and discovery into a simple process:

1. **Asking.** A deep and meaningful quest—especially one that calls us into the unknown and toward something different and new— always starts with a question. Sometimes these questions are front and center, easily discernible; other times they can be obscured. Paying attention and investing time and energy to clarify and refine the questions that motivate us into the unknown is a vital first step.

2. **Seeking.** Once the question comes into awareness and we accept the call to answer, we naturally begin looking for ideas and solutions.

3. **Making.** This is where we build, break, bend, and/or blend things together into potential solutions.

4. **Having.** In this phase, we "live with" and experience the progress, process, and results of making.

5. **Sharing.** Here, we bring our visions, ideas, solutions, and products to others.

6. **Celebrating.** Together we rejoice in the benefits, value, and outcomes that we've generated.

7. **Being.** Finally, we become anew. Being completes the process and transforms the way we approach successive quests.

There is so much to learn from this approach. Here, the processes of envisioning, learning, creating, and sharing come together as both individual and community-based activities. This path contains phases that are often left out in others, such as *having*, where we simply experience (have) what we have created. In this busy world we live in, especially in Western cultures so focused on achievement, how often do we pause to simply have and enjoy the fruits of our progress without consuming, striving, or controlling? To let them seep in, percolate, and filter through us before we take our next step?

Like Campbell's journey, the visioning path also includes *celebrating*, which brings in the joyfulness that comes from exercising our potential to create. Finally, the *being* phase highlights a core truth: quests and journeys of discovery change who we are and who we are becoming. Transformation comes from learning through discovery and creative participation.

Notice the similarities in these two different depictions of the path of discovery. In each, there is exploration of the unknown—bringing illumination, ideation, and learning. In each, there is the generation of something new. In each, there is a drive toward an outcome that brings value. And both depictions highlight the elements of self-awareness, celebration, and personal transformation. Together, these pathways illuminate the kinds of experiences you're likely to encounter on journeys of discovery, across the threshold into the unknown.

I can't help but wonder how things might have been different for me or for the team on the Creative Leadership project if we had taken time to understand that, in fact, we were on a hero's journey of discovery into the unknown. What if we had stopped to clarify the questions at the root of our quest? What if we knew in advance that we *would* lose our way—and talked about how we wanted to work together when that occurred? What if, instead of blaming each other when we got stuck in the "pit," we paused to simply *have* the progress we'd made and see what wanted to emerge next? What if we took a more iterative approach to making and sharing our ideas and solutions—instead of aiming for perfection right out of the gate?

I invite you to study each of these core depictions of the dynamics of discovery in greater detail and learn from others who have been out there on the frontier of the unknown. Understanding the shape your pathway may take will help strengthen your footing.

Insight Two: Don't apply rules for execution to journeys of discovery

Execution is fundamentally different than discovery. Yet most of the rules and practices we use to get things done today (in businesses as well as our personal lives) exist to support execution. The rules of execution cherish standardization, repeatability, control, compliance, structure, and predictability. We set clear goals with known endpoints and milestones and define discrete roles for different people to play. We develop plans and we plot our path to and through these markers of progress. We define metrics to evaluate success and performance— and we make promises about where we'll be and how much we will accomplish by a specified time. We develop elaborate plans to help us manage the change we seek—the move from "here" to "there"—when we will arrive at our defined goal.

Dr. Seuss's book *Oh, The Places You'll Go!* offers a window into how different it can feel—and what is at risk—when you set out instead on a journey of discovery. Using simple rhyme, he shares messages of hope, anticipation, and expansion, but also warnings of hurdles and hang-ups, confusion, loneliness, and darkly lit places where you might get hurt. And through his wisdom, Seuss brings us right to that place of decision on the journey where we must choose whether to move forward or not—and whether what might be won on the journey is worth the cost of what may be lost.

Though he was writing for kids, Dr. Seuss captured a simple truth: in discovery, there is both danger and excitement in the unknown—in the places that are unmarked or dimly lit. You can't know where you'll end up when you start, and you can't always plot and plan your course or manage the change you seek. That's what's so exciting (and scary) about embarking. In discovery, you need a trusted guidance system more than a detailed map or plan. Some call this a "north star," in reference to the way sailors in the northern hemisphere would use the stars to guide them out on the open ocean. Whatever you call it, this guidance system becomes your reference point to help determine whether you're on or off course. In discovery, you need a fluid exchange of leadership and followership instead of discrete roles and responsibilities. Stories of meaningful value and benefit are more important motivators than predictions of return on investment.

If you are like most people who work in companies and institutions, you're probably more familiar with the rules of execution than with the hallmarks of discovery. In execution, evaluating the risk of proceeding is not as relevant because certainty is part of the game plan. The system is set up to control for predictability and repeatability and to seek value at scale. Don't get me wrong: these fundamentals of good management and the tools of execution are core to delivering business objectives. And execution doesn't mean staying stagnant. Over the last few decades, "continuous improvement" has become part of execution. There are frameworks, processes, templates, and best practices for building improvement into the system, enhancing productivity, streamlining operations, eliminating waste, capturing efficiencies, and managing change.

But on a mission of discovery, you will need different capabilities and tools. You will need to confront the question of what you might lose—both by embarking and once you are on the way. You must surrender to the emergent. And you must have a deep faith that what may be lost will be superseded by what might be won—even though at the start, you cannot know how that will manifest. While you can be assured those gains will come in the form of learning, deepened relationships, greater self-awareness, and the generation of new value, you cannot know how and when that value will emerge, what form it might take, and how you will be changed in the seeking. You will need to practice opening to the possibility of getting lost. As poet David Wagoner says in "Lost":[9]

> Stand still. The trees ahead and the bushes beside you
> Are not lost. Wherever you are is called Here,
> And you must treat it as a powerful stranger,
> Must ask permission to know it and be known.
> The forest breathes. Listen. It answers...
> The forest knows
> Where you are. You must let it find you.

In discovery, what you don't know becomes like the "powerful stranger" who is here all the time—who must be joined, honored, and learned from. Different values come to the forefront (curiosity, play, learning from mistakes, vulnerability, transparency, courage, surrender), while other values recede into the background. Trust and shared purpose help you listen to and interpret the landscape and set and adjust your course. As you traverse the unknown, you will practice becoming finely tuned to the emergent and learn to hold on to your agendas more loosely.

In discovery, you also make use of different behaviors, practices, and tools. Your interactions with others, the way you make decisions together, and the kinds of conversations you have all shift, in ways that promote co-creation and interdependence. Loosen controls to enable shared ownership, shared leadership, and shared followership. Evolve your operating principles and apply new rules for activities like seeking funding, resourcing your efforts, complying with constraints, and assessing, reporting, and rewarding progress.

In discovery, it's also critical to set expectations and to contract appropriately (not just with others, but with yourself). Whenever your circumstances call for an adventure into the unknown—whether you're embarking out of necessity, out of a personal desire, or on the request of others—knowing what to ask for, what to promise, and what *not* to promise can make all the difference.

Remember: what's being asked of you is different than what you likely do day to day. Treating a request to discover the same way as a request to execute is a painful error. You'll need to articulate what will be different and contract carefully, identifying and discussing known constraints and risks—and talking about what you'll do when new risks and constraints show up over the horizon. Talk with others about the potential for failure and how you will share learning from both successes and failures. Develop a shared sense of just how far from the status quo you're aiming. And don't forget to contract for the possibility of returning to recontract timelines, deliverables, and resources like budget.

Insight Three: Pay attention to how you participate

Over time, active participation combined with self-awareness breeds wisdom and trust. By consciously participating in the process of discovery—where you bring your whole self to the twists and turns, the joy and pain, the moments of courage and of weakness—you will develop a deep and unshakable faith in your potential to enter the unknown, find your way through, and emerge transformed. This is how you will learn: by paying attention to both the conversation in your head and the way the landscape of your journey shifts and changes in relation to your aims, intentions, and desires. You will learn by venturing forth not just once, but over and over: by becoming a student of discovery, exploration, and the unknown.

On your journeys of discovery, you must cultivate a mindset of experimentation instead of achievement. It will make all the difference to view your efforts as an experiment—all in service to learning and better, more conscious decision-making. You'll develop a kind of freedom that helps you find new and different allies, pause now and then to reflect and assess progress, and continue to push out into the frontier beyond what's known. And when you do find yourself stuck in the pit—in the deepest and darkest Swamps of the unknown—a mindset of experimentation will help you get moving again. This is the benefit of conscious, self-aware, and accountable experimentation.

Right now, you're likely on any number of hero's journeys in both your personal and professional life. What are you learning? How might these different journeys be related and nested together? How might they point to new opportunities and futures that want to emerge?

If you search inside yourself, how would you say your experiences are helping develop the kind of faith you'll need for future journeys into the unknown? I encourage you to observe yourself along the way. Avoid getting caught up in drama of the journey you're on. Unfortunately I can't say I did this well in Europe on the Creative Leadership project. If I'm honest with myself, I was pretty unconscious during that experience. I lost sight of why I was there and how my experiences were informing where I wanted to go and who I wanted to become. I missed the opportunity at the time to look at the big picture—with the tools of accountability, self-awareness, forgiveness, and self-loving—and contribute from a place of courage, humility, and service.

SO MANY gifts can come from exploring the dynamics of discovery and reconnecting with your spirit of adventure. First, exploration returns you to the world of mystery, play, and wonder—a world that we crave but that seems less and less attainable as the obligations, routines, and pace of life increase. There are benefits to wellness, engagement, affinity, and happiness. Next, the fruits of discovery benefit you individually as well as the people in your life and the organization you work for.

When discovery combines with conscious creativity and learning, the results are remarkable: innovation and the generation of new value follow. Finally, as the rate of change quickens around you, your active engagement in conscious discovery and creativity will provide a core of stability and strength amid the chaos. You will be better positioned to learn quickly from mistakes and new information, to actively shape (and reshape) where you're headed, to explain why it's important to you, to understand what's changing and what's *not* changing, and to share more of yourself as the journey transforms you.

ASK YOURSELF...

Now, at the end of this chapter, take time to pause and reflect on the following questions.

Three Truths About the Unknown

- What is changing in your work and life that's calling for a different future?

- How might you meet these challenges with a greater sense of agency, creative accountability, and vulnerability?

- What clues might signal that "what you seek" (your hopes, dreams, and aspirations) is also "seeking you" (reaching back to help you)?

The Dynamics of Discovery

- What would it take for you to leave the comfort of the familiar and go into the depths of the unknown?

Insight One: Learn from others who blazed the trail

- What hero's journeys are you on right now in your personal or professional life? How is your creativity showing up (or not) in the way you might hope?

- What is the core question at the root of your quest?

- What are you learning about who you are—and who you are becoming?

Insight Two: Don't apply rules for execution to journeys of discovery

- How would you describe the balance in your life between execution and discovery? Which situations and circumstances could benefit from a more exploratory approach?

- If you were to write new rules to enable more exploration, what would you change? What might you engineer in—and engineer out?

Insight Three: Pay attention to how you participate

- How do you typically navigate situations where you don't know how things will turn out (e.g., jump in and figure things out along the way, wait for clarity of direction before venturing forth)?

- What can you do to strengthen your confidence—and deepen trust in yourself—to help you greet the unknown with passion instead of trepidation?

Keep Going!

• • •

Find out more about differences and similarities between popular descriptions of the creative process and the process of innovation. Go to **creativetogetherresources.com** or scan this QR code:

Flexing Your Superpowers

• • • • •

THE JOURNEY to bring creativity forward in your work and everyday life starts as an inner journey. It's about you—shifting into the new story, claiming your potential, and consciously bringing your creativity center stage with you as you make decisions, take action, innovate, and learn from what emerges.

Once your creativity is activated, four Superpowers come into play: 1) Creative License, 2) Questions, 3) Seeing Beyond, and 4) Learning. These are special gifts that animate and amplify the dynamism of creativity in your life. They are also critical for navigating the tests you'll encounter on any creative quest into the unknown. Learning how to flex and strengthen them will help you play, adventure, discover, and create in ways that transform both you and the world in your sights.

Superpower One: Creative License

• • •

Most every week, our Creative Leadership team gathered in one of the small towns near Lausanne, Switzerland, to learn new concepts from Josef. On any given day, he might teach us about stress and its relationship to creativity or disclose how "microfield evaluation" works and how to use it to diagnose forces that drive behavior. He might explain "transcalar self-similarity" or the factors contributing to Creative Leadership. It was heady stuff, and somehow, we had to find ways to turn these extremely obtuse and complicated concepts into services that the firm could sell to clients.

After one of these weekly sessions (and a lot of "talking *about*" things), I decided to act. After all, in my consulting practice back in Laguna Beach, I specialized in designing fun, engaging tools and materials that brought complex concepts to life. And it had been a while since our team had produced anything concrete. The partners of the firm were gathering in a few weeks; it would be great to have something tangible for them to see and hold in their hands—something that could help explain in everyday language how the key concepts of Creative Leadership fit together.

I took a risk and designed what I called a "learning wheel"—a playful tool for engaging with the concepts we had been exploring. I wrote the content, sketched out the design specs, had the wheels printed, and brought them to our weekly session two weeks later, just in time for the partners meeting. To my dismay, Josef was furious and deeply offended. By inventing this tool and presenting concepts in an interactive way in everyday language, in his mind I had cheapened and debased his content. Worse still, I had taken initiative without permission.

What I did—and was reprimanded for—is what I call Creative License, your first Superpower. Creative License has been given other names: some call it poetic license, others, artistic license. But Creative License is not limited to a particular domain like the arts, literature, or sciences. It's at the root of innovation in any domain. Fundamentally it's about courage; you exercise Creative License when you claim the freedom to invent, alter, combine, bend, deconstruct, and play with possibilities and constraints. Instead of seeking permission, you authorize yourself to choose where and how to apply this license. You don't ignore constraints, conventions, and rules. Instead you claim your creative right to address them in novel ways: to speak up and make suggestions, improvise, take risks, and think differently. You might even take the path of *least* permission.

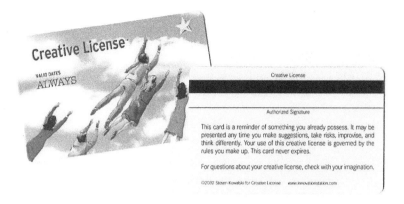

Does it sound risky? It is. One reason Creative License is a Super-power is that it has the potential to shake things up. There can be a price to pay for the choice to proceed without permission—especially when you are playing around with "the rules." If things go well, your efforts may be greeted with accolades by some and muted applause from others. In my case, Josef was angry. After the partners reacted positively to what I had produced, he reluctantly approved. But if taking Creative License generates uncertain or shaky outcomes—especially at first—you may find yourself facing tough opposition.

That's why taking Creative License is a courageous act. You invent despite self-doubt and with full knowledge of the risk you're taking in the face of constraints both real and perceived. You choose to act in the face of resistance, honor your own voice, and potentially risk your reputation and brand in service to living out your imaginings and convictions.

Claim *your* Creative License by practicing five actions that amplify your potential.

Action One: Speak up

Your ideas and unique perspective are valuable assets when you work on something new and different, wrestle with uncertainty, or improve results. The questions that follow can improve how your ideas are received when you speak up and contribute:

- How might your idea resonate? Does it feel timely, desirable, and relevant to potential users or customers? Be sure to assess the timing, calculate readiness for disturbance, and weigh the risk/benefit ratio to help ensure that your ideas serve the circumstances and purpose of your quest.

- Does the way you share your idea appear to make others "wrong" for how things are currently done? Check to make sure that you are offering ideas with curiosity and in a way that honors everyone involved.

- Are your ideas tied to your sense of identity? If they are, when your ideas are rejected, you can feel rejected. Practice detaching your ideas from your identity—giving the gifts of your suggestions freely, without expectation.

Action Two: Improvise

In creative activity, at any number of moments you will not know what to do next. That is the nature of creative work. You are going into uncharted territory without a clear path. But too often, people stop when they don't know what to do next. Sometimes the next best action is to improvise: to think on your feet and make up an answer or solution based on your experience, knowledge, and wisdom. As you improvise, you engage in playful irreverence—a kind of mischievousness. You play with the rules. Boundaries become more permeable. You're more focused on experiments and iteration than on achieving outcomes exactly as you have envisioned them.

When you improvise, your choices set off a chain of events that can bring surprise, possibility, and opportunity. "Happy accidents" frequently occur. With Creative License, you're open to serendipity and you're an opportunist—noticing possibilities and seizing them. You're like a jaguar that knows when to pounce, when to wait in stealth, and when to rest. The key is to adopt a growth mindset when you improvise. That means you apply whatever you learn from improvising to your next step—whether or not things work out as you'd expected.

Action Three: Reframe

Every day you will be faced with circumstances that challenge you. Many of these challenges will push your buttons, triggering old habits of reaction that diminish access to your creative potential. Emotions can well up and obscure your view of novel responses. But remember: this is exactly the kind of situation where creativity is needed. Your Creative License empowers you to look at these challenges in new ways. Instead of indulging your habitual response, get curious about how you might take an alternative point of view. Challenge your assumptions. Practice empathizing with people who raise your ire. Make up a different story about what is happening and why. And then, look back at yourself and your circumstances and find a different path forward.

Action Four: Take risks

Exercising Creative License is not for the faint of heart. If you want different results, you need the courage to leave the safety of the status quo, break with tradition, admit you don't know all the answers, and stick your neck out anyway. However, it can be helpful to distinguish between a risk that is truly unknown and one you might call a "smart risk." Both may be needed on a creative journey into the unknown. Smart risks are based on the foundation of your current expertise, the available data, your knowledge, and your assessment of the probability of success. These risks are easier because they make sense.

But there will be other times when you'll have to take a chance you can't really explain. These risks are harder. You will need guidance from a strong internal barometer—a deep faith that whatever happens, you will be OK. Not because it will turn out the way you'd prefer, but because you know that your gift—your creativity—will help you navigate through whatever you discover. I encourage you to take Creative License even when it requires this kind of a leap of faith.

Action Five: Think differently

Your creative purposes are open-ended: there is no one right answer. To get to the best possible answers, try different angles and break out of routines of thinking. If you typically plot out a path before acting, try jumping in without a plan. If you tend to plow forward and see what happens, try strategizing a bit first. If you like spreadsheets, try drawing a picture. If you like to think things through on your own, ask people around you for their perspective instead and seek to understand how they arrived at their view. If you think more linearly and sequentially, practice noticing patterns and seeing relationships between things. If you wait for ideas to be "baked" before sharing them, take a risk to put out a messy fragment of an idea and see what happens. Most of all, have fun flexing your Creative License to amplify your potential.

Superpower Two: Questions

• • •

At first, Questions might seem too simple for a Superpower. We ask questions all day long. And likely you've noticed how many questions I pose throughout this book and at the end of each chapter. That's because asking questions—though seemingly easy—is at the heart of initiating and sustaining a creative quest. But there is a distinct art in asking *powerful* questions—questions that can change the trajectory of your creative journey. What makes a question powerful? I've asked this of hundreds of people over the years. The most common responses I get are "It's open," "It makes you think," "It challenges assumptions," or "It helps people focus."

All these are true, and yet the two most important aspects of a great question are that the question fits the circumstances and that it is asked with a curious mindset. Great questions help move things forward because they are poignant and relevant when they are asked. The intention behind the question is genuine curiosity, learning, and positive intent. In many ways, asking a great question resembles the way Michelangelo described his process of sculpting. He famously said, the idea is there, locked inside. All you have to do is remove the excess stone.[10] A great question unlocks value in the moment and reveals something that was previously obscured.

At the heart of this Superpower is a deep understanding of how questions work. Different questions yield different types of answers. The questions we ask focus energy and attention in a particular direction. The type of answer is literally coded into the structure of the question. By understanding the answers different types of question are likely to evoke, you can become more intentional about which questions you ask and when. Explore the six types of questions that follow. As you do, reflect on times when you used these questions effectively—and times when you may have used them ineffectively.

Type One: Yes or no questions

Yes or no questions are invaluable for getting things done—for decisiveness, prioritization, and strategic focus. Sometimes—like in an emergency—you need to hear, simply, yes or no. Other times a yes/no question calls forth an opportunity for courageous authenticity that brings needed clarity to relationships and interactions with others. But this type of question is commonly misused when we face the unknown. Yes/no questions during discovery can shut down further inquiry and stifle exploration of alternatives. Think of how different it is to ask, "What resources do we need?" (open-ended) rather than "Do we have the resources we need?" (yes/no). You may be so accustomed to misusing yes/no questions that you don't even notice.

I challenge you to use yes/no questions carefully. Practice for at least a week answering yes/no questions with a simple yes or no. It's harder than you think. We're so conditioned to guess at what's behind the question that we embellish our answers with explanations and rationales. Instead, simply answer yes or no, and wait for others to ask any follow-up questions. Notice when you are asking yes/no questions and pay attention to the answers you get in return. Practicing will help you learn the power of this type of question as well as how to use it more appropriately.

Type Two: Leading questions

We all have been on the receiving end of a leading question. "Don't you think that Shaina is right when she says we should... ?" "Wouldn't you agree that... ?" "Isn't it wrong to assume... ?" I encourage you to cut leading questions out of your repertoire completely. These questions, by their very nature, are the opposite of what people report makes a question great. They are crafted to tell you the answer you're supposed to report back. They are designed to box in your response, shut down alternatives, and build a case of support for a particular position. When asked by someone in power, they carry weight that can be especially damaging to creativity, exploration, and discovery.

It can be tricky to answer a leading question differently than with the expected answer. People often remain silent when one is asked, or they give some subtle indication of agreement through their body language. But there may be times when you're called to demonstrate courageous authenticity: to speak up, challenge the asker, stand on principle, and hold your ground if you disagree. "What if Shaina is not right?" "Can we explore this further before deciding?" and "How might we reframe our options?" are examples of curious questions that can help diffuse a leading question. Make your decision carefully about when to answer and how—and work diligently to eliminate leading questions from your own repertoire.

Type Three: Action questions

Action questions help move ideas into implementation and achieve desired results. "What is the next step?" "Who is accountable?" "When do we expect to achieve our milestones?" "Who should we consult with and inform?" These kinds of questions are probably very familiar to you—and it's likely you've become adept at asking them. That's because we all get rewarded for getting things done. But you might default to them even when they are not appropriate.

The challenge with action questions comes when you want to explore, adventure, and discover. Remember that all journeys of discovery require some measure of unknowing. If you ask action questions too early, you can undercut exploration and the value that comes from not knowing. In your rush for clarity and some measure of certainty, you may prematurely jump to action questions to limit ambiguity. Instead, get curious about what is driving the use of this type of question. Is it simply habit? Is it fear? Are you overwhelmed? Who might you be trying to please? Get curious and ask a good insight question instead.

Type Four: Insight questions

There is a set of questions that yield greater depth of understanding about whatever you are focused on. They provoke reflection and contemplation, and often can't be answered as quickly as action questions. "What is it we don't yet understand?" "How will my ideas impact the status quo?" "What are we missing?" "What is my vision of breakthrough?" "If we're successful, who will benefit and how?" These types of questions are the ones people identify most when I ask, "What makes a question great?" That's because they are so refreshing in our world of speed and action.

Insight questions help uncover root causes and influencing factors. They are essential for taking an enterprise and systems view: for seeing a situation, problem, or opportunity from multiple perspectives. They open spaces for wonder and curiosity—especially when you ask them in the spirit of learning. Give them time to breathe. And as you do, look for the deeper insights that arise when you pause to understand things.

Type Five: Divergent questions

Divergent questions open up possibility and prompt ideation, exploration, and expanded thinking. They are best asked when the field is open and all options are on the table without concern for constraints. The most famous divergent question could be, "How might I/we... " This question was popularized by the folks at IDEO in the process of Design Thinking. It generates an open field of possibility that calls creativity forward. One thing to keep in mind is that asking *how* is different than asking *what*. "How might I... " will orient your exploration toward answers and solutions.

As an alternative, you can also ask, "What if... ?" to activate imagination and explore options without constraints. Asking "What if... ?" does not necessarily point toward a solution. Instead, it asks you to

exercise your imagination—to illuminate consequences and implications. "What if I try a different approach?" "What if my skills are losing
their value in a changing world?" "What if I reimagine the value I can
bring?" These questions are powerful because they create tension. For
that reason, they can be both exciting and disturbing. Check with your
intuition to help you identify the best timing and forums for asking
"What if... ?" questions that may be controversial.

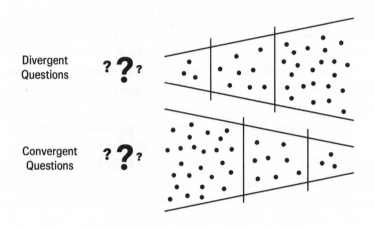

Type Six: Convergent questions

While it's important to generate enthusiasm for possibilities, it's
equally important to narrow options and focus on the highest priorities and best solutions and approaches. This means asking questions
about feasibility, viability, and impact in service to making effective
decisions. "What are the trade-offs?" "What unintended consequences
might result from this or that option?" "Why wouldn't I want to take
this particular course of action or decision?" "What different scenarios
might result, including worst-case scenarios?" "How might my biases
be influencing our assessment of different options?"

Because convergence naturally involves pruning and narrowing,
these questions can feel like a downer. They can shut down exploration if they are asked too soon or unintentionally diminish the effort
you have expended to come up with possibilities. But convergent

questions are critical for turning ideas into value—for meeting possibility with constraint. Here, your intention to catalyze will make all the difference. Ask convergent questions with true curiosity. Carry the enthusiasm from ideation forward—but turn it into excited anticipation for the value that solutions will bring. If you think it might be too early for convergent questions, hold back.

NOW THAT you have a better sense of how questions work, the next step in flexing this Superpower is to consciously break your habits. Yes, we all fall into habits—asking certain questions across multiple situations even when they may not be appropriate.

What kinds of questions do you typically ask? I have a habit of asking provocative insight questions even though they may be disruptive and ill-timed. You might ask action-oriented questions and miss the opportunity to dig deeper for insight. Or you might know someone who regularly asks questions that narrow options—unintentionally dampening enthusiasm. Maybe you keep questions to yourself, rarely asking them unless it feels safe to do so. Whether you are naturally a skeptic, an enthusiast, a dissenter, a systems thinker, a detail person, or a visionary, you will likely have favorite and habitual questions that you ask.

Habits are hard to break! Become a student of questions. Listen to yourself and listen to the people around you. Notice what kinds of questions you ask and when you ask them. Notice the ones in your head that you don't voice out loud as well as the ones you ask without thinking. Pay attention to your motivation and the intent behind your questions. Curiosity, accompanied by a great question that is well timed and posed with positive intent, is powerful indeed.

And now, practice. Try out different kinds of questions in different settings and take note of the response. Practice at home as well as in professional settings. Commit to using this Superpower as a source of positive forward movement—to ask questions with the intent of learning, improving, supporting, and clarifying. As you practice, you will learn how to better use this Superpower to amplify your creative potential.

Superpower Three: Seeing Beyond

• • •

Seeing Beyond is one of your most important Superpowers, yet one of the most elusive. It is important because it directly connects you to the source of new ideas and new possibilities. Innovating and changing the status quo is all about looking past what exists today to imagine, invent, and evolve something different. But Seeing Beyond is elusive because the "apparent" is so tangible and prominent in our lives; we're surrounded by artifacts of the familiar and immersed in routine patterns and habits. Our day-to-day lives are shaped by structures that constrict and constrain us in ways we no longer challenge.

Think of the house or apartment you live in. The walls, floors, ceilings, hallways, open spaces, doors, and windows all shape your movement inside of, and into and out of, the house. You don't challenge the walls and test them to see if they'll give way. You don't question the doorways. Unless you are in the midst of a remodeling project, you simply accept the structure, live in your home, and move around within the pathways its shape allows. The apparent operates in a similar way in our lives.

The apparent is also alive in ways that are not as tangible as the walls and doors of a home. Each of us has actively constructed an invisible world of what is apparent in our minds and memory—as facts and interpretations—based on what we've learned and experienced. We use this web of constructs to decide what's possible, to assess what's changeable, and to predict what we think will happen tomorrow. Your beliefs, assumptions, and values are like the walls and doorways inside your mind that shape the movement of ideas and give room (or not) to new possibilities. They have a profound impact on whether you try, test, push, experiment, and question what you "know for sure, that just might not be so."[11]

For years, as I've worked with people to develop this Superpower, I've discovered three distinct practices that form its core: 1) *Looking near* to see what is right in front of us that we, and others, are missing; 2) *Looking clear* to see through our filters, beliefs, assumptions, preferences, and biases; 3) *Looking far* to see around the corner and forecast and imagine alternative futures. Each of these three practices has enormous power to generate opportunity.

Practice One: Looking near

In one of my all-time-favorite Gary Larson cartoons, a man in a karate uniform is intently focused on chopping a piece of wood that's stretched over some bricks. He's so focused on the task that he doesn't notice an entire brick wall just about to crush him from behind. This cartoon is a powerful reminder that when I am focused, my ability to notice other things is limited. I can easily miss important details about what is right in front of me (or behind me) that I am not aware of.

Failing to see what is right in front of us might lead to an impending mishap that would be obvious with just a few yards of perspective. We also might fail to connect things. Consider for a moment that our human ancestors created the first wheel over 5,100 years ago. It's at least that long ago based on radiocarbon dating of the oldest wheel found in the Ljubljana marshes of Slovenia. So, why did it take until 1972 for a patent on luggage with wheels? We were able to put a human on the moon and develop the foundations of the internet before someone thought about putting wheels and luggage together.

We also might pass up an obvious opportunity because we are fixated on our plan. We pass people by who might be untapped allies with great insights. We miss "dumb" ideas that are floating around but not explored. Or we may fail to recognize that we are pursuing the wrong goal—one that will not yield desired results. Other times we pursue the right goal—but do it in familiar or traditional ways that no longer work effectively.

On journeys of discovery, missing these clues can lead you down dead ends, take you off course, and leave value on the table. The trick is to gather alternative perspectives and step back even a few metaphorical yards from your own view. That's when you're more likely to notice if familiar tools and approaches are obscuring an easier or better option. To look near, practice these activities that amplify your creative potential:

- Put yourself in unfamiliar territory. "Get out of the building" and take a different perspective. Observe things as if you were visiting from another planet. *From this perspective, what looks strange, surprising, and interesting to you?*

- Pause, reflect, and take a meditation/relaxation break. *What more can you see once you have refreshed your energy and perspective?*

- Transform the ordinary into the extraordinary. Like Andy Warhol when he turned a row of Campbell's tomato soup cans into a work of art, practice seeing anything and everything with passionate interest, open eyes, and an open heart.[12] *What's ordinary in your world that could become something extraordinary?*

- Set aside all the ideas and solutions you've already had. *How long can you suspend ideas or solutions before "not knowing" becomes uncomfortable?*

- Make fun of what is most revered and/or considered untouchable. *What do you notice in reaction to even the suggestion of this practice?*

- Seek the simplest possibility. *How might over-complications be obscuring what is at the heart or core of something you care about?*

What you are focusing on might be pulling your attention away from opportunities right in front of you. Are you focused on executing and achieving goals? Are you enamored with solutions you've already identified? Are you overly focused on protecting boundaries and turf? Staying curious and using these practices for looking near can be a fantastic source of opportunity and possibility. What other ways can you activate this practice?

Practice Two: Looking clear

Years ago, I was flying into Los Angeles for a conference. As the plane descended, I noticed a dense, hazy brown smog covering the entire metropolitan area. The sun was glinting off it as if it were solid. On the ground, the air seemed thick—even though the sun was shining through. At lunch that day, I commented to a friend about how thick the smog seemed and how obvious it had been from up in the air. He replied, defensively, "What are you talking about? It's a beautiful day!"

I was surprised at how willing he was to argue that I was wrong and that it was, in fact, a beautiful day. It was a striking example of how the frame we see things through shapes what's in the picture, what is unseen, and what we might not even want to see. That frame is made up of a collection of biases, filters, attachments, assumptions, expectations, beliefs, mental models, and judgments. The more we confirm, through our experiences, that our frame is serving us, the more solid it gets and the more it obscures what else might be possible.

Clearing out the smog that's formed by our unconscious frames is a lifelong pursuit. It's tough work because, for us as for my friend, the smog has become invisible. We've stopped noticing. And like so many people who believe they are not creative, the smog of our old story obscures the truth of a new story about our creative potential. Without an unexpected or traumatic event that provides perspective, or someone to point out a different way of seeing things, we may fail to notice these inner mental structures and fail to understand their consequences.

And there are consequences—not only to what you see and don't see, but to the decisions you make. I saw this so clearly some years back when I worked with the leadership team of an internal service organization within a large corporation. This group was so oriented toward pleasing that they couldn't say no when their customers asked for something. They agonized over every detail to provide the most perfect solutions—stopping themselves from taking risks or trying something new out of fear of how customers might react. What I noticed, from the outside looking in, was that complying and pleasing had become go-to tendencies. It was even biasing which people they hired to join the group.

The first step in looking clear is to become curious about what is clouding the clarity of your view. What are some of the old stories, unquestioned interpretations, untested assumptions, and non-negotiables that may be obscuring new opportunities? What do you take for granted? What are you sure is true, which might actually be an interpretation? How are your unconscious biases influencing what you're attracted to, what you shun, and what you believe is possible? I encourage you to spend time reflecting on questions like these on a regular basis to help reveal the smog that might have accumulated in the frame of your view.

The next step is to clear away that smog. Practice listening—deeply, and with your whole self. Listen with more than your ears; listen with your heart, your eyes, and your undivided attention. Listen to the stories you tell. Do they open possibility and opportunity or shut them down? Do they promote fear or control? Listen for when you're defending a rule or arguing against a possibility. And then, practice asking questions. Ask "What if...?" and "Why not...?" questions to surface alternative perspectives. Ask insight questions to dig for root causes and to understand how your filters came to be, how they are influencing your choices, and how they may be limiting the activation of your creative potential.

Practice Three: Looking far

Remember I said that Seeing Beyond is both important and elusive? As tricky as it can be to look clear, looking far can be even more elusive. It's hard to see around the corner. The future never provides us with firsthand information. We must infer, guess, and anticipate what might happen over the horizon and how trends and clues we can see today might collide and disrupt things tomorrow. This is what the Pixar team was up to when they worked out different scenarios for Carl in the movie *Up*—imagining alternative futures that may or may not occur.

Looking far requires that you pay attention. Then you notice when the signals and signs, the fragments of information, the wonderings, and the obstacles you encounter point to something likely to happen down the road. Maybe you notice a trend or pattern that seems odd. An emerging technology might hint at disruption on the horizon. Maybe you have an inkling that a social trend might collide with diminishing resources in the ecosystem. Whatever the clues, when you've got your purpose squarely in your sights and you're paying attention, these signals are gifts. But you must have a curious eye—watching carefully while you step into the unknown. That's when you're better able to generate value from what you notice.

- **Notice every moment.** Remember our three core truths: 1) there are multiple possible futures ahead of you; 2) you have agency in helping shape what happens, but you are not in control; and 3) the outcomes you imagine are reaching back to help you realize them. In fact, the clues for what's coming are all around you—right now. What catches your eye throughout your day? What might it signal about what's ahead? Spot the clues right in front of you about the future that is reaching back to you. Practice looking with "hungry eyes."[13]

- **Look through wide-angle, macro, and telephoto lenses.** Do you typically look for the big picture, pay attention to the details up close, or seek to bring the long view into focus? Using each of these lenses—and rapidly switching between them—is incredibly valuable when you're in discovery mode. Through a wide-angle lens you can see across boundaries and look for the higher principles that underlie dynamics. You spot clues that illuminate the big picture: the ecosystem of interconnections, interdependencies, and networks that might influence the future. Alternatively, a macro lens provides a view of detail, magnifying fine distinctions that can illuminate what might otherwise go unnoticed. And through a telephoto lens, you see further ahead than you're typically able. You can strategize, chart your direction, identify milestones and markers for progress, and scope out likely "oases"[14] where rest and recharge make sense along the way.

- **Avoid multitasking.** In our modern world, with multiple devices and the accelerating barrage of inputs and obligations, multitasking has emerged as a strategy for managing it all. But multitasking is no friend of creativity and discovery. In fact, it's a fallacy—we're just rapidly shifting our attention. And there's a "switching cost." You will miss connections, details, and clues that point to future opportunities and emerging possibilities. You will also make mistakes. Take, for instance, one occasion when I was on the phone talking with my mother. I was at work and the emails were piling up. When she started talking in depth about someone I didn't know, I took the opportunity to respond to an email. Suddenly, I heard my mother say, "Great! We'll see you in three weeks." I had inadvertently said yes, I would come to Florida to visit, without realizing what I was doing. Avoid multitasking—especially when you are seeking value that may be hiding in between things, out of sight, or in scattered fragments that don't yet make sense.

Seeing Beyond kicks into high gear when attention is mixed with curiosity. Despite how challenging it can be, you *can* learn to look past the familiar, past the things you take for granted, and step aside from your habits and routines to reveal opportunities and breakthroughs. Can you imagine how many other innovations like wheeled luggage are all around you right now? Seeing Beyond is at the heart of creativity. It is a critical Superpower on any journey into the unknown.

Superpower Four: Learning

• • •

Your fourth Superpower is Learning. Creativity, transformation, and learning go hand in hand. Individually, all three result in the birth of something new. Together, these forces are at the root of all successful journeys of exploration and discovery.

With creativity, new forms, solutions, and possibilities come forward in response to problems and opportunities we face or design for ourselves. In transformation, new ways of being emerge. We are reshaped, reborn, and made anew through the integration of experiences, tests and obstacles, and encounters with allies. In learning, new meaning is generated as we construct knowledge and wisdom in the space between what we already know and what we encounter. Through exposure to people and to new concepts, and through participation in experiences, we build understanding that enables different choices and more effective action. Learning is an active, generative process of weaving and revising our web of knowledge.

When learning is most powerful, it is "indelible"—connected to a deeply meaningful purpose, to our pursuit of competence and our sense of identity, and to meaningful progress toward desired aims. This is the kind of learning that resulted from my three-year European adventure on the Creative Leadership project. In the face of struggle and adversity, joy and discovery, and success and failure, I learned lessons that are forever woven into the fabric of my being: lessons about myself and how I respond to ambiguity and uncertainty, as well as lessons about the barriers and enablers to creativity and innovation.

The funny thing is, we're learning all the time—in every moment. Most of the time, though, we're simply not paying attention and so the learning goes unnoticed. On journeys of discovery, however, you can't afford to be asleep at the wheel. Your openness to learn—and your awareness of what's happening while you are learning—will have a profound impact on the outcomes you attain. In many cases, the learning in and of itself will be one of the greatest gifts of your quest, though you might not realize the full implications until later.

Activating this Superpower requires awareness. You need to pause along the way to take stock of what you've learned and how it's changing the way you see the world. This can be especially challenging if you're making progress and "succeeding." When we achieve the goals we set for ourselves, it's easy to move on and skip the step of pausing to *have* the value and impact of what we learned. When we fail at something we care about, we often want to turn away and avoid looking deeply at what happened and why. Here again, we miss out on some of the richest by-products of adventuring into the unknown.

As you flex this Superpower, activate these five elements that amplify Learning.

Element One: A learning mindset

When I became a manager for the first time, I remember being terrified that people would find out I had no clue how to manage. My strategy was to act as if I *did* know—which was a disaster. Mostly I ended up repeating all the mistakes that I'd experienced when I was being managed. What I didn't have was a learning mindset. Instead of being curious when things didn't go well, I tried to avoid the situation. Instead of reflecting on the consequences of my actions, I blamed others. Instead of asking for feedback, I made excuses for my behavior. And instead of experimenting and trying out new approaches, I stuck to my guns and defended my ground. A learning mindset would have made all the difference, including humility for what I didn't know, openness to new ways of doing things, willingness to "unlearn" things I was convinced were true (but weren't), and self-awareness about who I was—and who I needed to become to be successful.

Element Two: Networks and community

Learning is fundamentally a social activity. Traditional views of learning typically focus on the individual. But learning takes place most naturally in interaction between people. We rely on others more than we know—as role models, troubleshooters, critics, approvers, teachers, and collaborators. That's why it's critical that you develop "responsive networks" to help you leverage the social nature of learning. These are both formal and informal networks: some are curated while others spring up organically. As you build these networks and participate in them, pay attention to how you are connected to others through a common purpose. Share ideas generously and provide honest input that contributes to creative outcomes. Find ways to strengthen connections and pay special attention to how you influence each other when you share expertise and wisdom.

Element Three: Experimentation and iteration

As much as I work in the arena of creativity and innovation, you'd think I'd be a master at experimenting and iterating. But alas, I tend to want things to be successful on the first try. This has really been a challenge for me over the years—and I'm still working on it. Why is it so hard? Part of it likely is my upbringing; there wasn't much tolerance for mess and unfinished things that weren't "right." Part of it is the environments I've been working in—critical cultures that demand all i's be dotted and t's be crossed. Whatever has led me to aim for "done" on the first try, it's no longer working. And so I've become a student of experimentation and iteration.

I've discovered that experimenting, iterating, and prototyping are so much more fun than aiming for perfect the first time. Try practicing any of the following approaches:

- Design a prototype of an idea or solution with the intent to fail and learn. By purposely aiming to fail, you test the limits, edges, and rough surfaces of a solution.

- Involve others earlier in the process—especially people who are outside your familiar circle. This means taking a risk by sharing something that's not yet finished or may not yet make sense to get input and to watch people struggle and play with it.

- Allow things to be messy while new connections, new ideas, and new solutions emerge.

- Be willing to start over, throw away parts of your creation, break things apart, and even stop the action.

- Be clear about the outcome that's driving your exploration, the hypothesis you're testing, the assumptions you've made, and what "done" looks like. How will you know whether to continue refining your solution or stop in service to other priorities?

Element Four: The Bump Zone

Along the path of learning, especially indelible learning, there is what's called (technically) the "zone of proximal development."[15] I call it the Bump Zone because that's where learning is amplified, and you get bumped forward in leaps and bounds. Here, your circumstances are pregnant with learning potential. There are more unknowns than you're used to. You're stretched outside your comfort zone—but not stretched so far that it shuts down your ability to think and process new information. The tension is critical: a window of opportunity opens that bumps you up to new levels of understanding and mastery.

You are squarely in the Bump Zone when you are at the center of purpose, possibility, and constraint. In that intersection, you know what you're committed to, but you don't know how you'll get there. The tension that's generated activates your creative potential. Then you can look beyond your own backyard to get exposure to new possibilities, new alternatives, and new options. You can allow yourself to not know in advance of moving forward and acting. You can find those people and experiences that bring you in proximity with important lessons on your journey. And you can learn (and unlearn) as you step out of the familiar.

Element Five: Learning to learn

Learning to learn is ultimately about self-awareness: paying attention to how you learn and how you can improve the power of learning. Get to know yourself as a learner. Do you learn best by listening and watching others, or by taking action and trying things out? Maybe you learn best by gathering information from reading and research. With a deeper awareness of your patterns and preferences, you can take charge of your learning process and consciously attend to and improve how you learn. When familiar methods are not yielding value, you can challenge yourself to try different approaches.

Learning is a vital Superpower because it's a force for change and transformation—an active process of "becoming." The key to activating this Superpower is self-awareness during action. You learn when you act and risk trying something new, while at the same time courageously reflecting on how experience sheds new light on what you already know. You learn when you relax your attachment to what you think is true. You learn when you step into unknowingness with an open mind and an open heart.

TOGETHER, YOUR four Superpowers—Creative License, Questions, Seeing Beyond, and Learning—amplify the gift of your creativity. You don't have to be a superhero like Wonder Woman, Superman, or Thor. What's exciting about these Superpowers is that they are available to everyone. Remember: it's not creativity that's special, it's *you*. It's how you bring your passions, your experiences, and your hopes and dreams into the world. With your Superpowers, you can animate and amplify the dynamism of creativity in your life. I encourage you to flex and strengthen each of them as you confront the tests in your path, and as you play, adventure, and create in ways that transform both you and the world around you.

ASK YOURSELF...

Now, at the end of this chapter, take time to pause and reflect on the following questions.

- Which of your Superpowers are more familiar? Which might require attention and practice to develop greater strength?

- Where and how might you practice?

Creative License

- What is your experience with taking Creative License? What happens when you claim permission, break the rules, and make up new rules?

- How might "courageous, playful irreverence" benefit a current project or endeavor?

Questions

- Which kinds of questions are your natural go-tos—and which might be helpful to add to your repertoire?

- What practices could help you bring more conscious choice to the questions you ask in different contexts?

Seeing Beyond

- What might be getting in your way of looking near, looking clear, and looking far? What can you practice to help focus your attention?

Learning

- In your work and life, where do you have opportunities to experiment and iterate? What small, scrappy steps can you take—and learn from—that will illuminate different options?

- What can you do today to stretch yourself beyond the familiar? What value might come from pushing past what feels comfortable and safe?

- What makes learning "indelible" for you?

Keep Going!

• • •

Check out my in-depth article about Learning to Learn—to help your team increase the speed and impact of productivity, work together more effectively, and innovate. Go to **creativetogetherresources.com** or scan this QR code:

5

Navigating Tests

• • • • •

I'VE SPENT much of my life experiencing and studying the hero's journey. More than twelve major moves over the years took me to completely new places. I've changed careers multiple times, shifting the focus of my work into new arenas where I had little experience. Through it all, I learned that on any journey into the unknown, there are common tests along the way. These include learning to trust yourself and others, getting stuck in "the pit" and finding your way out, struggling with the will to persevere, having the courage to become vulnerable, and fighting forces that thwart the realization of your purpose.

I'm also deeply familiar with the kinds of tests we all face as we activate creative potential to spark innovation. And there's an overlap—a common set that are likely both when you express your creative potential and when you venture forth on journeys of discovery in our modern world. These are the five tests we'll explore here: 1) the Blank Canvas, 2) Mistakes and Failure, 3) Time and Timing, 4) Obstacles, and 5) the Swamp.

Each of these tests has a "villain" who acts to undermine your creative expression and your progress through the unknown. If you pay close attention, you will notice that these villains are actually different manifestations of the ultimate villain: *fear*. Depending on the test, fear may cloak itself as self-doubt, as impatience, as protecting, as your Inner Critic, or as control. Each of these manifestations of fear is best met with one or more of your Superpowers.

While no heads-up about these tests will take the place of the learning that comes from direct experience, I hope this chapter can serve to guide and coach you. Then, as tests appear, you'll be more prepared to meet each one with awareness and tools for navigating through.

Test One: The Blank Canvas

• • •

Back in 1981, I was really struggling. I had worked hard to get into Brown University, the school of my dreams. For three years I studied art, philosophy, semiotics, and communications. While I believed I was learning and growing, I felt lost. I yearned for something deeper. I felt like I didn't know who I was or what path I wanted to pursue. One of my professors even remarked, "If you ever find anything that works for you as a career, it will be a miracle." Without much keeping me there, I decided to take a year off. Secretly, I wasn't sure I would ever return.

I headed out to California. I took a couple of "crappy jobs" and ended up as a retail salesclerk in an art materials store in Venice Beach. It made sense, given my fine arts studies, although the owner of the store couldn't figure out why someone who had attended Brown wanted to work in his store. I was grateful for the job.

Oddly enough, the store was named after the Tibetan mystical power called Ashe. This word describes the space of mind before the first thought, the first gesture, and the first mark or stroke on a blank page or canvas. In this space of mind lies confidence and compassion when approaching the blankness. Back then, I didn't give much thought to the store's name or what it meant. Upon reflection, I don't think I demonstrated much Ashe in my life back then. Most of the time I felt scared, like I didn't have a clue. Little did I know how powerful this theme would become in the many moves and changes I would experience over the years.

In actuality, the blank canvas is an illusion. Even at birth, we already bring experience to whatever we face. As we move through the landscape of our lives, we continue to build expertise, wisdom, intuition, skill, and knowledge as we face new challenges and opportunities. Why, then, do we shrink from the blankness of the unknown? I've learned it is fear that immobilizes us when we face what seems like a blank canvas. Facing this fear is one of our greatest tests as we seek to activate and express our creative potential. If you're like me, this is not a comfortable place. That's why Ashe—the confidence and compassion you bring here for yourself—is so critical as you take action.

There are two primary ways a blank canvas can appear in your life:

1. **Disruption and opportunity.** Sometimes, the blank canvas shows up in the form of unanticipated disruption. Something happens that you haven't consciously asked for or chosen and you find yourself face to face with the unknown. It could appear in an extreme way, like when a global pandemic erupts and completely changes every expectation of normal day-to-day life. Or maybe it shows up in a more personal way, like when your employer announces a reduction of jobs at work. Or you discover that a loved one has cancer. Other times, the blank canvas shows up as an unexpected opportunity. You get a call out of the blue from a recruiter with a job opportunity. Maybe you stumble across an idea that no one else has thought of and you see its potential. In these cases, some form of surprise catches you off guard and requires that you act into unknowingness—despite your fear.

2. **Of your own choosing.** On other occasions, you generate the conditions that give rise to the blank canvas by embarking on a path you set for yourself. You might choose to switch jobs, go back to school for an advanced degree, or volunteer to work on a challenging project at work. Maybe you leave a job to start your own business, start a family, or move to another continent to join a team (as I did). These are examples of chosen adventures, where you've consciously signed up for a creative quest. Fear of the unknown is likely to arise here as well.

The canvas shows up both as disruption and opportunity, and through active and purposeful choice. While it may be tempting to feel like a victim in the disruption—or to lament a choice that thrusts you into the unknown—the trick comes in meeting the challenge with creative accountability. Sometimes it's hard for me to remember this when I get caught up in struggles, desires, expectations, and obligations. I forget to meet my fear of the blank canvas with Ashe: with conscious confidence in my creative potential, my Superpowers, and compassion for myself.

How is the blank canvas showing up in your life? Are you greeting it with Ashe and with creative accountability? Are you stuck in fear of the unknown? Is your potential waiting, untapped, for you to bring it forward? If you are standing in front of what feels like a blank canvas, paralyzed by fear, you are failing the test. And you're not alone. Millions of people are suffering from CDD, simply by forgetting that in every moment we have access to our creative potential. The antidote to fear of the unknown is a deep faith in your creative potential.

Whether you realize it or not, your life is unfolding as an expression of your creative potential. But you are likely disconnected from the power of your creative potential if, on a regular basis, you encounter any of the following:

- Your attachments, commitments, obligations, and the consequences of your decisions feel like they're imprisoning you.

- You find yourself repeating the same activities, going through the motions, following familiar patterns, and feeling like a slave to the clock.

- You wonder why you're doing whatever it is you're doing—and wishing there were something more.

I know this place well. I've stood before this kind of blank canvas, immobilized with fear of the unknown. In one extreme instance, I stayed for years in a job where I was unhappy. Every day I faced the blank canvas—wanting to make changes and find something better for myself but afraid to act. I was so afraid to splash the paint and make that first mark, to take that first step toward something new without knowing what would come next.

Not all of your blank canvas tests will be as deep or as far-reaching as rethinking your career or making a life-changing move across the world. Ultimately, however, the test of life as a blank canvas is the most important of them all. Look around you right now and really see what you've created. Do you like it? How are the big and small strokes you've made on your canvas playing out? What has emerged from the choices you've made, the consequences of those decisions, and how you are working with what you've spun into motion? How is it playing out day to day? Are you connected to your power to create something new, or do you believe you're stuck in what you've generated?

One of your most awesome responsibilities is to face the blank canvas and dare to make new gestures and new marks. But, as I've stated, the villain lurking here is fear. Fear could cause you to turn away and avoid facing the canvas at all. The uncertainty evokes a sense of danger—especially if the stakes are high for making the wrong choice or if marks on the canvas seem irrevocable. Accurately assessing the real (rather than perceived) danger will go a long way to diffusing the fear of what might be lost.

Use your Superpowers of Creative License and Learning. Creative License, applied here at the threshold of blankness and the unknown (whether you're making your first stroke or the five thousandth), brings courage and agency to this test. You confront the fear with the freedom you claim to invent, alter, combine, bend, deconstruct, and play with possibilities and constraints. Instead of seeking permission, authorize yourself to act, decide, and to "splatter your paint" and see what happens. Learning helps bring all the wisdom from your past to put this, your most current unknown, in perspective. It helps you decide which ideas and solutions to pursue, and how to go about inventing, adapting, overcoming obstacles, reframing, and making stuff up. That's where Ashe comes in.

Test Two: Mistakes and Failure

• • •

There were so many times in Europe, working with Josef and the team, when I believed I had made a colossal mistake. I remember calling my family and telling them as much after only a few days. But I had made a big bet and I decided to stick it out. There were benefits, for sure— but for the most part, it was a disaster. We made mistake after mistake along the way, and in the end, like the team before us, we failed.

I hadn't been willing to say that out loud until I began writing this book. Failing, I've learned, is hard to admit, especially when a lot is at stake. But we make mistakes and we fail all the time. Companies have "Million-Dollar Clubs" where, to join, members made a mistake or failed in some way that cost the company more than a million dollars. There are "rubber-chicken awards" for well-intentioned projects that didn't work out. And I regularly hear people say, "We have to celebrate failure." Why go to so much trouble to normalize mistakes and failure? Why is there so much embarrassment, shame, and blame surrounding this very common experience?

I became determined to dig deeper and to understand this most human of tests and why we are so inhumane with ourselves when it happens. As I explored, I discovered that dealing with mistakes and failure is a critical test on any creative quest. As you cross into the unknown in pursuit of innovation, you will explore pathways that won't work out. You'll have to turn around. You'll get lost and need to stop. You'll join with associates and find out they are not the best traveling companions. You'll pass up others who would have been. You'll make decisions to pursue things that look good but aren't. And you'll decide not to go in directions that might have worked out. It's all part of the journey.

Take time to think about what mistakes and failure really are. How do you define mistakes and failure? How are the two outcomes similar and how are they different? Both share certain characteristics:

- Something happens that produces an unexpected and undesirable result. For example, after everything I'd invested in moving to Europe, I didn't want our Creative Leadership project to crash and burn. But it did, and it was a messy failure.

- It can be hard to admit and take ownership for what happened. This undesired part of the result is at the root of our tendency to avoid facing the outcome directly and confronting what happened. Vulnerability, courage, and compassion are required to honestly face the result.

- Some measure of error, miscalculation, misinterpretation, false expectations, untested assumptions, or an unaddressed flaw ends up contributing to undesired outcomes. In many cases, it can be challenging to tease out your responsibility in these choices and decisions.

- What happens could be seen as blameworthy, or it could be seen as praiseworthy.[16] When unintended or unexpected results arise from a violation of—or disregard for—laws, rules, regulations, and standards, we consider them blameworthy. When they come from smart risks, experiments, and exploration, we could consider them praiseworthy. But often, we treat praiseworthy failures as if they were blameworthy. The Million-Dollar Club is full of members who made mistakes or failed, but who remained employed because the results were praiseworthy—even if costly.

- There is learning potential in what transpired—whether you mine that potential or not. Both mistakes and failures can illuminate new insights and ideas, deeper awareness, and new opportunities. Without reflecting on what happened, you risk losing the one thing that is most valuable: the gift of learning. Through learning, you can avoid making even more costly mistakes in the future.

These are aspects that both mistakes and failures have in common. But there are also some differences worth noting:

- We tend to think of mistakes as more singular occurrences—not as consequential, though some can have huge implications. Failures tend to have a more cumulative feel—the result of multiple mistakes, errors, and unanticipated results.

- Mistakes have a less final feel, like an accident that happens along the way, in the flow of a bigger effort or process. Failures often feel more final, implying that something has been declared done or over—like the ending of the Creative Leadership project in Europe. Even though we made many mistakes along the way, in retrospect I wouldn't call the whole adventure a mistake. But I do call it a failure.

- Mistakes are usually more obvious, while many failures can be subtle: you can fail by falling short of expectations, by not living in the integrity of your values, and even by not recognizing your creative potential.

Think of a time when you failed at something you really cared about or made a mistake that put you in a tough position. *How did you feel?* Here, the villains you will encounter are judgment, shame, and blame. Judgment says things like "You're wrong" and "That was stupid." Shame happens when you feel that you are bad—disgraced, humiliated, and guilty of something embarrassing. And blame says things like "It's your fault." Together, these three villains would have you believe that by failing, you've done something disgraceful and blameworthy. While it may be true that in some measure you are at fault, that doesn't necessarily make you a bad person. The challenge is that these villains exaggerate. They make declarative statements that may not be wholly true. Together, they point the finger and seek to diminish you.

Be diligent about your villains. Don't fall into the villains' trap. Many practices can help, including mindfulness (reflection, compassion, meditation), humor (making the villains look foolish), and curiosity (using questions to explore what's true versus what judgment, shame, and blame would have you believe). These practices will help you "psyche out"[17] the villains and give you a clearer path to navigate through the test of Mistakes and Failure. And to get the most out of the experience, your most powerful Superpower is Learning.

Through learning, mistakes and failures become part of the evolving story of who you are and who you are becoming, instead of a stain of shame. Don't celebrate mistakes and failures—celebrate learning from them. Here is a model I developed as a guide for learning from failure:

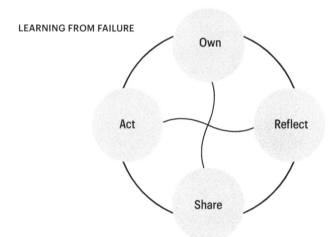

LEARNING FROM FAILURE

- **Own what happened.** Acknowledge and take appropriate accountability for mistakes and missteps early. Make it safe to discuss mistakes, failures, and unexpected results. Proactively talk about the kinds of failures that might occur given the nature of the risks you are taking. Demonstrate courage, vulnerability, and humility.

- **Reflect.** Adopt a learning mindset. Get curious and invest time to dig deeper for root causes. Look clear to see through your biases, filters, and assumptions to understand what happened. Get input and perspectives from diverse sources. Distinguish between praiseworthy and blameworthy failures.

- **Share insights with others.** Use the opportunity to build collective expertise. Openly share your analysis of the root causes of failure with others. Strengthen trust by demonstrating vulnerability and showing that it is safe to discuss unwanted outcomes. Acknowledge others when they share what they have learned from mistakes and failures.

- **Act on what you've learned.** Determine how best to proceed: stop, pause, pivot, or adjust. Apply insights to improve knowledge bases. Make changes that will improve future performance, including changing your behavior, circumstances, and approaches. Find opportunities to experiment with different ways of doing things based on what you've learned.

Keep in mind that these are not necessarily steps in a linear process. Depending on the nature of the mistake or failure, you may have to act first if there is urgency in correcting what went wrong. You might start with owning what happened, then go to action, and then to reflection and sharing. In some cases, sharing will be your vehicle for forgiveness and ownership. The beautiful gift that awaits you is not only new wisdom—it is the deepening awareness and evolution of your identity. If you avoid mistakes and failure to protect your sense of identity, you miss out on using these opportunities to reveal your humanity and vulnerability to yourself and to others. Learning from them is a courageous act.

Test Three: Time and Timing

• • •

The first time I heard the song "Time Is a Healer"[18] was when I listened to Eva Cassidy's album *Songbird*. The song celebrates the power of time to mend broken hearts because "love heals the wound that it makes." Besides being profound as a statement about love and letting go, the song speaks to me about the power and mystery of time. Time can be both a precious gift—as in the song, bringing release and relief from pain—and it can be a ruthless thief, stealing away our dreams and possibilities.

Because time can both give and take, it can be a tricky test on your journey of discovery. You'll need to respect its power and mystery—without giving up your own creative power and agency—and float freely between your aspirations and the realities of life that time keeps track of. It's important to distinguish between two ways this test can show up: 1) as the fickle trickster *timing*, known to the ancient Greeks as Kairos; and 2) as the indiscriminate consumer *time*, known as Chronos. Ultimately, timing will mess with your desire for control, while time will stir up fear. And control or fear will swamp your creativity most every time.

Timing

Not long ago, I was interviewing candidates for an open role in my team. I asked, "What are two or three things you're curious about that have nothing to do with your work?" I like this question, because it can help give me a sense of how broad and diverse people's interests are, whether they make time to follow their curiosity, and if they pursue interests outside of the workplace.

That morning I was interviewing Natalie and asked her this question. After a moment, she shared that recently she'd discovered pottery quite by accident—and was really taken by how, from a lump of clay, something beautiful (and maybe functional) would emerge. She explained how pottery helped her practice letting go and letting the form come forward without striving and without expectations of what it should become. I was excited by this, as you might imagine.

The clay, she discovered, has a lifespan—a period when it is most workable, able to be manipulated, shaped, and molded. Too early and it might be soft—not able to hold its shape. Too late and it might dry out and become flaky or brittle. In her explanation, Natalie took me right to that moment when ripeness yields the sweetest fruit. I appreciated the depth of her insight and her use of this example to explain how she approaches her work with a keen sense of the way Kairos plays with us, and we play with it.

Timing is about the right or opportune period during which our efforts are at their optimal malleability. When someone says, "It's an idea whose time has come," they're talking about right or optimal timing. It can be remarkable to notice how things happen: how opportunities show up, how people and support appear, and how ideas for solutions start showing up. While timing might not unfold according to your preferences, there's a funny way the conditions around you rise up to meet your needs.

This is where the villain of control enters in. We're all seeking some measure of control to help bring order and meaning to the chaos of life. We walk through our lives with agendas—those plans we carry around for getting things done. In and of themselves, agendas are simply a part of being human and of living our lives with intention and planning. But on a journey of discovery, you are not in control of the timing. If you become more focused on achieving your preset plan than on noticing what is happening around you, you might ignore the signs that say, "The road ahead is closed. Rethink your route." As hard as you try, you can't force it. Instead, be clear about your purpose and watch for signals that the timing is right.

You can also prepare to capture opportunity when it shows up. This is what I call "strategic stealth." You have a vision for breakthrough, and you wait, ready to pounce when the timing shifts. This dance between waiting and action is a compelling part of the test of Timing. Listen inwardly to the subtle urgings from your intuition to discern when to pause, when to press forward in the face of heavy winds, when to wait, and when to take advantage of good weather. The challenge is, we forget we're not in control and we act like we are. It's painful to try to force or push your agenda through before its right timing.

Time
The second aspect to this test is about time itself—what the ancient Greeks called Chronos. Here, I'm talking about time in the linear, sequential sense. We all know, in this jam-packed world we live in, that time is limited and never stops marching forward. There are

only so many hours in a day, and there's a lot to do. There's what I call "maintenance"—the work of just keeping up. These are tasks, by and large, that we *must* do: taking care of a leaky faucet, going to the dentist, taking the kids to school, or fixing a flat tire. When something goes wrong in your day—a "hurdle," as one friend calls it—it can throw a wrench into the schedule. If you're like me, time is allocated tightly across my day—there's not much give in the schedule.

At the same time, there are a great deal of things we'd *like* to do. When I ask candidates what they are curious about outside of their work, many of them say, "I wish I had more time to explore." Time consumes moment after moment, stirring up the fear it will run out before we get to the things we really value or dream of. Time generates pressure in your life when it gets between what we must do and what we want to do. That pressure—combined with the sheer volume of obligations, maintenance activities, and unexpected hurdles—typically forces out time to explore.

I often hear people say, "I need extra time to be creative." This is where I want to make a clear distinction. Creativity is not a separate activity that you have to stop everything else for. It's a potential that gets activated when you occupy the intersection of purpose, possibility, and constraint. It's there with you whenever you're called to do something different, bring a new solution into being, or generate a new possibility. You don't need separate, extra time to be creative. Creativity can be activated anywhere and at any moment, integrated into whatever else you're up to.

What *can* require additional time is when you implement ideas that depart from the familiar and routine. You're not making time to be creative—but you might need to carve out time to build something new. Exploring an opportunity and finding you've gone down a dead end can add time. Making mistakes and failing can appear to delay your efforts and add time (though in the long run, learning from mistakes and failure can accelerate progress). Pursuing your ideas by testing, prototyping, and implementing them does require the investment of additional time. But you can no longer use time as an excuse for not *being creative.*

Three common villains show up as you face the test of Time and Timing.

1. **Impatience.** I am an impatient person. But ultimately, wanting what I want when I want it produces pain and suffering. Impatience generates stress when I'm separated from what *is* happening because I think something else should be happening. And impatience generates disappointment—in myself, in others, and in life itself when things don't happen in my preferred timing. But opportune timing has its own plan. Acting on impatience often leads to mistakes and failures. This is where your Superpower of Seeing Beyond comes in. Practice looking clear to see beyond all the assumptions, desires, and expectations that drive *when* you think something is supposed to happen. Practice looking far to put your preferred timing into the bigger picture. And practice looking near to identify things you can do today to prepare for when the timing is right.

2. **Inertia.** Generating new value involves making stuff up and then adjusting it, elaborating on it, tearing it up and starting over, and deciding when it's "done." In this process, there isn't much that can take the place of trying something out in real time. Some people call it prototyping. Others call it throwing spaghetti at the wall and seeing what sticks. You must *do* something. And this is where the villain of inertia can settle in. We talk about what we want to do instead of doing it. It's pure avoidance, fed by fears like being exposed or being wrong, and tendencies like perfectionism that make it hard to iterate.

   When you find yourself talking about what you *could* do, experiment instead. Push past the fear and take a risk. Test your idea by building a small, scrappy version of it to see what happens. Apply your Superpower of Creative License to make something up and improvise. Let go of your need to be right or perfect, smart, savvy, or safe. True safety comes from having trust and confidence that what you learn will lead you to your next step.

3. **Stress.** People often say that stress is one of their greatest personal and professional challenges. In addition to the effects on

your health and general well-being, stress takes a heavy toll on your potential to see new opportunities, imagine possibilities, resolve conflicts, make decisions, and act with agility. Time is one of the most common of stressors. Maybe you're late and feeling the crunch. Maybe you've made a commitment and it looks like you're not going to meet it. Whatever the circumstances, stress arises when your relationship with time becomes taxing.

Even though it can be debilitating, the truth is that without some stress, there is no reason for your creativity to show up. Stress opens a window of opportunity. In a way, it's like the clay when it's at its optimal malleability. In these windows, the likelihood of creativity blossoms, as stress motivates you to invent something to alleviate its impact. But as stress grows, the window for creative expression closes when it becomes too great for clear thinking and action. Pay attention to the shape of your window of opportunity. Does it open and close quickly? Is there more space between the moment when time stress begins to impinge on you and the point at which it becomes overwhelming? With practice, you can reduce the negative impact of stress on your creative expression.

While there are multiple strategies for dealing with each of these villains, your primary tool is your Superpower of Seeing Beyond. To build a healthy relationship with time, practice looking past the limitations of Chronos and the fear it can stir up. Instead, pay attention to what is possible in the time you have and create into that space. Practice seeing beyond the fickleness of Kairos and the disappointment it can bring. Instead, learn to playfully engage with the delay, surprise, and mystery as you bring creativity to your pursuits and your dreams.

Test Four: Obstacles

When I led a team that was developing an approach for working flexibly, two people fascinated me. Sandy worked in a part of the business that was highly regulated, globally distributed, and very complex. She was keenly aware of all the constraints in our path: the legal and financial constraints, and the implications of different work arrangements on benefits and taxation. Sandy believed that *any obstacle could be overcome* with the right approach. When we exchanged ideas, I felt inspired and my hopes for making lasting, meaningful change were lifted.

Sonia worked in another part of the business that was also highly regulated and embroiled in a great deal of change. Like Sandy, Sonia was primarily oriented to constraints and had a nose for sniffing out all the obstacles we were likely to encounter. But Sonia focused on the reasons why a given obstacle would likely *lead us to fail*. The contrast between how each of them approached obstacles couldn't have been starker. Sonia acted as if obstacles were like a dark cloud hanging over us, limiting our range of options and diminishing any real hope for a solution. When she shared her knowledge about what might get in our way, I felt deflated and downtrodden.

What would the most important people in your life say about you? Are you more like Sonia or Sandy? I guess there's some of each in all of us. But working with both of them at the same time—on the same team— helped crystallize what I've come to understand about obstacles.

Insight One: Obstacles test your resolve and strength of purpose

Your commitment will make all the difference. With a clear intent, inner alignment, and a meaningful purpose, obstacles will make you stronger. You learn about yourself: about the fire in your belly that motivates you and leads you to go out on a limb even in the face of perceived danger. But without resolve and commitment, obstacles can easily be used as an excuse to give up, abandon your journey, or downgrade your aspirations.

Insight Two: Obstacles test your flexibility and fluidity

Are you more like Sandy, flowing around obstacles, or are you more like Sonia, letting obstacles stop you from moving forward? Think of a mighty river. It flows over smaller rocks in its bed and flows over some of the boulders. But occasionally, there's a giant boulder that it must flow around. A whole bunch of large boulders can dam it up—until the river builds enough strength and depth to flow over the dam. Like the river, you can flow over small obstacles and past larger ones, and, by persistence over time or with a sudden explosive disruption, you can move even the mightiest obstacles.

The more fixed you are on a particular pathway to get to your goal, the more rigidly you will approach obstacles. You're like a giant log floating on the water. Logs get stuck up against boulders. Instead, be like the water, which can flow around, over, and under anything. Being water means you recognize when your ideas, assumptions, and expectations are acting as a block. And you let go. You let yourself flow in another direction—while keeping your eye on the purpose of your quest. Obstacles, especially the big, seemingly immovable ones, are there to strengthen and transform you—and to teach you if you let them.

Insight Three: Obstacles test your access to possibility thinking

Any obstacle encountered on the path toward a meaningful purpose brings you close to the center of the intersection of purpose, possibility, and constraint. With your obstacle, you have two of the three forces: purpose and constraint. What's needed to complete the intersection is possibility. Does the obstacle inspire you to find new opportunity, reframe traditional ways of thinking and acting, and generate new value? Does it call you to invent a new approach, a new set of possibilities, or even a new energy of activism to change something that is no longer serving your creative purpose?

If you're more oriented toward constraint, you may find yourself like Sonia—challenged to think outside of the mental models that generated the obstacle in the first place. You might find yourself questioning your purpose and wondering if it's worth all the effort. If you're more oriented toward possibilities, you may find that it's easier to generate a wealth of ideas for working around an obstacle or moving it out of your way. In both cases, once you have ideas for alternatives, you can dance in the spaces between possibility and constraint to test your ideas, reshape them, and see how they evolve.

Insight Four: Your Inner Critic is likely to show up

Your Inner Critic is the voice of fear and self-doubt. It's the voice of judgment[19] in your head that chastises you and stops you from taking risks. It says things like "That will never work," "That was stupid," "Why bother," and "It will never be good enough." We all have an Inner Critic; it starts out with the purpose of keeping us safe, but ends up stifling learning, experimentation, and creative exploration.

If you are like everyone else on the planet, you're familiar with the voice I'm talking about. One of the favorite places for the critic to appear is when you encounter an obstacle—especially one that might threaten your competence, your success on something you care about, and ultimately your sense of identity. Here, the Inner Critic might show up as one of the following:

- **Declarations**, made as statements of truth, and typically delivered with a level of certainty and force that is meant to arouse fear of not heeding the warning. The critic often laces declarations with righteousness and a sense of blame to increase their effectiveness.

- **A victim mindset** that enforces the belief you are at the mercy of others. Here, the critic might craft stories about the undesirable consequences you'll face when others react, or suggest that others are to blame for the circumstances you find yourself in. Making you the victim is one way of protecting you; if you're a victim, you can't be blamed for things being the way they are.

- **Exaggerations and impossibilities** that amplify its warnings and heighten fear about the risks ahead. If you hear statements like "never" and "always," you can pretty much bet you're hearing the voice of the critic in your head or in the room. These warnings are meant to stop you when there is potential for mistakes, failure, embarrassment, or loss.

These methods are designed to protect you from risk. But on a journey of discovery, when you venture into the unknown, your safety comes from your creative potential—not from staying with the familiar. The Inner Critic will dampen your curiosity, cause you to second-guess a course of action, and instill fear into your decision-making. And by now you've figured out that the critic can come from the voice inside of you as well as the voices of others. When you're confronting your Inner Critic, you have three basic choices:

1. To stop, as the critic would urge you to do.

2. To get hooked into responding, meaning that you're arguing, defending, or explaining to the critic (never a good position to be in, because the Inner Critic doesn't respond to reason).

3. To use one of your Superpowers, like Questions.

The first two choices lead down a dark path. Giving in to the critic strengthens the power of its voice in your life. That's because the critic would love nothing more than to position itself as your ally. It wants you to think that you *need* it. Beware. It will always warn you away from the risks that lie in the unknown. But if you let it, you are also allowing it to warn you away from the potential for creativity, for learning, and for transformation. And if you get hooked into responding, you feed the critic: now you're playing on its turf.

The best choice is the third. When you're working to get around an obstacle, and you hear the Inner Critic, use your Superpower of Questions to make a sincere and curious inquiry—and deflate its power. Ask questions to explore possibilities and capture learning value from an obstacle. And use questions to reframe the obstacle as an opportunity.

REFRAMING THE CRITIC

Declarations	————————▶	Questions
Victim	————————▶	Responsible
Impossibilities	————————▶	Possibilities
Clouded/Exaggerated	————————▶	Objective and Discerning
Holding Back/Fear	————————▶	Experiment to Learn

When you reframe an obstacle as an opportunity, you look, listen, and inquire through different lenses: with curiosity, humor, and mindfulness. You stand courageously inside the constraint or obstacle and look for new perspectives, new ideas, and alternative solutions. To do this, you can also practice your Superpower of Seeing Beyond—rising above and looking beyond your immediate circumstances. You become detached from what you are reframing, and at the same time deeply committed to something new. You must also be grounded in the fortitude of your purpose to see obstacles as negotiable—as "movable." Then, even when obstacles may stop others, you are still able to look around and beyond them.

Test Five: The Swamp

• • •

When multiple tests pile up in life and work—especially when the villains of fear and control abound—you may find yourself in what I call an inner Swamp. That's when it feels like you're stuck in mud and quicksand. It seems like there are monsters, or dark water of unknown depths, and tangles of undergrowth that make it hard to move forward. There are no clear signposts to help find a way out or even forward. At any moment, you might be attacked by creatures lurking nearby. The potential for danger in every direction makes it tempting to stay put out of fear of what's ahead. But there's also danger in not moving forward. And one of the biggest challenges in the Swamp is that it's hard to know how big it is and how long you'll be there.

I was in the Swamp so much of the time when I worked on the Creative Leadership project in Europe that it almost began to feel like "home." I felt trapped, lost, and alone. I felt ashamed that I couldn't break through our team's destructive patterns. Obstacles stopped me in my tracks. And I felt like a failure. My Inner Critic mocked me: "You're stuck? You—the guy who talks all the time about how creativity is always with us? *You're* lost? You're a fraud."

But as I quieted the critic and acknowledged that I was in the Swamp, I felt an immediate sense of relief. That's because avoiding an inner Swamp takes a great deal of energy. It's like trying to hold a big, inflated beachball underwater so no one can see it.

As you cross the threshold into the unknown, you can imagine how multiple Swamps might overlap and combine. This can generate what I call the darkest Swamp—that place of hopelessness, despair, and grief that comes when it all seems too much, when you're weary and overwhelmed, deeply disappointed, and it seems like there's nothing left to do but give up. Maybe you've already given up. This darkest Swamp is a place where you can easily lose sight of the gift of your creativity. What do purpose and possibility mean here, anyway? You might decide the gift of your creativity wasn't what you thought it was after all, and you might let it drop into the muck and mire. You might stop trying to cross the Swamp and just settle into it like a new home.

I've been there, and I've witnessed it firsthand with clients, partners, and colleagues. Some just decided to pull the plug on their dreams and goals. Others stopped taking care of themselves or fell back into habitual destructive behaviors. Others were devastated by the realization that they had committed years of their life to something that didn't work out. Still others became weary of trying to hold things together.

Often people decided that just being in this Swamp confirmed that they weren't creative. They succumbed to a destructive belief: "If I really was creative, this wouldn't have happened. I wouldn't be here in the first place." While some still had a glimmer of hope for something different—by magic or miracle—most had abdicated their own potential and power to create something different.

Ultimately, the Swamp was not my home—and it is not yours. You don't have to accept that this Swamp is all you get, what you deserve, or what you should learn to live with. While it may feel hopeless to struggle and press forward, you must act. To cross the Swamp and find your way to a place where you once again trust yourself and your creativity, you will have to leave where you are. You might need to slay a few dragons and confront some scary monsters—including some of your own making. You will have to challenge your attachments and your sense of identity. You will have to pivot, reinvent yourself, reframe your vision, enroll new or different allies, and shift your priorities. This is one of the most important tests you will face: realizing that this Swamp is not where you belong and rising up with accountability as you reclaim your gift of creativity.

So, how do you make it across inner Swamps? The way through will be different for each of you. But there are some keys I've discovered over the years.

Key One: Your reaction is critical

As one teacher of mine used to say, "How you deal with the problem *is* the problem." But in the quicksand, and in the tangle of self-judgment, fear, anger, doubt, and helplessness, this just sounds like psychobabble. Why fight or even try to get out? What comes next might be just as bad if not worse. Unfortunately, however, there's really no way forward without self-awareness and without acknowledging and owning whatever measure of helplessness is active inside you. Listen to the story you're telling yourself and others about your circumstances.

For me, this was a painful realization about my experience in Europe. I was so stuck in being the victim—and so convinced of what had been done *to me*—that I lost access to my Superpowers for positive change. I couldn't see beyond my victim story. The questions I asked were all about why this had happened to me. When I challenged the rules and took Creative License, there was "againstness" in my actions and I was filled with bitterness. The only thing I was learning was that I was paralyzed by fear. In a way, I had turned my Superpowers against myself. Confessing all this was hard, but it *is* the first step.

Key Two: Choice is the crucible where change is forged

Choice—the decisions you make moment to moment—is the place where you either generate more tangle and darkness or awaken to new possibilities that give rise to different outcomes. This might mean choosing to surrender and stop striving and controlling. Or it might mean choosing to reach out for help, to listen to someone who's been supporting you, or to do something you've been avoiding. You might choose to let go of being right for the benefit it could bring to a relationship in jeopardy. Whatever that choice or decision, the key is that you are moving toward something you want instead of moving away from what you don't want. You're moving toward greater accountability. You're moving toward advocating for yourself. You're moving toward others who nourish you. You're moving toward a deeper understanding and acceptance of who you are and the truth about what's going on. You're accessing wisdom—from within yourself and from others—instead of "fixing a problem."

At first, it might not be obvious you're making progress. But each choice you make to move toward instead of away will build momentum—and you will cross through. Don't get me wrong; there can be a lot of bumps on the path out of the Swamp. But as you bring more awareness to your choices, you're on your way out.

Key Three: Service to others is one of the quickest ways out

I can't fully explain how this key works, but it does. Serving others—and sharing your energy, compassion, creativity, and loving with them—opens up a heart connection. You're not there to fix them, but to raise them up and support them in becoming more fully themselves. Not for them to see what you see or believe what you believe, but to inspire them in their own visions and dreams. Not to create for them, but to catalyze and nourish their potential to create. While it might be the last thing you feel like doing in the depths and tangles of your Swamp, it is one of the most effective ways of moving forward—even when you don't have a clue what that might mean in terms of your own direction.

Look around you. Who could use a hand or some loving-kindness, acceptance, and care? Who might benefit from recognition, support, or being included? Whose venture could use some of your "social capital" (the goodwill you've built up that can be leveraged to sponsor others)? Who could benefit from the offer to brainstorm ideas?

Not all your Swamps will be of the darkest kind. But crossing one and using the experience to deepen your practice of self-awareness, conscious choice, and service to others will reinforce your faith that you will find your way through.

ALL THE tests—the Blank Canvas, Mistakes and Failures, Time and Timing, Obstacles, and the Swamp—offer opportunities to learn. They are vital stepping-stones on your unfolding journey toward a more conscious, fulfilling, and creative life. And they are inevitable when you aim for innovative results that depart from the status quo. Each test you encounter and pass through, and every instance where you activate one of your Superpowers, serves to strengthen your connection with your creative potential. I encourage you to embrace these tests with gratitude instead of reluctance, with agency instead of submission, and with courageous vulnerability instead of self-protection. Look clearly at what shows up in your way. When tests appear, my hope is that you are more prepared to greet them with awareness and with tools for navigating through. This is how you cross the threshold and become anew.

ASK YOURSELF...

Now, at the end of this chapter, take time to pause and reflect on the following questions.

- What might have to shift and change so that you see each and every test as an opportunity to practice returning to the center of the intersection of purpose, possibility, and constraint?

Test One: The Blank Canvas

- How might you bring greater confidence and compassion to your experience at the threshold of uncertainty?

Test Two: Mistakes and Failure

Think of a time when you made a mistake or failed at something meaningful to you.

- How did you manage your inner response? What did you tell yourself about what was at stake? How did you take accountability?

- What did you learn, and how has that changed you for the better?

Test Three: Time and Timing

- How effectively do you navigate the give and take of Time and Timing? What could be different?

- In which arenas (e.g., at home, work, on a particular project) can you practice letting go of your agenda and attempts to control the timing of how things unfold?

Test Four: Obstacles

Think of a specific situation or circumstance where you are venturing into the unknown.

- How is your Inner Critic showing up as you face obstacles in this situation?

- What might be different if you moved your critic into the background, and brought your Superpowers into the foreground?

- What would have to be true if this obstacle was, in fact, an opportunity in disguise?

Test Five: The Swamp

- If you could fast-forward into your future and share a bit of wisdom—something you'd like yourself to remember when inner Swamps arise—what message would you send to help you cross through?

Keep Going!

• • •

Giving into the Inner Critic strengthens its power. I spoke with Michael Ray, co-author of the seminal book *Creativity in Business* and professor emeritus at Stanford University's Graduate School of Business, about how to psyche out the critic. To see the video, go to **creativetogetherresources.com** or scan this QR code:

What kind of experiences can trigger inner Swamps? Find out at **creativetogetherresources.com** or scan this QR code:

6

Stepping Across
the Threshold

●　●　●　●　●

E VERY DAY, when Phil's alarm went off at 6 a.m., Sonny and Cher
sang, "I got you, babe." It signaled the terrifying fact that yet
again, Phil had woken up on the very same day as yesterday.
As he opened his eyes and heard that same song morning after
morning, Phil knew he was stuck. He would encounter the same
people, the same circumstances, the same problems, and the same
opportunities.

Every day was a repeat of the same day for Phil in the movie
Groundhog Day. If you've seen the movie, you'll remember that Phil
didn't take it very well. First he sunk into despair and helplessness. It
was like living in a prison. Then he began using his situation to take
advantage of people. Since he knew what was going to happen next,
he could manipulate things, trick people, and get what he wanted. It
was a game—and at first, Phil was a cynical, selfish player.

But slowly (very slowly, since he was not particularly self-aware),
Phil began to realize that what was different about each day was what
he brought to the day. He realized he wanted to create new opportunities in his life that he couldn't get through helplessness, arrogance,
control, or selfish ambition. He discovered that things went better

when he brought his authentic self forward. He discovered that he could connect with people, learn new skills, improve his life, generously give of himself, and love others deeply. He discovered that he could create different outcomes when he wanted to. Phil broke the spell once he found the truth of who he'd always been—a curious, loving, generous, and creative man, standing at the center of all the possibility in his life.

You, too, are at the center of all the possibility in your life. *It starts within you.* It starts with what you believe about what's possible in your future. Is it going to be like the same day over and over, with CDD shutting your creativity down? Or are you living into the truth that at any given moment, 1) there are multiple possible futures ahead of you; 2) you have agency in helping shape what happens, but you are not in control; and 3) the outcomes you imagine are reaching back to help you realize them?

There's a fourth truth too. Just the other day, I heard a friend say, "Abandon all hope of creating a more perfect past." As he uttered these words, I realized another truth about creating your life and creating in your life: you can't go back and change anything about what has happened to you on past journeys. You can't change how you felt, what you decided about yourself back then, and how that has shaped what you bring to this present moment. You can't create a more perfect past. But you can learn from the past and use it to shape who you become in the future and what you know to be true about yourself. You can rewrite the story of who you are as a creator.

You are a creative person. This is the journey we've been on together in our first adventure—to support you in claiming full ownership of the creative potential that is your birthright and understanding that every day you step across the threshold into the unknown in small and larger ways. Even if, like Phil, you feel trapped in routine and years have gone by without you feeling connected to your creativity. Even if, like my friend the lawyer who thought he might have lost his creativity, you've been living with a narrow definition of creativity that separates you from your potential. Even if you're in pain or in a painful situation: feeling squelched by rules or exhausted by the collection of obligations and responsibilities you've taken on. Even if you know you're a creative person but forget to pay attention—like I did when I got swept up in the drama of the Creative Leadership project.

Whatever your circumstances, every day you are *creating your life* as you move through your moments, days, weeks, and years. You are making choices, gesturing to the world with your actions, succeeding and failing, making mistakes, finding new paths, gathering experiences and learning from them, and becoming more fully who you are. Every day you are writing the story of your unique contribution and mark on the world around you. You bring this creative potential to whatever you're doing as you actively pursue meaningful purposes that call you to venture into the unknown.

Trust Yourself as Creative
• • •

Take a moment to pause and reflect on all we've explored together. Take a deep breath and simply pause and listen inside as you let these truths seep into your inner spaces:

- You are at the center of all possibility and potential in your life.

- You are gifted with a most precious, inexhaustible, and sustainable creative potential.

- As a creative being, you can rebound, adapt, invent, and even disrupt your world—bringing new solutions to the challenges and opportunities you care about.

- You can meet any challenge with creative accountability—changing your circumstances if you feel stuck or don't like what's happening.

It's one thing to know you're creative, and another thing entirely to trust it, implicitly. I invite you to step into your future with this kind of trust. Even if you feel stuck or unsure of where to turn or what to do next, your creativity is there for you. While you're caught up doing routine activities, your creativity is there for you. While you're planning and working and resting and achieving, it is there. There are no qualifications, conditions, or comparisons. Creativity doesn't go away or diminish because you're not aware of how you are using it. You don't have to strengthen it and you can't lose it—even if you forget it's a part of who you are.

Your creativity doesn't care where you apply it. But you can become more practiced at leveraging its power, and you can consciously activate it. You can direct it and focus it whenever you embrace a meaningful purpose that requires discovery, invention, and innovation. You can actively apply it to the challenges, barriers, and struggles you face. Then you enter the unknown places with a deep faith in your potential to invent new solutions, new possibilities, and new opportunities.

Trust frees up energy to realize possibilities. With trust, you cultivate new practices for navigating the tests and obstacles in your way. Instead of falling prey to the many villains that arouse fear and try to prevent you from exploring the unknown, you greet them with all your Superpowers. Circumstances that might otherwise stop you, scare you, or diminish your resolve become stepping-stones for learning and transformation.

This was part of Phil's journey in *Groundhog Day*. As he began to see each day as an opportunity to become anew, he blossomed. He invested in himself and his future. He studied the piano and became a skilled musician. He learned how to create beautiful ice sculptures. He started helping others and found joy in connecting with people through service. He learned from his mistakes and failures—not to exert power over others, but to become a more compassionate, loving, and generous person. In his humility as a creative learner, he found happiness and self-love.

You have the opportunity, like Phil, to transform your future into a deliciously courageous adventure. Use everything we've learned and practiced together to generate a kind of creative tension—an energetic field where possibility, conscious creativity, and vulnerable receptivity spark together to bring forward what wants to emerge. Even if that might be different from what you think should happen. In this new future, focus on the learning and not the events. In this future, take accountability for your role at the center of the journey's unfolding. In this future, become the transformation that changes you and the world you live in.

This doesn't mean that adversity won't reach your doorstep. You will be tested over and over in big and small ways. Trusting your creativity doesn't mean that doubt won't still come around for a visit from time to time. There's no promise that everything will fall into place—especially in the timing you might prefer. It doesn't mean you won't get lost or ever feel stuck again. It doesn't mean you won't be afraid or feel helpless or in despair. And it doesn't mean that you will always be safe.

What trusting your creativity *does* mean is that even when you find yourself in dark, swampy places, you can rely on your creativity and your potential to invent ways forward. Trusting means you have a profound faith that you will figure things out no matter how messy, painful, or chaotic they get. Trusting means that when circumstances call you forward into the unknown, you know that you will *create* your way forward.

So how do you develop a deep and unshakable trust in your creative potential? It basically works the same way that trust develops in personal relationships. When you say you trust another person, you base that on your experience with them over time. You find them reliable and credible—and you know that they look beyond their own self-interests to ensure that everyone benefits.

The same is true for trusting your creativity. You strengthen a sense of reliability every time you simply notice that it's there when you need it. You strengthen credibility when you consciously and actively direct it to meaningful purposes and witness its power in action. And again when you get lost and create a way out or find a simpler solution. Finally, you build trust when you ensure that others also benefit from the value you've generated. Trust strengthens as you open each door that emerges, one by one, and pass through.

Starting today, I encourage you to pay close attention to how your creativity shows up in your life. Bring more awareness to how you can consciously direct and focus it on the challenges you face. Watch for ideas to break the mold, modify what exists, combine things, and build new solutions. Take note of the urgings you have to explore a particular course of action. Then follow through. Pay attention to your inner conversation as you become aware of different constraints. Observe what gets in the way—inside of you in the form of beliefs, assumptions, and feelings as well as outside of you in the form of resistance and blocks. As you test your ideas—and they meet with viability and feasibility—notice how new ideas show up for how to adapt or change your approach.

You will find your creativity is unfailingly reliable, inexhaustible, invested in your success and the success of others, and fundamentally trustworthy. As your trust strengthens, your sense of the risk associated with entering the unknown—not knowing how things will turn out—will shift. You'll hear yourself saying, "I've got this. I don't know what's going to happen or how it will turn out, but I know I'll be okay. I know myself and I'll figure it out." The focus shifts from knowing with certainty what will happen, to a deep trust that your creativity (not all the other strategies you may have employed to keep you safe) is what you can rely on to figure things out as you move forward.

Tell a New Story

● ● ●

In the movie *Groundhog Day*, as the same day wore on and on, Phil's story about who he was and who he wanted to become changed. In the years that followed my return from Europe, my story also changed. After our team crashed and burned, I felt scorched. In my story of what happened, Josef manipulated and controlled us—all in the name of "creative leadership." In my story, he pitted us against each other, bullied away any threat to his power, and sucked the creativity out of our souls. I was angry—and I wanted to reveal him as the most uncreative imposter who ever claimed to be an expert on the topic of creativity.

This was the story I told about what had happened for a long while after I returned. I told it to myself—and I told some version of it to my friends and family. But my story changed over the years. I began to get perspective and see things from different angles. I reflected and sought answers. If, as Joseph Campbell says, heroes get the adventure that they are ready for, why did I call myself into that adventure? What inside of me was seeking this particular journey? What did I learn through the tests—and through the anger, resentment, and shame—and how has that changed me?

The answers weren't easy to swallow. As I reflected, my experiences exposed a long-held view of myself as a victim—powerless in the face of authority, resigned to simply comply, afraid to disturb any conditions that provided a measure of security, and stuck in a pattern of pleasing others over standing up for myself. As I peeled away the layers with greater accountability and awareness, I simply couldn't tell the same story anymore. Not just because I came to peace with what happened, although that was one benefit. It was because the learning I garnered from venturing into this experience had changed me.

Our team's failure—and all that came with it—transformed who I knew myself to be before I left. And slowly, my role in the story changed from that of a victim to being an accountable participant. I came face to face with my own fears of being an imposter. Josef changed from an evil man into a catalyst for my transformation. I stopped judging the partners in the firm. I found compassion for them as I found compassion for the frightened, bullied boy I had once been. And I came to see my teammates as allies to my learning instead of accomplices to the crime.

So, how might your story change with your newly found awareness of the strength and power of your creativity? What might be different in your life if you knew you couldn't lose your creativity? What risks might you take? Your answers to these kinds of questions shape what I call your *story of opportunity*. This story is the manifestation of beliefs about yourself and your relationship with your creativity. It shapes the way you participate in creative activity. It shapes how you collaborate with others and influences how you access opportunities and practice.[20]

Because your story both shapes and is shaped by activity, practice, and participation, it can become crystallized and may persist despite your attempts to change it. That's why it is so important that you listen carefully. Your story is a window into your mindset, and into what you believe about yourself and what's possible for you. Pay attention to a few key elements—questions and clues to what might change in a new story about a more creative future.

Listen to the stories you tell about the range of opportunities available to you and how you are meeting them with your creativity. In the story I tell about the Creative Leadership project, for example, I can see now that there were endless opportunities to bring my creativity forward. Every day there were big and small opportunities to design products, help our team function more effectively, or even invent a new model for the consulting firm as an experiment—if only we had thought of it. There were opportunities to try things and learn—whether we succeeded or failed—and to play with the system, experiment with different resources and ideas, and see what response we got to our products. In the moment, we missed most of these opportunities. I missed them. But they were there.

In your story, how does opportunity show up? Do you invent opportunities by following your curiosity, seeing beyond the apparent, and going after them? Or do you wait for opportunities to be granted to you when others invite you to join them or assign them to you? Do opportunities show up unexpectedly—and if so, do you capture them or do they pass you by? Maybe you experiment and lean in, or you wait to get a sense of whether things might work out before venturing in. Listen carefully to the ways you describe the options, choices, and opportunities available to you and how they came to be. Listen for expansiveness or limitation. Listen for how you describe your measure of agency to capture opportunity.

Listen to the stories you tell about the blocks and obstacles that get in your way. As we encounter opportunity and possibility, we can let so many things get in our way. In my story, the opportunities to express my creativity on the Creative Leadership project were enveloped in a morass of interpersonal dynamics, politics, and personal trade-offs where I prioritized "not rocking the boat" over challenging the status quo. I enjoyed the benefits of how things were set up—the lavish accommodations, travel to new places, and fancy dinners. Eventually I settled into some measure of learned helplessness and decided there was nothing I could do. In the story I told, "I tried, but eventually I gave up." *Trying* allowed me to justify giving up.

What gets in your way? What keeps you from meeting opportunity with anything less than your full creative potential? Are the blocks and obstacles coming from outside of you? Are you greeting these tests with your Superpowers or letting obstacles be the reasons why you can't move forward? Maybe the blocks are coming from your inner life—the way your own willingness, motivation, drive, and commitments hinder creative pursuits. Are the purposes you're engaged with meaningful to you? If not, what are the trade-offs of rocking the boat? What might you lose and what might you gain? Listen inside to the conversation you have with yourself—as well as the story you tell others.

Listen to the stories you tell about your access to knowledge, resources, and experiences. Would you say you are in a resource-rich environment? How does that impact and influence the choices you make? Or maybe you are hampered by a lack of resources. Is someone keeping the resources you need from you? Do you have to invent workarounds? Maybe you struggle to find information that would help you make informed decisions.

Listen carefully for whether you are expressing from a place of victimhood or from a place of accountability. Like me back on the Creative Leadership team in Europe, it can be easy to suggest that you are not able to follow your curiosity, adventure into the unknown, and express creatively because of a lack of something you may expect. Maybe, like our team, you don't believe you have enough autonomy and freedom. Or maybe you believe you're lacking the time or the resources to "be creative." As you listen to your story, and as you begin to imagine a new story, pay close attention to see if you are claiming or denying the creative potential that is always with you. Make "choosing not to express your creativity" part of your story when that's true—instead of suggesting that something was lacking that limited you.

Listen to the stories you tell about the consequences of creative expression. In our Creative Leadership project, every time I tried something new (especially when it was "unsanctioned"), it felt like I got reprimanded. Back then, I didn't even bother to consider how I might be contributing to that outcome. What happens when you invent new things and take a risk to try something different and potentially controversial? In your story, what are the consequences of success? Does anyone notice? What gets rewarded and by whom? What happens when you fail or miss the mark? Who supports you and who has tended to suppress your creativity? Pay attention to the story you tell about how others react when you challenge the status quo, work to bring about change, speak up, and bring your ideas to others. Seek to understand your role in these outcomes.

The most important part of your story is what you have decided about yourself and your creativity, based on the consequences of taking creative action. Here, you have the most leverage to change your story. You can make new decisions that take accountability for the past, while at the same time affirming a different choice going forward. The colossal failure of our team in Europe, for example, could never diminish my gift—only my beliefs about it. When you hold a potential-based definition of creativity, the consequences you have experienced no longer mean anything about whether you are creative. They are simply opportunities to learn about yourself and this incredible potential you have.

Now it's time to leave your old story behind and create a new story. Ask different kinds of questions. Listen for and seek out opportunities to create something new where something *now* isn't working. Find the strength and power of your creative potential and express it through the channels around you. Change the channel if you don't like what you're seeing. Activate your Superpowers. Follow your curiosity, clean out the closet of your biases and filters, and pay attention to the short and long view.

Ask Different Questions

• • •

As you deepen trust in your creativity, the questions you ask will change. This may be one of the most visible outcomes of your new story. New questions arise as you shift how you frame your circumstances and how you greet them with proactive, creative accountability.

When our Creative Leadership project was ending—in the last gasps of breath right before we disbanded—the questions I asked came from a place of victimhood and blame. I was seeking support for my positions and for the "againstness" I felt: "Can you believe what they did?" and "What would you have done if you were me?" Other questions were focused on escaping my circumstances. "What should I do? What would you do?" I was grasping for answers—from myself or from anyone else who would listen—to *fix* my situation. My questions were reactive.

Over time, after I returned to the States, I started to ask different questions, questions that sought greater insight, awareness, and creative accountability. "How did I contribute to the failure of our project?" "What did I learn about creating with others?" "How did villains like fear and control get in my way?" "What could I do differently in the future?" Instead of reactive questions, these were questions about moving toward something new—about new avenues and possibilities to explore. I was relearning to follow my curiosity into the unknown. And I emerged with a quiver full of different questions to help me focus and direct my creative potential.

As you rewrite the story of who you are as a creator, you, too, will experience a shift:

* **Away from control and toward exploration.** In this, our first adventure, we've talked about how the desire for control—and the way this desire gives rise to striving—can diminish the expression of

your creative potential. When the purpose of your questions is to gain some measure of control, you'll notice an overwhelming focus on what to *do*. You'll hear yourself asking action questions about fixing things, solving problems, alleviating pain, and reducing risk. You might ask about how long things will take, when you'll know, or who has the answer. But as your questions shift to exploration, you'll start asking more open-ended, insight questions. You'll ask "What if... ?" and "How might I... ?" questions to test hypotheses, involve others, and experiment.

- **Away from protecting and toward courageous authenticity and transparency.** When you are protecting yourself, your questions will likely set you apart from others. You might ask questions about fault or blame, questions about fairness and if you're being treated differently from others, or questions that put others down. As your questions shift toward courageous authenticity and transparency, you will build up relationships instead of tearing them down. You'll ask questions that seek deeper truths about topics that seem undiscussable or non-negotiable. These might include, "What's truly possible here?" "What seed can we plant together?" and "Why is this important to us?" If you notice you are holding back, you might ask, "What's at the heart of this issue?" or "How does what's happening challenge my sense of identity?" Through your questions, you'll become more inclusive and more empathic— while at the same time standing in the truth of your point of view.

- **Away from individual winners and losers and toward value for the broader ecosystem.** When you're focused on your self-interests or seeing things through the lens of scarcity and competition, your questions will likely set up an "us versus them" scenario. You might hear yourself asking about how to win, gain turf or territory, get the upper hand in a situation, or get ahead of others. You could be asking questions about how you or your situation compares to others. But as you shift to seek value for the broader system, you'll hear yourself asking about interdependencies, the broader welfare of the community, the longer-term sustainability of ideas and solutions, and what you can do to serve broader goals. These questions might include, "How can we bring out the best in everyone involved?" and "What will serve the highest good?" or "What might promote the long-term health of the entire system?"

- **Away from enforcing and toward attracting.** When you're focused on the rules, you'll tend to ask questions that reinforce approved processes and ensure that people act within prescribed procedures and conform to existing policies. If the purpose of your questions is to protect boundaries and keep yourself and others inside the lines, you might take the role of a watchdog. As your questions shift toward attracting others, you'll notice that instead of policing, you inspire—drawing others to you and toward common, irresistible goals and aims. You'll ask questions that clarify purpose, principles, and values, like "What is most meaningful about this?" and "What shared problems can we solve?" You'll seek out a compelling vision of breakthrough that acts like a magnet pulling you into your future. People will want to go toward this vision, instead of feeling like they're forced to.

Notice how these questions shift from reactive ones that protect and control to questions that generate possibility and energy. What you listen for in the answers will also change. You'll begin to catch yourself when you're giving away your power or promoting a victim position. You'll notice if you're looking for someone to rescue you or if you're making excuses, letting fear guide your choices, or giving your Inner Critic too much airtime. The tone of your inner self-talk will become a signal if you slip back into a more reactive orientation.

I invite you go back and review the section in chapter 4 on your Superpower of Questions. Take stock of the questions you are asking and write down a few you've heard yourself ask over the past week or two. And take some time to reflect on the questions at the end of this chapter. *What story are you promoting* by your questions and through your answers? In the weeks to come, pay close attention to what you are asking of yourself and the world around you.

Take Your Gift into the World

• • •

Up until now, the journey we've been on together has been between us: just you and me. It hasn't been about a group of other people you work with. We've focused on just you and your relationship with your creativity. That's because the transformation to a more conscious, creative life starts within you. It's an inner hero's journey without a final destination, as ever deeper insights and lessons are discovered. It's a process of opening doors and passing across the threshold: getting lost or stuck and forgetting and then remembering again; succeeding and failing and then remembering yet again. Over time, as you participate with your creativity and witness it in action, you learn to trust this most precious gift as a way of being. Over and over, you emerge out of the chrysalis of reaction and limitation and take flight into more creative approaches. It's a daily practice, not an achievement.

Claiming the gift of your creative potential and flexing your Superpowers brings you into the center of possibility in your life. It's your choice and your fundamental accountability. I invite you to pause now and simply receive this gift. Find a way to let it seep into your inner spaces and your being. Stay with it for a time without moving forward. Experience simply having this gift and all that it means in your life.

When you're ready, it's time to take your gift and the new story of your creativity out into the world around you. Claiming your creative potential is the foundation for more effective co-creation—for sparking innovation in the new world of work. In our next adventure, we will focus on the outer world of work and explore what it means to *be* the gift as you navigate the spaces, structures, and systems that are part of your work and business pursuits. We will shift to explore what it means to create together with others—to bring your gift forward with the people in your work life—in the context of a rapidly changing business landscape. This is your next adventure—your next hero's journey.

ASK YOURSELF...

Now, at the end of this chapter and the conclusion of Adventure One, take time to pause and reflect on the following questions.

- What are your deepest insights from exploring this first adventure?

- What has shifted in both your inner experience and your behaviors out in the world?

- Of all that we've explored, what has challenged you the most?

Trust Yourself as Creative

- What do you believe about yourself as a creative being?

Tell a New Story

- How is your story (about who you are as a creator) changing with greater awareness of the unlimited power of your creativity?

- What might be different in your life if you knew you couldn't lose your creativity? What risks might you take?

Ask Different Questions

- How are the questions you ask of yourself changing? What's different about the questions you are asking others?

- How do your questions honor the power and presence of your creativity? Do they demonstrate proactive, creative accountability?

Take Your Gift into the World

- What practices can you bring into your daily life to consciously participate with your creativity and witness it in action?

ADVENTURE TWO

GETTING CREATIVE TOGETHER

"The uncovered heart reveals both vulnerability and strength. Its strength lies precisely in that ability to open itself to itself, with an elegance and grace that invites the hearts of others to do so too."

BARRON, Montuori, and Barron, in *Creators on Creating*

PROLOGUE

• • • • •

I T WAS early October, and I was finishing up one of my seminars on Creativity in Business. Of all the work I do now, convening these sessions is among the most rewarding. There's gratitude and grace when people come together to reclaim their potential and awaken conscious creativity. Sometimes I work with groups of leaders; other times I help reinvigorate the way teams co-create new value. This time I was working with a diverse group of professionals from all walks of life.

Late morning on the last day, we were taking a short break. All the participants were enjoying the sunshine on the patio just outside our conference room. It shone into the room and lit up our circle of chairs. As I started to prepare for the next series of conversations, I could smell the cool sea air mixed with lavender from the garden. I had come to relish these quiet moments in the room by myself in between convening the group.

Just then, Andrew burst in with a funny expression on his face. He was normally reserved and buttoned up; it was easy to see something was stirring. His glasses were off-kilter and he tripped on the carpet as he came inside. "I hope I'm not interrupting. Do you have a minute?"

"Sure," I said, putting down my notebook.

Andrew looked at the ground and straightened his glasses. "I don't want to go back."

He was talking about returning to his job; he'd worked for the last sixteen years as the deputy treasurer of a fast-growing county government in northern Oregon. During our time together, Andrew had shared about how dead he felt inside sitting at his desk day after day, processing claims, making sure regulations were followed, coding bills, and preparing financial reports. "I'm stuck," he said. "I can't stand going in every day, but I only have four more years before I'm eligible for my full pension."

He had already stayed years beyond the point where the work felt interesting or even mildly meaningful. For a long time, he'd been living every day believing that he wasn't creative. Now, in that room with me, he spoke with determination. "How can I go back to the same office and sit at that same desk? How can I work for my asshole manager? I don't want to do it for four more years."

I realized this was a conversation the entire group would benefit from having together. After checking with Andrew, I invited everyone to rejoin the circle. As we settled in, Andrew kicked off the dialogue about returning home and to his office. "My colleagues are just going through the motions," he said, "like I had been before this seminar." After a pause, he continued. "My manager is so steeped in rules and regulations. There's only one right way to do anything." He shifted in his chair and looked down at the ground. "I have to get out, for my own health and sanity," he said. "I want to do so much more with all this potential—to work on things that feel important to me." He let out a long, slow breath like he'd been holding it in for years.

Andrew's vulnerability opened a space for each of the participants to reflect on how they wanted to take the gift of their creative potential into the world, now that they had claimed it more fully. "I admire your courage," Mark said after a few moments. "Actually, I'm looking forward to going back. I've got so many things I want to try out now with the other teachers and with the kids." Mark was a science teacher at a middle school in Los Angeles where he'd been teaching for three years. "This seminar opened up my eyes. I don't think I'll ever look at the kids or my work in the same way."

Regina spoke next. "I want everyone on my leadership team to go through this experience. I'm going back with all these new tools and I'm going to shake things up." Regina had recently been promoted into a senior director role overseeing the Procurement department at her company. "I want to be a different kind of leader," she said, looking straight at Andrew. "We've got to find a way to cut through the bullshit politics and the resistance to change. Maybe we can kick some ass if we're all on the same page." I imagined she wanted Andrew to know that there were managers out there who really did care.

There was a long pause. I looked around the circle to those who had not yet spoken and noticed Lily fidgeting with her notebook. Over our time together, Lily had revealed how much she loved her work as a biostatistician in a mid-sized life sciences company near San Francisco—but that she didn't think it was creative. Outside of work she participated in all kinds of artistic projects. That's where she felt creative. Now she had come to realize that there was no separation—the creative Lily outside of work was the same creative Lily at work.

"I'm not even sure I'll have a job to go back to," she said, as if she felt my gaze. "Everything is changing in my department, and we're on our third wave of restructuring. A bunch of my friends have already been laid off." She looked directly at me with surprising intensity. "I see how my creativity is always with me whatever I'm doing. I know I'll be okay whatever happens at work. But waiting to hear if I still have a job is the hardest." She crossed her arms. "And I don't want to see any more of my friends go."

One by one, as we prepared to close our time together, each member of the group shared about their hopes and fears. They all were at powerful inflection points in their journeys. Each of them—with their own talents, perspectives, challenges, and dreams—had claimed their gift and come to realize the true nature of their creativity. That day, they woke up and came together in our circle as the fully accountable, creative people they had always been. They woke up inwardly, as well. And they asked, "How can I bring my potential forward more effectively at work?" "Can I go back?" "Will anyone else be able to understand?" Each of them, in their own way, wondered how to return into the same systems and structures at work when nothing else had changed but them.

In those final hours of our seminar, I shared a few themes that have emerged over the years through my work:

- **It's a choice to go back.** With all you've learned, you choose, consciously, to return through familiar doorways, like Mark when he walks into his classroom every morning. Or, like Andrew, you might seek out new doorways that lead somewhere else. Maybe the doorway hasn't changed, but now you're choosing to bring your Superpowers and your creativity forward. Some places will be more receptive; others will be dismissive and unforgiving. Whatever the outcomes, it's your choice to return and create—and to keep entering through familiar doorways and through new ones that show up along the way.

- **Your allies and mentors—and how you work with them—will change.** As you take your gift out into the world, you will learn to collaborate differently with people. How will things be different for Mark as he engages students in learning? Who will come along with Regina in her quest to "kick some ass"? Some people won't be able to go there with you. But that's OK. By sharing your gift, you will awaken the gift in others. There will be new mentors, new friends, and new colleagues who get it. The ones who don't will test you in ways that strengthen trust in your creativity.

- **Your relationships with all the bosses and leaders in your life will change.** Mostly, you'll stop giving your power away. Instead of feeling that management is stopping you, blocking your creativity, or slowing things down, you'll take accountability, speak up, give feedback, and get involved. You'll change your story. Lily can let her boss know how challenging it is to focus during such uncertainty. In her new role, Regina will have the opportunity to help shape what I call the "tone at the top"—the example leaders of any organization set by their behaviors and decisions. You'll find ways to influence the leaders of your organization to move things forward. And if you find yourself working for an asshole, like Andrew did, you can choose to do something different.

- **You will encounter new and different tests.** In addition to the tests we explored in our first adventure (like navigating the Blank

Canvas or Time and Timing), there are new tests to face as you bring your creativity forward inside social systems. You will have to cross different Swamps—places where you may feel stuck in the trappings of bureaucracy, hierarchy, and organizational politics. These kinds of dynamics are not going away. They are deeply entrenched in how companies, school and healthcare systems, governments, and academic institutions survive. But they are at odds with the expression of your creative potential as you work to change the status quo. Though these challenges will test you in powerful ways, they don't have to stop you from inventing with others inside social systems.

- **You will change the system.** Your voice, your creativity, your Superpowers, and your unique perspective will change the shape of the organization you're in—even if you can't see it. Think about Mark and his seventh-graders. Mark will never see the consequences of his impact on the students he teaches. They'll go on to become who they become—in part because of his influence. But he won't see it because whatever awakens in his students will play out over time, after they've moved on. It's similar with you in the system. When you keep your gift alive and bring promise and possibility into your world, you will transform things in ways you won't even know. Sometimes you will get to witness the transformation and sometimes you won't.

In our first adventure, we explored your inner relationship with creativity and worked to rewrite the story of who you are as a creator. Now it's time to realize the benefits of your inner work and turn your focus outward—taking your gift into the world to co-create more effectively with others. That requires letting go of the illusion that you can create alone.

Like Andrew, Mark, Regina, Lily, and so many more, you are poised to head out into the world on a new hero's journey, together with others. That's what this next adventure is about: *getting creative together.* You'll learn how to navigate the systems you're in and stay true to who you are. You'll practice applying your creativity to spark innovation, co-create with others, share leadership, and navigate the Swamps that show up along the way. And you'll awaken to a deeper understanding that creativity is not a solitary act—it is an experience that must be shared.

The good news is that you are a creative being. You want to apply your gifts to meaningful purposes out in the world. You want to discover, invent, and innovate. While you may enjoy some places in your life where things are more structured and certain, you were born to play, to make things, experiment, learn, and progress. You want to make things better for yourself and for others. So, how do you survive and thrive in the systems that you work in? How do you keep that spirit of play, adventure, and discovery alive inside these systems? As the business world changes, how can you collaborate with others more effectively in pursuit of a better future? Let's see what we discover in this, our next adventure together.

Identifying Your Creative Style

. . . . .

WHAT DOES it feel like when you are doing your best work? Who are you partnering with and how are you collaborating together? Are you working more independently or as part of a team? What kinds of projects are exciting—where you feel like you're making an important contribution? Are you starting up new ventures or improving existing products and services? Maybe you are simplifying things in ways that add value or developing a new idea or technology. What do you look forward to?

Now think about the other side of the coin. What circumstances do you dread? What sucks the energy out of your desire to do your best and make a difference? We all know it can be difficult to experiment and innovate in the context of organizational systems, large or small. We've hinted at some of the challenges of hierarchy, bureaucracy, and the "bullshit politics and resistance," as Regina would say.

Despite these tests, there are advantages to creating "inside" an organization. You're part of a kind of village—and there is strength in belonging. We need connection, kinship, and community to stimulate and activate purpose and potential. Inside social systems there is shared purpose. There is a network of ideas, resources, support, technologies, people to learn with, and in many cases a bigger mission to connect with. These elements support and nourish creative potential.

At the same time, we crave independence and autonomy. We want freedom to explore and experiment and test ourselves. We want to see ourselves as individuals—distinct from others—with a unique and valued identity. But it's easy to confuse this need for individuality and freedom with the idea that creativity is a solo act. It is not. In fact, *it's an illusion that we can create alone*. Your gift of creativity gets activated in relationship with the external world—within social contexts and systems.

Whether you realize it or not, creativity is a shared experience. While creating alone might be glorified in our mythology (think of stories of the inventor working alone in a basement or attic), it's difficult when you try to go it alone. If you do, you lose connection to the source of ideas as well as all the ways community and collaboration make those ideas better, more relevant, and easier to implement and sustain.

So, how can you harness all the best of belonging—without getting mired in the rules, politics, norms, and practices that can diminish the realization of your creative potential? How can you follow your curiosity and shape the future, while taming (instead of fighting) the monsters that live in the Swamps of social systems? How can you rewire the way you bring creativity forward into organizations that are experiencing rapid, complex change and disruption? The first step in this journey involves knowing more about what I call your Creative Style.

Over the years, your experiences and actions (and the beliefs, assumptions, and expectations that built up around these) have formed your style. It's the constellation of strategies, preferences, habits, and practices you typically use when you create in the world—developed over time—as a co-creation between your external and internal world. But if you're like me, your Creative Style formed without much conscious awareness.

Through our early years and into adulthood, we learn about ourselves, about life, and about other people. We learn how social systems work and what happens when we bring creativity forward within these systems. We learn if it's safe to be ourselves and what happens when we take risks, step out of line, and make things up. In the socialization that happens through our family and schooling, we learn how to get things done, what gets rewarded, and what gets us in trouble. This kind of learning—how to succeed, stay safe, and make our way as a member within social structures and systems—continues well into college and our early job experiences.

As we enter the world of work, these lessons become amplified in our choices about where and how to work. We learn to follow rules primarily designed to replicate the familiar, retain control, and serve the rule-makers more than they serve us. To succeed, we navigate hierarchical structures and "color within the lines" even while we're being asked to think outside of the box, challenge the status quo, get "agile," and innovate. We're evaluated and rewarded for delivery and execution against goals and performance metrics. Promotional norms favor fitting in, loyalty, and playing the game.

Think about the different systems and organizations you've lived and worked in—all the way from your early family years through your current work situation. These life experiences have shaped your Creative Style. That means it's durable, but I want to be very clear: your style is not fixed. It's not a trait, like a personality trait. It's malleable. You have agency to adapt and change it.

Through my doctoral research[1] and subsequent practice, I've discovered four core Creative Styles that people form in relationship to social systems: the Soloist, the Rebel, the Entrepreneur, and the Collaborator. These four styles are not exclusive: you have some measure of strategies and practices from each of them, though one might have been front and center, up on the "stage" of your awareness for a very long time. Nor are the styles fixed, as I've mentioned. You can rearrange their configuration "in the theater." But knowing which of these styles is dominant—and how the other styles show up—can bring great insight into how you create together with others.

DIFFERENT CONSTELLATIONS
OF THE FOUR CREATIVE STYLES

■ Soloist

□ Rebel

▨ Entrepreneur

▨ Collaborator

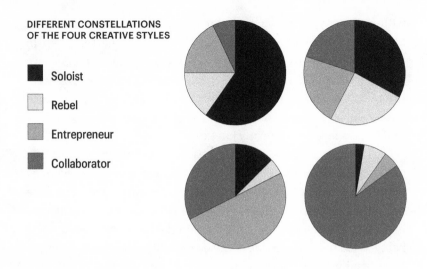

Some of the practices of your Creative Style will support the effective expression of your creativity in the new world of work, as organizations evolve and change. Others will not. When you come to understand the patterns, habits, and behaviors of your style, you gain access to new choices and new possibilities. Before we consider adapting your Creative Style, let's get to know it better.

Style One: The Soloist

• • •

I talked with Lily a few weeks after our seminar ended and she returned to work. "Things got messy with the restructuring," she said on the phone. "I thought I was going to keep my head down and just keep quietly doing my best. But I got a great idea, and I just couldn't let it slip by." Lily told me about some new, exciting work she'd started: shortening the time it takes to generate insights from the data she and her colleagues work with.

"There are so many opportunities to adapt our approach to storing and accessing data," she said. "Most of the people I work with just want to keep doing it the way we've always done it—and they're protecting the systems they built." But having multiple systems that didn't talk well with each other made bundling, aggregating, and analyzing data much slower and more difficult. Lily really cared about making things better in her work—for herself and others. Focusing on this project was Lily's way of bringing her caring and her creativity together—and delivering something within a defined scope.

Lily is a classic Soloist. She tends to define boundaries around what she can own and control—and she creates within those boundaries. Because of this, Lily thinks of her ideas as "hers," rather than as something that emerges from interactions with others. Like most Soloists, Lily is less interested in creating outside the scope of her domain or sphere of influence. She prefers to work with others when it's necessary to progress her goals, when she must comply with organizational procedures, or when she believes it will benefit those in her care or the outcomes for which she is responsible. In classic Soloist fashion, Lily would follow rules and regulations publicly, but bend or break the rules more privately, within the confines of her project.

Like Lily, Soloists create their own path. They are rarely satisfied with following the manual or textbook, but instead go above and beyond to keep things fresh and interesting. It's in her nature to follow her heart about the right thing to do. Because she has control over her sphere of influence, she can do that inside boundaries where she has agency.

Most Soloists share the products of their creativity as completed ideas, rather than including others in their creative process. Because they regularly come up with novel approaches within their domain, they are often viewed as stimulants to the creativity of others. When people see the Soloist's ideas and how they work, it gives them ideas for how they could do something similar or how they could adapt the solution. At the same time, however, Soloists benefit from collegial sharing—using the ideas of others to spark new approaches, strategies, and the novel use of different materials.

Soloists can inspire others—opening windows of possibility, generating new options and choices, and showing that ideas and solutions can work. There are, however, drawbacks to this Creative Style:

- Soloists can generate a lot of extra work for themselves, others, and managers by going it alone. In addition, managers are often challenged to adjust systems to the variety of different approaches Soloists generate.

- Soloists express a high need for autonomy and freedom from administrative control, which means others must adapt to them. They thrive with managers who do not check too carefully on what they are doing or look over their shoulder.

- Their pursuit of autonomy can lead to jealousies and rivalries. Colleagues may become irritated or resentful if they don't experience the same freedom, or they may feel compelled to work harder because of the high standards Soloists typically set. When others are not interested in going the extra mile, Soloists stand out.

Despite these challenges, Soloists are generally perceived as an asset to the organization, contributing to a more stimulating and enriched environment and bringing valuable gifts to the systems they create in:

- Soloists generate lots of ideas and possibilities, based on deep technical and domain expertise. They know the landscape of their "sandbox" and understand both the fundamentals and the spaces of opportunity.

- Because they are focused more tightly within arenas they control, they can play more deeply in the realm of possibilities, while limiting constraints. This empowers them to act with Creative License—taking risks; adapting methods, processes, and tools; and inventing and disrupting in new ways.

- Soloists can adapt an idea that works in a different context and make it relevant and resonant in their world, and then offer it to others.

- Soloists are often motivated by a deep sense of service. Sometimes that is focused on advancing their domain of expertise. Other times it is directed toward helping people in their care, improving conditions, and creating experiences for others that help them grow and develop. Soloists care deeply about making a difference through their ideas.

Are you primarily a Soloist? At my core, I am. There are many Soloists working in all kinds of different organizational systems. You might be a consultant out working on a client project or an independent contractor moving from project to project in our increasingly fluid gig economy. Maybe you're a driver for one of the on-demand rider applications like Lyft or Uber. You might own a small business, or you could be a classroom teacher. Maybe you're a research scientist, working in your lab, or a university professor, working with a measure of autonomy that enables you to own some organizational territory: your work, your scope, and your outcomes. Or, like Lily, you might be an employee in a corporation who—while working effectively with others—still prefers to have defined work that you can own.

Style Two: The Rebel

• • •

I knew going into the seminar that Andrew wasn't happy at work. So it wasn't really a surprise that he decided he couldn't stay in his old job. On a call about a month before the seminar, Andrew shared many of the frustrations he had just making basic improvements to the systems and processes the county used to comply with regulations and ordinances. He longed to make broader changes—to overhaul the way payments, transfers, billing, and collections were managed.

Unfortunately Andrew's manager shot down his ideas at every turn, claiming that the changes would be too disruptive and might threaten compliance. But Andrew knew that his proposals would ensure a *higher* standard of compliance than was currently the case. "My manager won't even give me a chance," Andrew said.

Andrew presents primarily as a Rebel in his Creative Style. And for him, the unfairness, dismissal, and lack of consideration for his ideas (and for his diligence in thinking them through) was like a punch in the gut. Like most Rebels, Andrew has a keen sense for the gap between the way things are and the way he believes things should be. Strong moral ideals shape his creative expression. The unfounded dismissal of his ideas motivated him to speak up and challenge his manager and the people he believed were protecting both the status quo and his manager's bad behavior.

For Rebels, this tension between reality and a more ideal state brings their creativity together with their sense of justice. The gap may even anger them, and Andrew was no exception: the conflict activated his creativity to make change. "There's so much we could do to make this place better," he said on the phone. "Not just the systems and infrastructure, but even how we treat each other." A whole host of issues, conflicts, and circumstances can raise a Rebel's ire. These situations act almost as a wellspring for ideas about how things could be different and better, how problems could be solved, and how situations could be righted.

Rebels are often described as people who may swim against the tide of popular opinion, marching to the beat of their own drum. This brings specific challenges and drawbacks:

- Rebels must be careful not to go too far into righteousness. They often set themselves up in opposition to conditions and other people. They are prepared to fight for what they believe, despite the cost to collegial and managerial relationships.

- Like Soloists, Rebels tend to view their ideas as "their own," though they may engage a small, trusted cohort of people for the exchange of ideas and to build strength and support for their positions.

- Their unconventionality can generate friction, and sometimes their caustic approach puts people off. A Rebel might say, "I couldn't care less about other people's opinions" and "Don't mess with me." They may believe they can do whatever they want despite rules and regulations.

- Rebels make waves, take risks, and are often a catalyst for change— yet at the same time, they can be viewed as a "problem" to be reckoned with. They might purposefully act as a thorn in the side of the status quo. Because of their fearlessness, Rebels may choose to be highly vocal about mistakes and failure.

At the same time, Rebels bring valuable gifts into the systems they live and work in:

- Rebels see gaps and are keenly attuned to what is out of alignment in a proposal, in a solution, or within a system or relationship.

- They naturally see how an idea either stays true to shared principles or undermines them. If their delivery of the message doesn't get in the way, this attunement can be critical in making decisions that communicate the best intentions and aspirations of the enterprise.

- Rebels are not afraid to speak truth directly to power and address the elephant in the room (or the "stinky fish on the table," as my European colleagues would say). While others stay silent—or share their concerns only with colleagues who are not decision-makers— Rebels will give voice to these concerns.

- Their ideas for improving, inventing, and disrupting often address both relationship challenges and task challenges. Rebels might just as easily come up with a way to partner more effectively as with a better policy, process, technology, or standard of care. Thus, the impact of their ideas can cut across a broad spectrum of impact and value.

Are you a Rebel? Do you share some of the strategies, preferences, and practices of Rebels? In her book *Rebel Talent*,[2] Francesca Gino describes how she has encountered Rebels in all walks of life. It's less about what you do and who you work with that makes your Creative Style like that of a Rebel. It's more about what activates your creativity, how you see opportunity in arenas like injustices and complacency, and the strategies you use to make change happen. Maybe you're speaking up to management—putting what you believe is right ahead of your own reputation. Maybe you're not interested in "playing the game." In fact, maybe the game pisses you off and you're more than happy to let people know. Maybe you're comfortable breaking the rules in search of what you believe. You might even wish that others would have the kind of courageous authenticity you show. "Maybe if more people would tell it like it is, I wouldn't get so much shit for doing it," Andrew said. You'll know your Rebel style is front and center if the gap between what is and what could be brings your creativity forward.

Style Three: The Entrepreneur
• • •

I met Mark down in Los Angeles a few months after our seminar. He told me about an exciting new project he'd started within the school district. I couldn't help but notice how his face lit up when he talked about creating the plan, identifying who to include, and figuring out how to garner support and funding. In his way, Mark was setting up a new venture—like he was creating his own business. For Mark, his creativity came together with a kind of "systems thinking" that helped him see new opportunities across the ecosystem.

Mark presents primarily as an Entrepreneur. If he were a Soloist, he'd likely focus his creativity directly on his classroom—the space in his world that is within his control and sphere of influence. If he were primarily a Rebel, he might challenge the other teachers and the principal to change things he believes are not as they should or could be. But Mark's creative focus gravitates instead to the broader system, to how things are organized and run, how things could be better from an effectiveness and efficiency standpoint, and how those involved could be better engaged and served. Mark is always thinking about what new ventures he can set up—projects, committees, policies, task forces— out in the broader system beyond just his work or area of expertise.

As I listened to Mark over lunch, I heard how much of his creativity was focused on the question of *how*. While the ideas and solutions generated by Soloists and Rebels may rank high on novelty in the eyes of others, the Entrepreneur's ideas may seem downright practical. That's because Entrepreneurs are builders and implement-ers. In classic Entrepreneur style, Mark talked about how he planned to forge partnerships with corporations, political stakeholders, and the teachers' union. And he shared how his methodologies were fluid. Sometimes getting things done would mean capturing public attention. Other times it might mean doing things quietly and subtly behind the scenes. Sometimes he might have to work alone. Other times he might need to enlist the help of others.

Like Mark, Entrepreneurs bring new ventures into existence with a strong sensitivity to how ideas for new technologies, products, ser-vices, and approaches will live and interact within the system. They're busy experimenting, changing things, figuring out what needs to be done, connecting people with similar interests, and checking on the progress of projects. Entrepreneurs mobilize support to finance proj-ects and figure out how to access resources and adjust budgets to fund their projects. They keep abreast of what's going on around them. "I've got my finger in as many pots as I can," Mark told me at lunch. "It helps me know how to get things done and who to work with."

Entrepreneurs are confident and self-reliant, combining their skill for identifying opportunities with skill in figuring out how to capitalize on them. Their confidence, however, can present certain challenges and drawbacks:

- Entrepreneurs tend to want to find and make their own way. They rely on their own judgment of what needs to happen and how to go about it. To others, they may come off as ambitious drivers—and if they are more focused on their own success than the success of the collective, their ambition can become a liability.

- Entrepreneurs can be wary of anyone who might claim to know what is best for them. They believe that local control and hands-on management contribute to success. That can make Entrepreneurs reluctant to follow the advice of others who make recommenda-tions that differ from their own vision.

- They may have difficulty working collaboratively. When ideas and approaches veer too far from their original vision—the one that they have passion for—Entrepreneurs can disengage and lose interest. Even so, Entrepreneurs are more likely to include others in the design of their creative endeavors than Soloists or Rebels. They recognize that getting things done within the context of the broader system means forming alliances, getting involved in politics, and working with others when necessary.

Despite these challenges, Entrepreneurs bring valuable gifts into the systems they work in:

- Where others might create a solution that only serves their part of the system—the part that is within their view or remit—Entrepreneurs tend to generate solutions that cut across parts of the broader system.

- They understand and can mitigate the challenges that could stop a solution from working longer-term, at increasing scale, and in different applications and contexts.

- Entrepreneurs are often keenly attuned to politics, influence, and persuasion—and they can apply their creativity to enroll people in their vision.

- Connecting their vision to value and benefits for the broader system comes more easily to Entrepreneurs and helps to garner resources and attract people to help them.

- Entrepreneurs are opportunists—spotting needs or gaps and putting together solutions to address them. If their idea or vision doesn't play out as hoped, they might simply leave to start up something new.

Are you an Entrepreneur? Maybe you find your creativity naturally activated by starting up new ventures, setting up projects that cut across boundaries, building alliances and coalitions, and moving around resources to achieve your goals and desires. Maybe you're keenly attuned to what motivates others, and you know how to influence people to garner support for your efforts. You might be a self-starter, creating new avenues for change and greater effectiveness. Like Mark, you might be driven by a vision for how new ventures could make things better for "customers." In his case, Mark envisioned a new way of learning science that was completely different than the norm. What's your vision?

BEFORE WE explore the fourth style, the Collaborator, let's review some similarities between these initial three. First, Soloists, Rebels, and Entrepreneurs tend to believe that creativity is a solo act—something that happens in their head or by their efforts. They also tend to struggle with the tendency to want to control outcomes. This can make it harder to join with others in a true process of co-creating. And while they are likely to have a keen sensitivity to the needs of whomever they see as their customers—whether that is an individual, team, or an entire system—they want to be the ones deciding which solutions meet these needs, how solutions should be developed, and how they should be implemented.

But creativity is a social phenomenon. Soloists, Rebels, and Entrepreneurs must figure out how to "own" their ideas and visions—in the sense of taking accountability for them—without controlling them as one might own and protect a possession.

A Different Kind of Style: The Collaborator

· · ·

My doctoral research, and the subsequent work I've done over the years, revealed a fourth constellation of strategies and practices that can develop in relationship to social systems. I call this Creative Style the Collaborator. But while it's easy to find any number of Soloists, Rebels, and Entrepreneurs out in the world of work, it's quite rare—at least in our westernized culture—to find people whose primary style is the Collaborator. At least at present, the Collaborator appears less likely to manifest as a primary style given our adherence to the old story of what creativity is and the way our families, institutions, and workplaces have been set up and run in the past.

Despite their rarity, I have met people who present primarily as Collaborators. Regina is one of these. We met many years ago, when she first became a manager and participated in a class I taught at her company. Back then, Regina doubted herself and her creativity—mostly because she didn't believe she generated a lot of ideas *on her own*. "I need to talk with people for ideas to take shape," she said. "When we work on it together, it starts to make sense and then I know how I can contribute." Through our work together, Regina reclaimed the gift of her creativity. And she learned to honor, instead of doubt, her Creative Style.

After her first promotion into management, Regina rose quickly through the ranks and was most recently asked to lead the Procurement department for the Americas. With her deep sense of humility, she always seemed surprised at how she'd been promoted. This isn't unusual for Collaborators; they tend to see themselves as part of a group, network, or community and rarely set themselves apart. While you can find Collaborators at all levels of an organization, they make wonderful leaders. That's because, like Regina, Collaborators are looking out for the interconnections: the way things fit together, the different contributions people and departments make and how that diversity adds value, and the intersections of everyone's ideas, together.

Unlike Soloists and Rebels (and even, to some degree, Entrepreneurs), Collaborators do not like to work alone. They are less territorial—less focused on protecting their turf—and more focused on the collective good. Collaborators understand the challenges of creating with others and the way individual freedoms might be limited in the give and take of ideas and perspectives. They prefer this approach and view it as an opportunity rather than a constraint. To a Collaborator, it makes no sense for one member of the group to claim personal responsibility for the products of creative activity. In fact, if someone does, it can be seen as a breach of trust.

For Collaborators, ideas come from all around us and are not "ours alone." They belong to the collective. Therefore, Collaborators can more easily adapt when ideas get batted around or plans evolve as ideas are implemented. Collaborators prefer to operate in relationship to a shared vision and strategy, where both serve to direct, inform, and sometimes, if necessary, constrain creative activity.

Regina exemplified all of this. In contrast to the previous leader of the Procurement group, she met regularly with her peers, partners, and stakeholders. She listened to their ideas, talked things over with them, and involved them in helping to shape the future vision for her department. She saw this network of relationships and interconnections as a creative "community of purpose," working on behalf of the company's mission. Like Regina, Collaborators believe that together they can do more, that interaction with others ignites and increases possibilities.

For Collaborators, *how* people work together is as much a demonstration of creativity as what may or may not be produced. Leadership is often shared, with people swapping roles and fulfilling different functions in the co-design of approaches, processes, policies, and improvements. Because one of the most valuable products of their creativity—this collaborative way of working together—is intangible, sometimes it can seem that they are constantly having to justify their value.

In fact, colleagues who are strong drivers in any of the other Creative Styles might mistake the Collaborator's desire to join with others for a lack of strength in driving for results. In a world obsessed with achievement, products, deliverables, and action, it can be uncomfortable when you can't attribute results to any one member of the team or network. But Collaborators understand that organizations, as living systems, flourish when all people are active participants and contributors.

Aside from the risk that Collaborators may appear to lack personal conviction, there are few drawbacks to this style. And Collaborators bring valuable gifts to the systems they work in:

- Collaborators tend to have a high tolerance for ambiguity based on a foundation of honesty and trust. This allows them to consider multiple solutions and alternatives, suspend judgment, and delay closure until action is necessary.

- They value connection over individual achievement. This enables them to align with the visions of others. As Collaborators create, they seek communion, relationship, and shared purpose over personal ambition and drive.

- Collaborators are oriented toward the co-creation of value with customers and partners—across boundaries. That helps to ensure solutions, approaches, and outcomes are developed with diverse input, in an inclusive process, and with a shared sense of ownership.

- Collaborators seek transparency as a default. Active resistance and protecting are contrary to their values, and they thrive when there is a generous exchange of knowledge and resources.

- It's easier for Collaborators to participate in an iterative, agile process of creating, adjusting, making decisions, and then adjusting again.

Are you a Collaborator? Maybe you've thought all these years that you weren't really "that creative" because you don't seem to have a lot of ideas on your own. Maybe you prefer working your ideas out with others, adapting them in relationship to an evolving vision that you co-create. Maybe it doesn't matter who has the idea—and you can't always recall how the idea came forward. Maybe you're sensitive to the presence (or absence) of a compelling strategy that guides the way ideas come forward and get developed. You might be focused on creating something intangible—a kind of community or network that has a life of its own. You might be connecting people who have similar passions and interests and who are working toward similar goals. At times, you might feel like the value you personally bring as a co-creator gets lost a bit in the collective. In the end, if you show up primarily as a Collaborator, what you're creating together will matter more than being seen as the hero with the idea.

The Rise of the Collaborator

• • •

A new world of work is emerging. The importance of—and need for—the Collaborator is on the rise. We're facing disruptive challenges across all walks of life. The increasing interconnectedness we observe in our society and institutions means we can no longer expect to succeed if we strive to operate independently. We have to *get creative together*. As the world changes, our social systems will evolve. I believe we will see more people emerge who express their creativity in the style of the Collaborator.

Meanwhile, it will become increasingly important for those of us who present as primarily Soloists, Rebels, and Entrepreneurs to adapt our Creative Style to succeed in creative ventures. That will be tricky, because we've learned how to succeed in the business world as it has been, and it's hard to think about doing something different and risky. It will take attention, energy, and perseverance to change these durable habits.

To help understand how things are shifting, let's consider some widely held assumptions and beliefs that have been prevalent over the past decades. Back in 1978, Gifford Pinchot III and Elizabeth Pinchot wrote an article called "Intra-Corporate Entrepreneurship"[3] where they first coined the term *intrapreneur*. An intrapreneur is someone who brings creativity forward to invent inside the context of a large corporation, business, or organization. Intrapreneurs pioneer, explore, discover, and innovate inside the system. They generate new value from the products of their efforts.

In the book *Intrapreneuring*[4] that followed the article, Gifford Pinchot proposed Ten Commandments that challenged professionals to show up every day with the kind of resolve that might get them fired, and to undertake any tasks to help a project succeed regardless of their job description. He encouraged people to honor their sponsors, but also to follow their own dreams despite any "orders" not to do so. Pinchot urged intrapreneurs to seek out others to help, gather "the best" like-minded people to work with, and keep efforts underground to avoid "the corporate immune mechanism." And perhaps most famously, he suggested that "it is easier to ask for forgiveness than for permission."

Can you hear the voices of Soloists, Rebels, and Entrepreneurs in these "commandments"? To many people, much of Pinchot's guidance will ring true even today. And many of his commandments have made their way into how we go about innovating within the system. But Pinchot's work was a product of the times. He was talking primarily to an individualist—working in a business world and workplace that was very different from how things are today.

Back then, the Soloist, Rebel, or Entrepreneur's preference to work independently, come up with ideas "by themselves," work around the system's rules (or despite these rules), and maintain control of their vision and its implementation might have been more effective. It was easier back then to follow the commandments.

Decades later, this approach for intrapreneuring is still alive—but it is fast becoming a recipe for failure. Take, for example, the case of Vicky, a Soloist at her core but with a strong Entrepreneur side. Vicky worked in human resources at the headquarters of a large multinational company. A few years ago, she agreed to lead a team charged with developing a new Leadership Framework for her company. For years, she'd successfully led teams to deliver solutions that helped the company stay relevant and progressive with their HR practices. It never occurred to her that her Soloist and Entrepreneur styles might not work—or might have a downside.

As she had done many times before, she organized the team and divided up the initial work of gathering research and intelligence on the topic. Everyone on the team was working on a different part of the puzzle—largely in isolation and in a shroud of secrecy. They vowed early on to protect their efforts from potential intervention until there was something coherent to share. Finally, the team put together a draft "framework," something they felt was ready to share.

Vicky presented the framework to a group of business leaders who had come together for a three-day meeting. In a stunning rebuke, everyone rejected the framework. "It felt dead to them," I remember her telling me later. "Like there was no energy or life in it."

It was a devastating blow, but Vicky listened carefully to the feedback and quickly developed a new version. When she presented it again the next day, the reaction was overwhelmingly positive. "They loved it," she gushed as she shared her new version with the team the following week. Not surprisingly, the team adopted this new framework. After all, the leaders had loved it, Vicky loved it, and it seemed to meet all the criteria for the solution.

The framework was celebrated as a success, and Vicky and the team were rewarded and recognized for their achievement. But now that the work of creating it had come to an end, it was time to hand the framework off to a new team to embed it into the processes, systems, and programs across the HR department. The problem was, the framework was created in classic Soloist style. It belonged to no one—except maybe Vicky. It wasn't a product of true co-creation. The new team certainly didn't feel invested in the framework—in fact, several of them didn't really understand it but were afraid to ask.

In the end, the Leadership Framework floundered and finally failed. Slowly, it disappeared from any of the places the new team tried to deploy it. It was hard for Vicky to watch all her work collapse as soon as she stepped away. But as the product of a Soloist approach, it simply wasn't sustainable. Vicky's story is just one example of the kinds of personal and systems-level failures that are increasingly likely when we rely on traditional tactics, seek solutions for discrete parts of a complex problem, and invent in isolation.

What if someone with the primary style of the Collaborator had led the same project? How might a Collaborator have built shared purpose among the team and across the organization? What might a Collaborator have done differently, when presenting the draft version to leaders? Once rejected, how might they have brought an updated version to life? What strategies and practices might have been different from someone who doesn't believe it's *their project* to own and progress? From someone who's more interested in joining others rather than seeking others to enroll?

We all need to bring forward the Creative Style of the Collaborator. The business world has changed radically since the Pinchots coined the term *intrapreneuring*. Work and life have globalized into a complex web of interconnectedness. We're all tied up in each other's business—and what someone does or what a system does in one part of the world impacts other systems far and near. News travels to all corners of the world in an instant. The disruptions, surprises, actions, and choices of people in systems all over the world are intertwining in ways we could not have imagined back in the early 1980s. What people create "over there" impacts and influences what's possible "here," in the systems you and I work in. What will happen next is unknown.

In this increasingly complex ecosystem, co-creating is fast becoming the best way to generate new value that is scalable and sustainable. Innovation will happen within and across networks as people collaborate on complex and interdependent projects. In the new world of work, different norms are emerging:

- **Collective ownership** is on the rise. Capturing value and holding that value for competitive advantage is slipping away as a primary principle for innovation. Co-creation of value with customers and partners—across boundaries and industries—is becoming more prevalent. The face of competition is changing. We will all need to learn to realize our individual and personal visions within the larger context of collective dreams and visions.

- **Trust** is fast becoming the most valuable currency when creating within and across systems. Credibility, reliability, fairness, connectedness, and intimacy—the hallmarks of trust—are all tempered by the perception of your level of self-orientation. That is, trust is impacted most by whether others believe you are more oriented toward your own gain, interests, and desires or more oriented toward the aims, interests, and desires of the collective. In a world where value is co-created, self-oriented people will not garner the currency of trust that is needed to work together in new and evolving ways.

- **Transparency** is becoming an essential ingredient for activating and accelerating creativity. Visible and accessible common standards, shared language, shared principles, shared data and evidence, and shared knowledge are like water flowing out of a faucet, giving life to fertile fields. Transparency breathes life into creation because it opens access within and across systems to anyone wanting to contribute.

- **Incremental and iterative** is the new style of moving creative output forward. The introduction of "agile" language, principles, and methodologies have forever shaped the landscape of how we work. In this approach, small groups of people with a shared purpose are the vehicle to make additive and incremental progress that contributes to the whole. Iterative design and development are critical to working collaboratively on big, audacious goals within complex systems. Mechanisms for gathering and incorporating feedback at regular intervals along the way are also a hallmark of this approach. The days of working in isolation and launching finished products, solutions, and services are over. It's about adaptation and evolution along the way.

- **Decision-making** is becoming more organic and distributed. Command and control are on the wane, which is a tough pill to swallow for managers and senior leaders across industries and enterprises. Every day I hear managers ask, "What's my role in this new world of 'agile' ways of working? If I'm not approving, assigning, directing, and evaluating, what am I doing? What does it mean to be a manager?" As I write this, I can only say that we're all still collectively figuring that out. But one thing is clear: the role of a manager is becoming much more like that of a coach and curator—someone who shares wisdom instead of someone who prescribes.

- **Rewards and recognition** approaches are undergoing a seismic shift. Currently, the tools and methods for rewarding and recognizing creative output are steeped in personal achievement and individual accomplishment, which lines up nicely with the values of Soloists, Rebels, and Entrepreneurs. But things are shifting—even as they are hard to change. More and more clients I work with are seeking new ways of rewarding teams, networks, and collectives—rewarding the whole rather than the parts of a creative venture or effort. Just watch the credits to a Pixar film, where *everyone* is acknowledged, and you will see the tip of the iceberg of what's to come.

WHY IS all this important—and how does it relate to you, to me, and to Vicky, Mark, Andrew, Lily, and others? The global changes we are witnessing are fundamentally transforming our ways of working. In turn, this is changing the landscape into which we express our creative potential and our Creative Style.

Creating together is becoming something different than it has been. Each of us will be called to move from an ability-based view of creativity to a potential-based view and to bring forward the strategies and practices of the Collaborator. To be successful—and to learn faster than you are making mistakes—intrapreneuring must become *a process of co-creation inside nested interdependent networks and systems*. Whatever your primary style, you will need to take the best of your gifts of heart, intellect, and will into a new kind of collaboration for a modern time. Then you can show up in the process of co-creation as a living example of conscious creativity.

ASK YOURSELF...

Now, at the end of this chapter, take time to pause and reflect on the following questions.

- Which of the Creative Styles shows up front and center as your primary style? How do the other styles show up "in your mix"?

- What experiences in your life have influenced the development of your Creative Style and how you use it to create within social systems?

- What might you take for granted about your Creative Style that may or may not be true?

Style One: The Soloist

- How does your creativity show up when circumstances are more within your sphere of control? How do you prefer to share your ideas and the solutions you generate?

Style Two: The Rebel

- What kinds of circumstances might compel you to fight for what you believe in? How does the gap between what is—and what could or should be—motivate you to take creative action?

Style Three: The Entrepreneur

- What challenges, needs, and opportunities can you sense across the system that are activating your creativity? What is your vision for a better future?

A Different Kind of Style: The Collaborator

- What kinds of circumstances attract you to join in and become part of a collective effort? How does your approach add value to complex, interdependent challenges?

The Rise of the Collaborator

- Which of the patterns, strategies, and behaviors of the Collaborator might be showing up in your Creative Style today?

- What benefit might come from bringing the Collaborator forward as you activate your creative potential?

Keep Going!

• • •

What life experiences have shaped your Creative Style? Go to **creativetogetherresources.com** or scan this QR code to find out:

2

Co-creating

· · · · ·

O N ONE of my monthly check-in calls with Lily, she told me how proud she was of the work she was doing to adapt her department's approach to storing, accessing, and using data. So far, she'd escaped the impact of the restructuring that was still going on across her broader business function. Her husband was thriving in his "not so new anymore" job, and the kids were doing well. Lily was making good progress shortening the time it took to generate reports and protocols using artificial intelligence. "What a surprise," she said, as she adjusted her camera on the computer. "They just recognized me at the annual managers meeting with a special award for innovation!"

Even before the award, people from across the organization had started calling and asking if Lily would share her approach, the name of the external partner she'd been using, and anything about the project she could offer. They wanted to learn from her and replicate her approach in their part of the organization. For anyone working in a large, complex system, this should sound familiar. It made perfect sense to Lily, as it would to countless other Soloists, Rebels, and Entrepreneurs. That's because all three of these Creative Styles are happy to share the output, benefits, and learning of what they've created— once it's completed and successful.

So often, when I hear clients talk about collaboration, they are really talking about it from the perspective of the more individualist styles of the Soloist, Rebel, and Entrepreneur. People think that collaboration means sharing what they're doing. This is the basest form of collaboration. It's transactional—not transformational. Yet it comes naturally to Soloists like Lily and me, as well as to Rebels and Entrepreneurs. We want to let people know what we're up to for a whole host of reasons: so they don't generate solutions that are at cross-purposes with ours, so they don't have to reinvent what we've already created (though this often doesn't stop them), so others can benefit from what we've learned, and so the progress that's been made can be recognized across the system. This kind of transactional collaboration might be good enough when you are in execution mode, but it falls short of what's required in a process of co-creation on journeys of discovery.

When you aim to co-create new value, you must look beyond just sharing the output of your creative activity. Here, people work together to *make* something—to generate new solutions in response to a shared purpose, opportunity, or challenge. It involves more than getting together to see what others are doing or acting as a sounding board for each other. It must be more than getting others "on the bandwagon" of one person or one group's ideas. Co-creating means that you are *jointly producing* a tangible product or solution that adds new value—something that you could not generate and produce on your own. This comes more naturally to the Collaborator than to the other Creative Styles.

What helps to build a strong foundation for co-creating within and across social systems—in our increasingly complex, networked, and interdependent world? A new set of commandments for intrapreneuring wouldn't make sense given the new world of work that is emerging. Instead, I propose five essential practices of co-creation that form a new platform for creating together. As you read through these practices, consider how you might evolve and adapt your style to contribute to effective co-creation.

Practice One: Develop a Shared Dream

• • •

Remember: a meaningful purpose activates your creative potential. But for true, conscious co-creation to thrive, it's not about having your own dream—your own idea that you push forward within the system. Instead you become a partner to something that is bigger than just you, something that requires a team or network of people and systems to achieve. You spend time crafting your mission together, setting collective priorities and areas to focus on, and determining together how far to aim from the status quo.

A shared dream—a common purpose—is the first step in co-creating. When your team, cohort, or network are all working toward a shared purpose, your collective creativity is activated and focused—even when you are working with others around the globe in different time zones or in a decentralized way. It is especially important if you are empowered to move things forward without heavy governance. Everyone is clear about the outcomes to be achieved. People empathize with each other. You honor and seek to understand each other's perspective.

Also, you must be willing to evolve your personal connection to shared purpose as it matures along the path you're walking together. Creative tension is generated by the diversity of perspectives that come from a mix of people with different life experiences. That might lead to an evolution of your shared purpose over the course of your journey together. Here, a spirit of inclusiveness can make all the difference, across siloes, industries, networks, and communities of practice. Then, when you are confronted with new ideas and different directions, it's easier to identify whether they will help enhance your shared purpose or not. If you get lost, you can return together to your shared purpose for new inspiration and guidance, for getting back on track and continuing the journey.

Once shared purpose is clear, your next step is to generate a "shared vision of breakthrough." This is a step that many groups fail to take in their journey together. When you're creating together, it's not enough to have "completion of the goal" as the mission to pull you through the inevitable discomfort, ambiguity, and uncertainty that will arise. You'll need a clear and compelling picture of what it's like in the future you desire—when you've achieved your quest. Even while you realize it may turn out differently than you imagine.

It's best when this picture is articulated in terms of the benefits and value that are being experienced and felt by people and by the ecosystems involved. What's different in the future when you've been successful? What does that make possible for specific people? What have they learned and who have people become? What has the system—and the broader ecosystem of systems become? What is the organization capable of that it wasn't capable of before?

Mark learned the hard way what can happen without a shared purpose and vision for breakthrough. Being a typical Entrepreneur, he had a strong individual vision for innovating the way science was taught in the school district. His first mistake was failing to develop a shared purpose, with a clear focus and aim. Even though he had successfully "enrolled" people into his vision, and his fellow teachers were enjoying working together in new ways, when Mark took his idea district-wide, beyond the scope of his own reach, it floundered.

Mark's second mistake was failing to craft, with his fellow teachers and partners, a compelling vision of breakthrough for what might be possible once this approach went broad. For example, how would success at the district level connect with what administrators cared about? What would be different in their world, and what would be possible that would help them meet their aims and purposes once the approach was implemented? Mark had failed even to articulate his own vision of breakthrough. That's because "changing the way science is taught" is not a vision of breakthrough. It's just a strategy without clarity about *why* anyone will benefit. Mark needed to take the next step of identifying outcomes—framed as benefits for people and the system.

The clearer the picture you can paint about the breakthrough, the more energy and juice it will have to pull you and others into and through the journey. Who is there? What are people doing? What did people learn along the way that transformed them? What's possible that links to people's deeply held values and motivations?

If the anticipated gain at the realization of your purpose is not meaningful or compelling enough, or targeted to different audiences, or inclusive enough for people to see how they will benefit, momentum will falter when things start to go sideways (as they will). And you will likely falter too. A clear and compelling vision of breakthrough ensures you—and the folks you're co-creating with—are fully committed to a shared purpose.

Practice Two: Explore the Unknown Together

In Adventure One (see especially chapter 3), we explored your individual relationship with the unknown. I invited you to greet the unknown with passion, instead of dread, and to develop a deeper understanding of the dynamics of discovery. Now it's vital that you take that strong foundation—including trust in your creativity, your Superpower strengths, your understanding of the phases you're likely to pass through on journeys of discovery, and all you've learned from tests in your life—and bring it to the process of co-creating with others.

First, consider who you are journeying with and how that serves your shared purpose. Do you have a diversity of perspectives, strengths, expertise, and Creative Styles in the mix? This diversity will be critical to see and sense new opportunities and to address constraints as you traverse the unknown. Who is part of your core group, and who are the allies, stakeholders, experts, and sponsors in your wider network? Who else might you include and how might new people join along the way? How are you engaging people? Take time to *consciously design* what "together" means, given the landscape of your quest.

Then carve out time to explore together. One of the biggest challenges to co-creation is that your time—and the time of most people you work with—is not your own. It's very rare for a team or network to be fully dedicated and free to work only on a new venture. That's because people tend to be hired to do a defined job, with goals for execution, action, and implementation. And often, doing the job you were hired for takes priority—with multitudes of tasks just to fulfill these obligations and expectations. On top of that, there are meetings, mandated trainings, and lots of other activities that come along with working in a bureaucracy.

All this reduces the energy available to participate together on new projects where outcomes are unknown and uncertain. But to co-create—especially on journeys of discovery—it's critical you find and foster an appropriate measure of freedom and devote time and focused attention to exploring together. You need space to ask divergent and insight questions—to understand dynamics, interconnections, constraints, resistance, and root causes. You need to "get out of the house" and find inspiration from sources beyond the familiar. You need appropriate autonomy to organize, govern yourselves, and figure out the *how* without being told. And you must anticipate that at some point—or at multiple points along the way—you will get lost or stuck in the Swamp.

Talk together frequently about where you are in the journey and about the tests that are showing up—both individually and collectively. One of the greatest gifts of co-creation is the support that is available when you consciously explore together.

With dedicated time and appropriate degrees of freedom, you and your partners can do the hard work of navigating the inevitable challenges, trade-offs, and paradoxes that show up on any journey of discovery. In his book *Know Yourself, Forget Yourself*, Marc Lesser suggests that the contradictions and paradoxes in our experience act as signposts that can help point us in a clearer direction.[5] In the unknown, paradoxes will test you, test your visions and dreams, and test your penchant for safety and certainty. As they test you, they will also illuminate spaces where new ideas can emerge. Consciously lean into paradoxes and use them to activate your creative potential. Build collective skill in embracing multiple paradoxes simultaneously. This is fast becoming an essential skill for navigating volatility, uncertainty, complexity, and ambiguity.

Of the five paradoxes that Lesser illuminates, one is of particular importance when you are co-creating: "Benefit others, benefit yourself." In creative collaboration, there's a shift from "value-capture" to "value co-creation." Capturing value is akin to protecting it as an advantage, apart from others and sometimes despite others. It's at the root of older conceptions of what it means to create competitive advantage.

Value co-creation, on the other hand, is an active process with partners, customers, and even competitors in service to higher goals that require different ways of working together. You share value and you share credit. You elevate your impact. In value co-creation, your efforts benefit both yourself and others, and may also bring value to the networks you work in and to society more generally. When you are focused on collective benefit, you can more easily release, let go, accept the will and vision of the collective, and trust that "what is" and "what is becoming" are better than what would be possible if you were creating alone.

Devoting time and energy to explore the unknown together will ensure that you and your partners can navigate through the paradoxes and challenges of co-creating.

Practice Three: Stand Together

● ● ●

Back in the late 1970s and early '80s when the Pinchots first brought the concept of intrapreneuring to light, they framed risk-taking as primarily an individual activity. Even today, taking risks is still largely seen as the bearing of personal risk—like standing behind a recommendation that might be unpopular or at cross-purposes with conventional approaches. Or it might mean bearing some uncomfortable measure of the potential for failure. In his first commandment, Pinchot challenges the intrapreneur to be "willing to be fired." For the Soloist, Rebel and Entrepreneur, Pinchot's commandment makes perfect sense. It feels risky when it's your idea, your vision, and your neck that's on the line.

But in co-creation, the risk is distributed across the team and network in a different way. There's strength in the network and in standing together across the organization. It's less of a personal risk when you challenge the status quo together and demonstrate a collective willingness to fail and learn. I found this to be the case when I worked on a new approach for working flexibly for one of my clients.

I was actively practicing a more collaborative style of creating—working to shed some of the old habits from my Soloist style.

The first thing I did was form a network of partners from across four different departments that had a major stake in the success of any approach for working flexibly: HR, IT, Facilities, and Corporate Communications. These four departments had never collaborated to co-create something together. Up until this time, it was unusual to even share what each other's departments were doing, and when that happened, it only happened at the highest levels of leadership. But I knew it was critical to the success of the initiative that we form a new and different way of working together. We were going to have to take some hefty risks to change the status quo. I also knew it was vital that I was not the leader or at the center of this network. I intentionally selected a Collaborator to lead the team—someone who could activate the energy and vitality of the collective.

By bringing the four groups together and ensuring everyone had skin the game, we shared in the courage it took to stand up for some of our more controversial recommendations. We shared in the risks because, instead of running in this race alone, we were all in it together. We quickly developed a shared purpose, a vision for breakthrough, and we built our network with allies, mentors, and sponsors from across the four organizations and beyond. The most satisfying outcome was not even the results we produced. It was starting a new way of working together for people in these four previously independent and siloed organizations. To this day, all four continue to co-create—to make things together that are better and bolder than what had been the norm before people started sharing risk and supporting each other to be courageous.

To leverage the power of your networks in co-creation, you will also need to think differently about sponsors. Here, sponsors are involved in the creative action. This is a departure from the intent behind Pinchot's commandment to honor one's sponsor, and it runs contrary to the current custom in most organizations. Typically, sponsors of goals and initiatives sit on the sidelines and simply act as overseeing representatives from a governing board. I've seen it over and over again. Someone from a leadership team is assigned as the sponsor, but it's hard to even get time on their schedule. They rarely know what struggles the team is encountering. And when it comes time to influence their peers on the leadership team, it's also rare that they stand up and truly "sponsor" the work they're representing. Often, when I begin to work with teams, most sponsors are detached, steps removed from the real work of invention.

But this is changing. As the "agile" mindset, principles, and methodologies make their way through organizational structures and influence the way we work together, sponsors are getting more involved. Teams call them in to do real work together when their expertise is needed to move things forward.

Regina is a great example of a new kind of sponsor—one who is empowering and accountable for her role in advocating for the team's needs as they emerge. On one of our check-in calls, she shared a story about a team she was sponsoring. "A couple of months in, the team realized the metrics we'd asked for wouldn't actually measure what they were creating. They had moved past our original request and started to see a new opportunity," she said. With Regina's involvement, the team quickly co-designed a new metrics dashboard. Regina was able to advocate for them with her colleagues on the leadership team to adjust the approach—even though the head of the department opposed the change.

When you're co-creating inside the system, the way you leverage allies and mentors will change as well. For Collaborators, everyone can be an ally—even those who test you through resistance and opposition. That's because anyone can contribute ideas, perspectives, watch-outs, cautions, and constraints that become contributions to a better, emergent whole. Mentorship can also come from anywhere and it is not level-dependent. In co-creation, we all have much to teach each other and much to reveal to each other through our different perspectives and life histories. Since our creativity is what's common, and our perspective is what's unique, the field for mentorship to emerge and thrive is opening.

Draw on your networks and stand together by generously exchanging knowledge and ideas. The tendency to hoard and protect our creative endeavors is a remnant from the past that must change if we're going to move into a more modern kind of creating together. Think of Pinchot's commandment to keep your work underground and out of sight. It's easy to understand where this comes from. We've talked about the mind-numbing impacts of bureaucracy on creative endeavors. We've talked about how it can eliminate variation in service to repeatability—and short-circuit experimentation and risk-taking in service to certainty. So it's not surprising that one of the commandments would recommend protecting new ventures from public attention.

But this is an old mindset that must change to keep pace with evolving dynamics in the business world. Hoarding and protecting cuts directly in opposition to the values of transparency, openness, shared ownership, and benefit for all. And it cuts directly into the kind of trust that can come from co-creating value instead of capturing and hoarding value. If you are to build a solid architecture for co-creating, you will want to open access across a broader network of people, technologies, and tools. That means being more inclusive: inviting others to join in and be a part of the process, involving more partners and customers along the way, and seeking to *join* instead of to hide and operate in isolation.

In the new world of work, resilience, strength, and boldness will all come from the power of a distributed network rather than from a single individual. Sheltering your creativity from the system only ends up reinforcing single points of failure.

Practice Four: Check Your Ego at the Door

● ● ●

There are so many ways that our ego—and our need to distinguish our self from others and protect our self-esteem—can show up amid the trappings of hierarchy, organizational politics, and bureaucracy. But over the years, I've observed that two ways in particular get in the way of true, conscious co-creation: proving and seeking credit.

Proving

One of the most powerful concepts I learned in my doctoral program at UCLA was the distinction between what educational psychologists call a "proving orientation" and a "learning orientation" to life and events. In a proving orientation, the focus is on delivering a masterful performance—so others see *me* as competent and proficient. Maybe in some cases I am proving it to myself, but in most cases, I am proving it to others. This is critical: a proving orientation is primarily other-oriented in the sense that it is focused on building evidence that supports other people's acknowledgment of your competence, accomplishment, expertise, contribution, and capability.

This was, for example, our overwhelming orientation on the Creative Leadership project in Europe that I described earlier in this book. On the project, each one of us sought to shine individually to prove to Josef that we were absorbing his teachings and becoming competent in his methods. His evaluation was paramount. We also sought to prove to the partners of the firm that we were making progress in ways that returned the investment they were making in us. This kind of proving orientation is extremely common—and you may recognize how you do this yourself. Any of the four Creative Styles might find that they have fallen prey to "proving," although it might look slightly different for each style.

A learning orientation, on the other hand, has a different aim. Here, the generation of new insights, the evolution of perspective through diverse experiences, and the acknowledgment of unknowing and both conscious and unconscious incompetence is primary. The aim is to *enhance* competence rather than prove it to others. In a learning orientation, failure, errors, unintended outcomes, and "negative" results are all part of the mix involved in growing from experience. People in a learning orientation seek out and actively invest in experiences that challenge and test their competence—for the sake of their own advancement and the advancement of others. There's a greater openness to experience, a different view of risk, and a dash of humility that suggests you can always improve.

For co-creation to reach its full potential, no matter which Creative Style is front and center for you and for each of your partners, you will want to adopt a learning orientation and let go of proving. This will mean moving from criticizing each other's ideas to tear them down or poke holes in them, to building on each other's ideas in a constructive, additive way. That's often heard out loud as a shift from "But... " to "Yes, and... " It signals that you are sharing ownership of creative output and letting go of ensuring everyone knows your specific contribution. Although it can be hard to do, in co-creation you need to let the differentiation of individual contributions recede in favor of the celebration of collective accomplishments and learning.

Moving to a learning orientation also means that together, you and your partners will work more iteratively, in shorter cycles of trial and error. You'll conduct quick experiments, develop prototypes, and generate iterations of work products. You'll seek feedback more frequently and stop to take stock of what has been learned and how it has changed you and your approach. The idea is to fail fast and learn fast together.

For Lily, this might mean that instead of waiting until her project was finished, she could have worked together with others to generate smaller increments of work along the way, getting input and incorporating feedback into successive versions. But this would have required that she "go public" with her effort in a way that she was afraid to do. It would have required letting go of some measure of control and reorienting her approach from proving to learning. And it would have required breaking Pinchot's commandment to "work underground."

Finally, co-creating from a learning orientation means that you see each of the members involved in co-creation as basically equivalent—that is, as having no more or less potential than you or any other member of the network or team. This is a critical step in the evolution of the mindsets of the Soloist, Rebel, and Entrepreneur. These Creative Styles are more likely to hold tight to the notion that creativity is an ability—and that ideas happen "in *my* head" rather than through collective experience and exposure. Over the years, many people whose ego identity is deeply rooted in any of these styles have argued with me that "some people are simply more creative than others." In co-creation, however, it's essential for that comparison to drop away. Each member of the collective is celebrated for the unique mix of experiences, talents, strengths, and learning edges that they bring to the expression of their creative potential.

Seeking credit

The second most common way our egos can get in the way of co-creation comes from our deeply ingrained, habitual need to define who gets credit for ideas and solutions, successful ventures, and the generation of value. This is one of the biggest stumbling blocks to true, conscious co-creation. For Collaborators, sharing credit is a no-brainer. But for Soloists, Rebels, and Entrepreneurs—especially those who hold a proving orientation—sharing credit can be an enormous challenge.

In my work with teams, I see this drama play out again and again, especially at the interfaces and handoffs between teams and departments. Those who hoard and protect credit or steal it away from others are seen as villains. Those who believe they are making contributions that are under-recognized and going unrewarded feel like victims. And those who come to their aid, illuminating the true "owners" and rightful recipients of credit, are viewed as rescuers.

THE DRAMA TRIANGLE

Villian   Rescuer

Victim

What if we could get off this Drama Triangle?[6] What would have to be different so that "who gets credit" is no longer an issue that separates people in a process of co-creation?

First, we would need to let go of our ego's hunger for approval and advantage over others. Each of us would need to value intrinsic rewards (like concern for the broader community and the desire to make a meaningful contribution) over extrinsic ones (like recognition and praise from others, financial rewards, or advancement/promotion).

Next, we would have to move away from a mindset of scarcity and competition (that is, when you win, I lose—and there's not enough to go around). In a world of abundance of possibility and opportunity—a world where everyone is gifted with creative potential—hoarding credit no longer makes sense.

Finally, we would each need to be incentivized to think beyond our individual remits and serve the broader system instead of only our own interests. Then inclusion and generous sharing can replace protection and control.

The value that any one of us brings individually typically pales in comparison to the value that's possible when our contributions combine with what others can bring. This might not make your ego happy, but it doesn't make it any less true. When ideas and solutions are co-created, it's easier to "scale them up"—to implement them for greater volume and for broad use across multiple applications. That's when they become increasingly valuable. But that's also when the boundaries between your contribution and those of others blur.

Practice Five: Foster Collective Accountability

● ● ●

What does accountability look, smell, and taste like when you're truly co-creating? Most of us wouldn't know. That's because the entire structure of how we chunk up work, define jobs, plan and deliver, drive for results, and implement our work today is geared toward more individualistic reward structures. Things are set up primarily for Soloists and Entrepreneurs to succeed.

If you're like most people who work in large and mid-sized businesses, you have a job description that outlines your accountabilities. You set individual goals and objectives. You likely have conversations with your manager about your individual contributions and you're rewarded for them as compared to others' contributions. The system is set up to promote comparison and to carve up and divide accountability into smaller and smaller individual packages.

This is the world of work I've grown up in. It is deeply familiar—insidious in its invisibility to us and in the separation that it generates. It's built into the way so many of us drive for and deliver results. Think of Vicky and the way she delivered outcomes as she built the Leadership Framework for her company. Vicky worked as a Soloist/Entrepreneur and she was rewarded individually for her achievements, even though the project ultimately failed. But her achievements were not viewed in the bigger picture; if they had been, it would have been obvious that the outcomes were unsustainable.

Vicky did little to build capability in others along the way. Instead of joining others in creative collaboration, she was an individual hero, heralded as highly accountable because she pushed forward and achieved the goal despite the obstacles. In the world that Vicky lives and works in, personal accountability is conflated with individual achievement—viewed through the lens of drive, decisiveness, value-capture, and advancement. And in many cases, it is also accompanied by ambition, competition, scarcity, and an "us versus them" mindset.

Over the years, I have noticed how this crisis of separation, selfishness, differentiation, and individuation is running rampant across our social systems. It's straining our creative potential under the weight of growing complexity, ambiguity, and increasing interdependence. Creating in the system—and in nested systems of interdependence—has gotten a whole lot more complicated. I am reminded again of that bumper sticker on the green pickup: "Help! I'm making mistakes faster than I can learn from them."

The value of accountability, when viewed as individual achievement, is diminishing and will increasingly lead to mistakes and failure. That's because we're less and less able to 1) see the whole picture ourselves, 2) see beyond the horizon for what's coming next, and 3) understand the implications and unintended consequences for individual intervention in a networked, global, and interdependent world. We need each other now more than ever to co-create the advancements and innovations that will power our collective, sustainable future.

A new perspective of accountability is needed that's seen in the context of the collective. In co-creation, personal accountability shifts from being about me and my individual achievement to being deeply and personally accountable for the *we*. The separation fades away. The ego-driven need for distinctiveness and differentiation from others diminishes. You see things in broader, wider, and increasingly more inclusive circles of interdependence and interconnections. Creative activity moves from implementing my ideas—at the expense of others' ideas or in competition for resources—to joining ideas together. Strengthening ties across the network takes precedence over creating "my part" through controlled and discrete successes. Individual action, intervention, and achievement meld into a belief that "we're all in this together."

Accountability within the context of the collective, then, puts a higher value on care for relationship, shared ownership, and community than on individual achievement. This shift will require a greater level of self-awareness, attention, and careful practice for the Soloists, Rebels, and Entrepreneurs among us. But don't get me wrong: this shift does not signal the end of personal accountability for your own inner journey to express your creative potential. Your voice, your unique perspective, and your contribution are all vital in co-creation.

You still need to take care of yourself and manage the obligations of what you've set in motion through your actions. There is still a dance between your sense of individuality and your sense of belonging. Ideas may still feel like they are "yours." You still have your own dreams and you need to own them. It's just that your ideas and your dreams will be *realized* ever more increasingly in the context of joining others, letting go of control, sharing and giving, and caring for the ideas and dreams of others as well as your own.

THESE FIVE essential practices of co-creation will help you build a strong foundation for a new, more modern story of intrapreneuring—sparking innovation *together with others* within and across the systems in which you work and live.

ASK YOURSELF...

Now, at the end of this chapter, take time to pause and reflect on the following questions.

Develop a Shared Dream

* What are the hallmarks of a shared vision for a better future?

* What's different when you co-create that vision together?

Explore the Unknown Together

* What behaviors might you need to shift to co-create more effectively with others?

* How can you carve out time and energy to explore the unknown—developing insight and understanding—before moving into action and execution?

Stand Together

* Who else can you bring together through networks, coalitions, and communities to strengthen the power and velocity of your shared purpose?

* Where can you step up and forward—and where might you have to stand back—to stand together?

Check Your Ego at the Door

* How can you contribute your ideas without taking control or taking over?

- How might a "proving orientation" be showing up in your life and work? What can you do to shift to a "learning orientation"?

- What would have to be true so that "seeking credit" is no longer an obstacle to co-creation?

Foster Collective Accountability

- What kinds of behaviors signal collective accountability in your life and work?

- What might be different if more people valued relationship, care for others, and community outcomes over individual achievement?

Keep Going!

• • •

For an in-depth article about best practices for teams engaged in co-creation, go to **creativetogetherresources.com** or scan this QR code:

3

Adapting Your Style

· · · · ·

PEOPLE WHO show up primarily as Collaborators are rare—at least from my research and experiences in US and Western cultures. Remember: it's not about whether you can collaborate when you're executing and implementing in the routine of your day-to-day work. Most of us can, quite effectively. And it's not about sharing what you're doing to stay aligned with others.

I'm talking about true, conscious co-creation—venturing on a journey of discovery that requires you to cross the threshold into the unknown, together with others, and embody the five practices described in the last chapter. In this kind of co-creation, those of us who show up primarily as Soloists, Rebels, or Entrepreneurs will struggle. That's why it's vital you know yourself and understand how any of the strategies, preferences, and practices associated with these styles have shaped how you create with others inside social systems.

You already know that I lead with Soloist as my core Creative Style. Next strongest is the Entrepreneur, and then the Rebel. And I have a smidge of Collaborator. I must consciously and persistently work at bringing the Collaborator style forward. It's not natural for me. You know about the challenges and failures I've experienced trying to intrapreneur in my habitual Soloist-Entrepreneur-Rebel way. Because I've learned how my core style can get in the way of co-creating, I've challenged myself to experiment and practice bringing the Collaborator to the forefront. I want to have a more powerful and sustainable impact as I bring creativity into my work.

Why would *you* choose to bring forward the style of the Collaborator? What circumstances and conditions are calling for you to co-create with others? What would call you to invest in doing something different? Why would you answer that call? And why might you choose not to answer it?

A lot comes down to how strongly your identity is connected to a particular Creative Style and the mix of practices that have served you in the past. That's what makes it seem durable and fixed—although it is not. What values, motivations, fears, and aspirations are attached to your current mix? Does the familiarity of your primary style offer a strong a sense of security? Have you linked your primary style and style mix with your sense of identity? And your mix is surely interacting with your Inner Critic. Your wily critic is likely to promote the idea that your current mix got you where you are today—and "messing with it" will screw things up.

But if you hear the call—and if you trust your creative potential—you can adapt and evolve your Creative Style to rewire how you create with others. For most of us, that will mean bringing the mindset and practices of the Collaborator forward. Are you ready?

If you are, the first step is to return to the descriptions of the core gifts and the challenges for each of the styles we explored in chapter 1 of this second adventure. Take some time to review these. It's easy to go directly to the challenges, but I encourage you to understand, explore, and strengthen the gifts while you also face the shadow sides of your style that get in the way. Keep in mind that some of the strategies and patterns of the Soloist, Rebel, and Entrepreneur overlap. Some of the challenges are shared.

As you develop an understanding of the interplay between gifts and challenges for each of the styles, consider how these challenges resonate with you—with your unique perspective and in the context of your life, your work, and your aspirations. Select a few strategies and practices for bringing the Collaborator forward. Keep your notes handy; after we explore ways to adapt your style, we will focus on developing your own Practice Plan.

Adapting the Soloist Style

• • •

Vicky's experience on the Leadership Framework project illustrates many of the themes that Soloists must face to bring the Collaborator forward into co-creation. For Soloists, so much of their approach centers on maintaining control and being the owner of the ideas. You can just imagine Vicky thinking to herself, "If it's going to be done right, I have to do it myself." It's a classic Soloist mantra. But what do "done" and "right" even mean? Who is the decision-maker when people are consciously co-creating? The Soloist will tend to believe that *their* criteria for a solution's "doneness" and "rightness" are the correct yardstick. Add to that any perfectionist tendencies, and you have a powerful force that's hard for others to join with.

That's because control pushes people away. There's less space for other people's ideas, alternative paths, and differing perspectives. There's less space for mistakes, dead ends, delays, and false starts. And there's less space for people to play together in the unknown, to be surprised, abandon conventional approaches, and explore mysteries. People will quickly give up trying to join in co-creation when a Soloist starts controlling. It's easier to just let them take charge—like Vicky's team did when she returned with her new version of the framework. Everyone just went with it, but in the end, it only belonged to Vicky.

If you find yourself resonating with this challenge, then to truly co-create—to let go into the collective—you will need to confront the sense of safety and security that you've learned to derive from control. It may feel unnatural for you to seek out people to join with. Because Soloists tend to create within their spheres of influence, it's not imperative that others join in. If you'd like to move the Collaborator into the forefront, your Practice Plan can include a conscious focus on learning to share ownership. Practice inviting others to join you, and practice joining with others more often. More deeply, you'll want to pay attention to what you value—and shift to place a higher value on collective ownership (for the strength and sustainability that it brings) than on the value and rewards of your own individual achievement.

Vicky's core challenge was control mixed with some measure of perfectionism. At the same time, she was caught in the trap of proving. She wanted to prove to others and to herself that she could lead the team successfully. She wanted to produce a result she could be proud of. Underneath it all, the team was there just to serve her vision. Her own sense of competence and mastery—and the connection she had made between competence and her sense of self-worth—made it difficult to let go into a process of co-creation.

If you find yourself resonating with this challenge, identify specific actions to add to your Practice Plan that will help you confront fears about what it means to "not know." Practice becoming aware of and letting go of the tie you've made between being successful and being worthy. Practice asking for help and shifting out of the proving orientation into the learning orientation. In a learning orientation, it's much easier to join with others to know more together than anyone could on their own. Soloists who find themselves needing to prove will have to let go of a sense of competence that is individually based—and reach for a new vision of mastery and competence that comes from being a part of a collective.

There's another way that proving can play out in a team context. In a team, Soloists are most comfortable when work is divided up. That's because Soloists like well-defined boundaries that carve up ownership and define the spaces for creative control. This is how Vicky set up her team—as a collection of individuals, all working on a piece of the puzzle. But as work becomes more complex, more interconnected and interdependent, and more global—spread across time zones and across functional boundaries—creating together in this old-school way is going to get harder and harder.

Co-creating is not just about carving up the work into discrete parts and putting them together. Robots are already doing much of that kind of work. Co-creating is about working it out together more holistically. If this challenge seems familiar to you and you want to include practices in your plan to shift your style, consider how you can intentionally design opportunities for "creative abrasion." That's when ideas and approaches rub up against each other and shape and influence different outcomes that arise from the friction. Challenge yourself to cast a wider net for input and involvement. Instead of avoiding dissenting views, fully leverage the disagreement, opposition, and resistance (if it shows up) to accelerate new possibilities. Find ways to include customers, partners, stakeholders, and "outsiders" earlier in the process for both co-development and for feedback.

Finally, let's explore one more focus area for Soloists working to bring the Collaborator forward. This involves serving and developing others along the way. By their nature, Soloists are not particularly "selfless." When they're creating, it's natural for Soloists to focus more on their own needs, challenges, and opportunities for development and learning. Thinking about developing and mentoring others might take a back seat.

Effective, conscious co-creation requires us all to look out for each other. Remember: Collaborators are more interested in collective success, shared learning, and generation of shared value than in individual gain. They are attracted to creating in a way that includes and benefits others while, at the same time, advancing their own aspirations. As you think about a potential Practice Plan, consider developing capability in others—rather than being the star who solves the problem, saves the day, or answers the question.

When you're co-creating, find out what others hope to learn from the venture. Spend time talking about your individual development "edges" and where they overlap into collective development needs. Find out how people like to receive feedback—and practice giving and receiving feedback frequently along the way. Be sure to conduct retrospectives to validate learning. And practice giving your knowledge and wisdom generously to the group—even though it might seem more natural to protect it. The assets of wisdom you've gathered are abundantly multiplied when you share them with gratitude and generosity.

Adapting the Rebel Style

• • •

The Rebel shares many of the attributes and patterns of the Soloist. If your core style is Rebel, you will likely find that themes from the Soloist resonate, like letting go of a proving orientation. You can fold any of these into your Practice Plan. But there are some unique aspects to consider when you show up as primarily a Rebel. Like Soloists, Rebels tend to believe that their idea of "right" is the best, most correct perspective. But for Rebels, there's a twist: right can easily become *righteous*. Where Soloists will most often create the change they want to see within their sphere of influence and control, Rebels might easily embark on a broader crusade.

This was one of Andrew's struggles as he tried to move ideas for improvement forward at the county treasurer's office. As a strong Rebel, Andrew naturally saw things that weren't working or that could be improved or overhauled. His creativity was activated by what was wrong, unjust, or unfair, what could be better, and what needed to be fixed. Like most Rebels, these ideas are important assets for making improvements, increasing equity, and advancing progress—just as they could have been for the treasurer's office.

But when Andrew met with resistance from management, he went on a crusade. Now, not only was he fighting for his ideas, but he was also fighting with management to change the way they treated ideas more broadly. For Andrew, it became a cause and a fight to the finish. He felt that he was advocating not just for himself, but also on behalf of all his colleagues. Andrew had become deeply embroiled in the first of Pinchot's Ten Commandments: "Come to work each day willing to be fired." His identity and sense of self-worth were wrapped up in winning the fight, and in righting the wrongs he observed.

Things got bad enough for Andrew that in the end, he chose to leave his position—even though he had to sacrifice some of the equity toward his pension. He had burned so many bridges on his crusade, it was simply too difficult to return to a productive working relationship with management. Even some of his colleagues—who at first were glad that someone was speaking up—distanced themselves from him as things became more and more contentious.

Though Andrew's case is extreme, if you show up as primarily Rebel, there are some key nuggets to consider. The first is that an unintended consequence of righteousness is alienation. Strong righteousness comes across as overly critical and arrogant—and it pushes people away. An "us versus them" mindset is divisive. And the judgment that accompanies righteousness sucks the creative energy out of what once may have been a great idea.

If you don't primarily present as Rebel, I invite you to think of someone you know who demonstrates a measure of what Andrew was serving up. It's hard to collaborate and even harder to co-create with someone who's on a crusade—unless you're all on the same crusade together for similar reasons. If you are a Rebel at your core, consider how you might temper your righteousness and judgment with a more sustainable, strategic approach. Use your Superpower of Questions to find out what others value, how they see the circumstances, what their level of commitment to change is, and what options are available as a collective. Use your Superpower of Learning to find balance and composure, and to discover how to maintain greater emotional self-control. Finally, consider how you can raise the cause up to higher principles and motivate others through purpose and vision instead of emotion and injustice.

It can also be difficult for Rebels to join with others on a journey into the unknown that is not of their own making—or where it feels like they might have to give up some part of themselves to belong. Rebels naturally react against the idea of complying. In fact, complying—and its association with being conservative or passive and with pleasing others—can be so distasteful that Rebels may actively avoid any creative venture that feels like it involves compromise.

If this challenge resonates with you, consider how you may be distancing yourself from others, and from a multitude of potential options, out of a need to refuse compromise. Activate your Superpower of Creative License—and all that Rebel energy that's geared toward breaking rules—and try breaking some of your own rules. Find ways to turn that Superpower inward, to break down your own patterns and biases and the non-negotiables you've worshipped. Let people in. Practice joining with others in their causes and creative purposes. Find and celebrate opportunities to compromise and co-create value that's shared by all.

Rebels—in their fervor for what should or shouldn't be—can also dampen their power to leverage obstacles as opportunities. Remember: creative potential is activated at the intersection of purpose, possibility, and constraint. Rebels typically have no problem with purpose. They're attuned to it and seek out causes quite naturally. They also may see multiple possibilities, like Andrew did as he sought to modernize the financial and reporting systems at the county treasurer's office. But Rebels can struggle with constraint—especially when constraints feel like they "shouldn't be there."

In Andrew's case, the constraining factors and forces of management hijacked his composure. His restraint flew out the window and he—like many Rebels—lost his ability to use constraints to fuel creative progress. If this challenge resonates with you, identify specific actions to add to your Practice Plan that will help you activate your Superpower of Seeing Beyond. Take stock of what really matters and practice looking past the small constraints that ultimately don't matter. Find ways to see beyond your own perspective and work with others to co-create solutions that address the most important obstacles in your path.

Adapting the Entrepreneur Style

• • •

Entrepreneurs share some of the same challenges as Soloists in bringing the Collaborator forward: they typically have a strong sense of ownership of ideas, a high need for control, and strong conceptions of what "done right" looks like. Like the Soloist, being the one who has the vision, the ideas, and the answers can be tied to their sense of identity.

At the same time, Entrepreneurs also share characteristics with Rebels: they're more likely to look for others to join them, rather than joining with others in a shared vision and purpose. Like Rebels, Entrepreneurs tend to have a strong connection to their ideas as a "cause"—although it's less common for them to turn that cause into a crusade. They don't necessarily judge those who choose not to join in or adopt their ideas and offerings. While they may not believe you are wrong for not joining, as the Rebel might, they may not invest much in the relationship once it's clear you're not on board with them.

While some themes are similar, Entrepreneurs also face some unique challenges in adapting their style. Mark faced two of these in his work to bring forward a new way of teaching science: the issue of scale and the challenge of sustainability. "I thought of it more like *my* venture than the product of any kind of collective effort," he said to me on a call. "And when it came time for it to grow beyond what I could manage, I had trouble letting go."

Mark's mix of Entrepreneur and Soloist styles had led him to a good short-term outcome—proving the value of his new approach within a small arena—but it hamstrung the shared ownership and commitment that was required to scale and sustain the solution. "I learned a lot from this," he admitted. "I have to think of me at scale—I don't need to do it all myself. I *can't* do it all by myself. It won't be sustainable if I don't involve others."

In a way, this might be a typical Entrepreneur response: believing that what's needed is a shift to think of "me" at scale. But I reminded Mark that "me at scale" is still *me* instead of *we*. At first, it was challenging for him to understand what I was suggesting. Mark still thought it was about driving his vision forward, but maybe engaging others differently or gathering more people to help, or investing more in "stakeholder buy-in." While all those activities might help from a change management perspective, what I am suggesting is an entirely different approach.

For Entrepreneurs to bring the Collaborator forward, they must make the shift from *me* to *we* and move into greater alignment and accountability for the collective. For it's in the *we*—the collective—that solutions gain strength at scale. Here, the challenge for Entrepreneurs like Mark (especially if they also have Soloist patterns and habits) will be in letting go of control, loosening the grip on executing or implementing their individual vision, and finding ways to embrace the dreams, visions, and ideas of others.

If this challenge resonates with you, identify specific actions to add to your Practice Plan that help you frame your vision in terms of collective benefits to others and to the system—and then find opportunities to build on what others might have already started. Not everything has to be started up anew. Initiatives that are already underway—even (dare I suggest) being led by others—can use an Entrepreneur's touch. Instead of starting something new, Mark might have explored what efforts were already underway that he could join and potentially influence. And while Mark might have given up some of the cachet of having his personal brand attached to leading the work, the idea—and the seed of what he envisioned—may have grown into a more sustainable, scalable solution.

Mark's story offers another window into the challenge Entrepreneurs can face around sustainability. When he took his vision district-wide, Mark was sure people would want to join in and adopt the approach more broadly. His first mistake was going it alone and driving to realize his individual vision. In addition to his desire to be seen—to make his mark (pun intended) and to enhance his personal brand—Mark chose to protect his vision from the "corrupting" influence of others. Different choices might have made it easier to inspire others about the benefits for students and teachers when science was experienced differently. Maybe he could have supported others' ideas for how solutions could be localized and customized once the approach went broad. He might have let his vision evolve into something that was more of a collective effort.

But Mark chose to protect *his* vision—to drive his own vision forward. The risk of opening things up to others is an ongoing challenge for Entrepreneurs. Joining with others means risking that things could evolve out of control or into a new direction. That's when many Entrepreneurs can lose interest and step away or let go entirely. Their interest and passion is what becomes unsustainable. "Why did they have to mess with it? It was perfect," Mark told me on a call one day. This is classic Entrepreneur.

As his vision went broad and was taken up by some of the decision-makers within the system, it naturally evolved. This is what he feared and why he protected his ideas to begin with. Eventually, Mark became increasingly frustrated and finally disinterested. He detached himself from further involvement and blamed the dilution of his beautiful vision on the short-sightedness and political maneuvering that happens in large, bureaucratic systems.

To move some of their individualistic tendencies to the back burner, Entrepreneurs must learn to drive for results in a new way. That means moving forward without such a strong attachment to the destination they envision. Entrepreneurs like Mark have to *want* to see their vision evolve rather than protect against it.

If this challenge resonates with you, identify actions to add to your Practice Plan that will help you practice 1) letting go of your belief that getting results means getting the results you want, 2) letting go of your need to have your personal brand enhanced by what happens, and 3) staying with the effort even when you notice you may be losing interest or getting frustrated by how things are evolving. Stay engaged just a bit longer than feels comfortable and see what happens.

Your Practice Plan for Enhancing Conscious Co-creation

• • •

Now that you have a better sense of the strengths of each Creative Style, and what each style might struggle with to move the Collaborator up onto center stage, you can put together your Practice Plan. Your practices will likely be most effective when they include these elements: 1) a mix of specific actions for embodying the five practices of co-creation, 2) activities that strengthen your gifts, and 3) experiments that can help shift habits of your dominant style. Andrew, for example, might work on letting go of righteousness and judgment—freeing himself to move toward something new. That way, instead of leaving in negative emotion, he can bring the Collaborator forward and make his exit a process of co-creation. Mark may want to practice joining others and being a partner in joint ventures that he didn't necessarily start up himself. Lily might practice including others earlier in her process—and letting go of her sense of ownership and the need for individual recognition—to develop solutions with others.

PRACTICE PLAN TEMPLATE

	Start/Continue	Stop/Do less of
Practices that support co-creation		
Practices that amplify my strengths		
Experiments for shifting my habits		

As you shape your Practice Plan, consider activities that can help you focus on the following:

- Let go of control and work things out together instead of having to "own" the outcomes yourself.

- Ease a sense of righteousness that can end up pushing people away.

- Quiet judgment and psyche out the Inner Critic, to open spaces of trust, transparency, and communion with others.

- Join others—standing together instead of striving to move forward your own agenda and vision—and scale your impact through co-creation.

Whichever you choose, identify *specific* behaviors to practice. What will you stop doing, and what will you start doing? And find ways to practice with others.

- Experiment, take collective risks, and improvise together.

- Ask questions that highlight collective opportunity and clarify collective intent.

- Look for shared value in unexpected places and unearth collective biases.

- Learn together.

THINK OF this as another phase in your hero's journey of creating together. Bring forward the kind of curiosity that comes as you realize that your style is less fixed than you may have thought. Talk about your style and your Practice Plan with the people around you. Find out what they are working toward. Commit to giving each other feedback and helping each other learn together. Share generously about your experiences and about what you are learning. *Co-creating with others* is the key to scalable and sustainable innovation in the new world of work. Together, you will transform your workplace, change your world, and invent your future.

ASK YOURSELF...

Now, at the end of this chapter, take time to pause and reflect on the following questions.

Adapting the Soloist Style

- What might be the most difficult belief, assumption, or habit for a Soloist to confront to bring the Collaborator forward?

- How can you widen your circle and invite others into your process? What would you have to let go of? stop doing? start doing?

- Even if Soloist is not your primary style, what insights can you draw from the challenges and opportunities facing them?

Adapting the Rebel Style

- What might be the most difficult belief, assumption, or habit for a Rebel to confront to bring the Collaborator forward?

- How could you diminish "righteousness" to connect more deeply with others? What would you have to let go of? stop doing? start doing?

- Even if Rebel is not your primary style, what insights can you draw from the challenges and opportunities facing them?

Adapting the Entrepreneur Style

- What might be the most difficult belief, assumption, or habit for an Entrepreneur to confront to bring the Collaborator forward?

- How could you shift from *me* to *we* to co-create more effectively? What would you have to let go of? stop doing? start doing?

- Even if Entrepreneur is not your primary style, what insights can you draw from the challenges and opportunities facing them?

Your Practice Plan

- How would you describe the strengths of your Creative Style? What might you amplify for greater impact and influence?

- How might a learning orientation and an experimental approach help you enact your Practice Plan?

Sharing Leadership

* * * * *

I N ADVENTURE One: Claiming Your Gift, I shared openly about the
learnings that emerged from our colossal failure on the Creative
Leadership project in Europe. I had taken an extraordinary leap
of faith to join the team, leaving everything familiar behind. The
promise of working together to illuminate dynamics at the intersection of creativity and leadership was exciting. It was at the heart of
what I thought of as my "life's work," and there was so much at stake.
That's why our failure was such a powerful crucible in my life.

I often wonder what things might have been like if we had worked
together in a process of conscious co-creation. What might have been
possible? What got in our way? As I reflect, one insight stands out: the
leadership dynamic that we all fostered, promoted, and allowed was
an unhealthy one. I'm talking about the way we all contributed to our
shared experience of leadership. We had many of the hallmarks of
traditional leadership models that have permeated organizations and
institutions for decades[7]—and the characters to go with it.

First, we had Josef, the expert leader who thought he was "in
charge." His focus was fixated on maintaining the power of position,
ensuring compliance with his will, and achieving results in the way he
believed was right. These fixations played out at the expense of relationship, collaboration, and co-creation. Then we had the partners of

the firm. Like many sponsors, ours were distant and uninvolved. They were primarily concerned about how the project would reflect on their own status. Finally, we had the team (including me), who subjugated themselves to the leader. We sought approval, asked for permission, and looked to Josef for answers. We complied. *I* complied. And we complained—to each other and to our sponsors—in ways that solidified our victimhood. Frankly, the leadership dynamic in our project stunk.

Even though it was familiar, the culture of leadership we generated was seriously dysfunctional. It certainly didn't model "creative leadership." In fact, it made creative leadership—as a co-created outcome—virtually impossible. This might be the most painful part of what I ultimately learned. I was caught in a reactive pattern of hierarchical leadership that involved an intricate dance of controlling, distrust, complying, victimhood, and protecting. We were all in the dance together, playing our roles without self-awareness and without conscious choice. We were reinforcing an old model of leadership.

I don't believe that our failure was unique. In fact, I've seen this kind of failure on the rise. Vicky's experience is a good example of how the old story of leadership might lead to failure. Mark's failure to inspire change at the LA Unified School District also comes to mind. Andrew's experience proposing improvements to a complicated and bureaucratic management structure at the treasurer's office is yet another example. There are countless more instances in the companies and institutions I've consulted to over the years. And on a more macro level, governments and public systems are failing to rebound from disasters, serve people, work together across regional and political divides, and to even deliver the basic outcomes they are responsible for.

My key takeaway is that the relationship between creativity and leadership must be fundamentally altered if any of us are going to co-create sustainable, innovative solutions in our companies and institutions, and for our world at large. We've already explored the need to strengthen co-creation as our primary mode of inventing from inside the system. Now let's consider how to fundamentally rethink and reshape the very construct of leadership we've collectively bought into. We must give birth to a new kind of leadership dynamic—one that will help us rise to the challenges of our lives and of our times. The first step on this journey requires us to become aware of—and release ourselves from—the old story about what leadership is and how it works.

Unbuckling

• • •

It was just a few minutes into the spaceflight, and the vibration was too intense to be normal. Ellie was being shaken and rattled in the most violent way. She couldn't think straight, but she knew something was wrong. She was terrified. The flight capsule seemed like it was breaking apart and might explode at any moment. But inexplicably, right in the middle of all the shaking, she saw it. Free of gravity, the necklace Palmer gave her before the flight had come out of her pocket and was floating—effortlessly—away from her.

Ellie struggled to understand. And then she realized: it was the chair itself that was vibrating so violently, the chair she was sitting in, which was bolted to the floor of her capsule. She quickly unbuckled the harness that was restraining her and floated away free. As she reached out for the necklace, the chair shook violently one last time, came loose, and smashed against the floor in a crumpled heap.

The chair wasn't even supposed to be there. It was not part of the original design of her spacecraft. The engineers had added it as a security feature out of fear, assumption, and ignorance: after all, there had to be a place for someone to sit, restrained for safety, on a spaceflight. There must have been a flaw and omission in the blueprint, right? But that's why the chair was shaking so violently: it didn't belong there. Ellie let go—and without it, she was free.

This was the scene in the movie *Contact*; Ellie was played by Jodie Foster. Though it's been years since I first saw the movie, there are many times when this scene—and the visceral feeling that comes from hanging on to structures that are not serving—has come back into my awareness. I'm reminded of it at critical junctures, where I find myself holding on tightly to something that's no longer needed. Or when I'm hanging on to something in my life that's there because

I think it's keeping me safe. I remember it when I've bolted myself into circumstances that have me shaking and rattled—when I need to let go to be free.

That's what I observe about leadership in many organizations and institutions. *Our collective construct of leadership is constraining us.*

I've been working in the arena of what's called "leadership development" now for almost twenty-five years. Over those years, I've watched the "seat" of leadership—the position of "leader"—increasingly become a constraint that's no longer serving the ecosystem. It's like the chair in Ellie's capsule. The hierarchical power and control that we've attached to this seat in our collective mindset has remained relatively unchanged, while the world has fundamentally changed around us. The unintentional consequences of the way most organizations, institutions, and governments "do" leadership is fast becoming one of the most challenging obstacles to creating together in the new world of work.

We must unbuckle ourselves from our construct of what it means to lead. Collectively, we need to come to a new and different understanding of what it means to lead—especially in the context of co-creating and inventing the future we aspire to.

My colleagues who work in the leadership development industry might disagree. In fact, their business—and mine, to a large extent—is founded on the very model of leadership I'm suggesting must change. We serve leaders with positional authority—even as we all work to help them be better in those roles. But the rules and structures we're buckled into were built for a world that no longer exists, except maybe in our collective memory. We need a new way of leading—one that amplifies our collective creativity as we meet the challenges of the future and shape that future.

Letting go

Unbuckling is a great way to think about letting go. It's such a physical experience, felt in your body. You literally go from restraint to freedom of movement. Like when you're getting out of your car after a long drive, or when your plane arrives at the gate and you're anxious to get up. Take a moment and put yourself there, in the moment of unbuckling. What does it feel like? For me, it feels good to let go. It feels like the time for being restrained is over. I'm ready to move on to my next action, my next adventure. For all sorts of good reasons— primarily for safety—restraint made sense. But now, I set myself free, get up, and walk away. It's easy, and relatively painless, because it makes sense.

What would it mean to unbuckle yourself from what you believe about leadership?

What if we've gotten it wrong all these years? What if leadership, like creativity, is actually a *potential*? What if, like creativity, leadership is meant to be shared—without comparison—and can't be depicted in a normal distribution along a bell curve or put into boxes in a chart? What if leadership, like creativity, has nothing to do with "ability" and everything to do with the circumstances that give rise to its activation—in whoever is called into it? What if it has nothing to do with a position, a "seat" in an org chart?

What if we've built this seat, this structure around leadership that has worked OK for a long time but isn't fit for purpose anymore? In the future that's emerging, conventionally held beliefs about leadership will increasingly separate us from our potential—instead of connecting us and supporting the collective and accountable expression of all of our natural potentials, including creativity.

I talked this over with Regina, one of the rare Collaborators I know who is also in a leadership role. We were sitting together in the coffee shop on her company's campus. "I was reluctant to take a leadership role," she told me as she set down her cup. She looked around to see who might overhear. "The power associated with my position really separates me from the team. As much as I try to minimize the impact, people look to me for the answers. The dynamic is there. I can feel it. But there are times I need to follow instead of leading. And times I don't know the answers."

Regina went on to explain how hard she was working to shape the leadership dynamic into a more collaborative one, where people at all levels are co-creating and sharing leadership together. "Many of my peers like divisions and boundaries. It seems to make it easier for them. They know what to do—and where their accountability starts and ends. My direct reports look up to me and to the leadership team for direction." Regina wondered out loud if there was something she could do to help ease people's fear of standing up and taking responsibility for decisions. This, she felt, was a critical step toward a more shared experience of leading.

Instead of associating leadership with a position—as most of us do—and then separating people by those who hold that position and those who don't, what if each of us could develop a deep and profound connection with our potential to lead? And what if then, when we were called to activate this potential, we could be truly free to lead from any seat and share leadership in a way that doesn't quite make sense yet in our current structures?

When I think about this, my mind goes immediately to *how* that would work, given the structures and processes we currently have in place in most institutions and organizations. Together, we would need to figure out what shared leadership means for who gets to be the decision-maker. We'd have to figure out what it means for how people are rewarded and who is involved in setting strategy, vision, and direction. What might happen to the org chart? What would all of us have to shift and change to take such a monumental step? What would we have to let go of and stop doing? What would we step forward into? I believe we would move toward sharing accountability from a more conscious systems perspective.

I invite you to unbuckle yourself, even for a trial period, and see what happens when you float away and free yourself from the idea of leadership as we've known it. The first step is to get curious about the construct of leadership you hold. Use your Superpower of Questions. Start asking insight questions about what's changing in your environment, and what's working and not working in how leadership is supporting these changes. Then, as you unbuckle, new and deeper questions will come forward—less about how it would work out there in the world and more about how it works inside of you.

These deeper questions include: "How am I being called into lead-ership—from any seat and in any moment—in my life?" "How and where am I *already leading* in big and small ways every day?" "What might activate my leadership potential today?" You can ask yourself: "In which contexts do I lead more effectively and where do I strug-gle?" "What's getting in my way?" "What are the lessons for me here?" And at some point, we will all need to ask: "What will have to shift and change in our social systems to activate and unleash leadership potential in everyone?"

Thinking differently

If you are in a formal role, like Regina, there may be a multitude of questions you need to explore to let go of deeply held convictions about leadership—questions like "What beliefs and norms guide what I do and what I don't do?" and "How do I know who I am 'supposed to be' as a leader?" As Regina and I talked over several months, we explored the rights and duties that her position afforded her. We also explored some of the downsides and personal challenges of being in the role. She asked, "How is my role connected to my sense of iden-tity? What does the 'seat,' the position, mean about me, about what I've achieved, and about who I've become? What would be different if I were truly sharing leadership? How might a new story of leadership change the way I think about the trajectory of my career?"

Regina found these questions to be valuable and insightful as she considered her attachment to a construct of leadership that is changing. The tighter your identity is intertwined with your relation-ship to the seat (whether you are in it or not), the harder it will be to unbuckle.

Maybe you're not in a formal leadership role. Maybe you aspire to one someday and you're working toward that. Maybe you lead teams in what's called a "matrix environment"—and you're acting as the project lead or "engagement lead"—but without some of the respon-sibilities that come with formal authority for people management. Or maybe you prefer to contribute as an individual, without aspirations to lead people or a department.

This was Lily's case. She didn't want a formal leadership role—at least not now, given where she was in the arc of her career and family life. All the same, Lily was interested in learning what she might do to contribute to a different kind of leadership dynamic. She wondered how it might help her change the results on projects she was working on—and so we worked together to explore her assumptions and beliefs about leadership.

We started gently, by looking around at Lily's context: talking about the role that leaders play in the company she worked for. I asked her questions that I also asked Regina, and now I'm asking you:

- What do you believe about the function leaders fulfill—and what does that mean about who *you* are, what you do, what's possible for you, what constrains you, and how you are supposed to behave?

- What do leaders do that helps you make progress on meaningful work—and what do they do that inhibits your progress?

- What if there were no leaders or managers? What would that mean? What would have to be different?

- What would have to shift in your mindset to step up and into leadership more fully when the circumstances call you into it? What would you have to let go of? What would you have to accept as new accountabilities?

- What has been the payoff of things being as they are?

I asked Regina and Lily to consider these questions, just as I am asking you to consider them, from both sides of the coin—from the perspective of someone in the role of leader and from the perspective of those who are led by that person. I'm asking you to begin to consider the ways in which you are attached to a shared construct of leadership. The tighter our collective identity is intertwined with the seat, from either and both sides of the coin, the harder it will be to unbuckle. The more we believe this construct serves us, and the more ingrained it is in our unconscious routines and habits, the harder it will be to awaken our collective power to share leadership fluidly, in a process of co-creation.

For the sake of unleashing your creative potential and the collective creative potential in your work and world, I'm inviting you to awaken your leadership potential. Then you can activate your leadership and creative potentials, together with others, to reshape your world so that anyone can lead co-creation from any seat.

Embracing a New Story of Leadership

• • •

Letting go of your long-held conceptions of leadership—and experimenting with different ways to express your own leadership potential—is a fundamental test on your hero's journey of creating together. Especially given that you are likely working in a world that will resist and even protect the old constructs. You will still have "leaders," "bosses," "managers," and "supervisors." You may even be one of them. No matter your role or experience, you have an opportunity to wake up to your potential and lead in new ways. Sharing leadership will require you to shift mindsets and behaviors and embrace a new way of leading inside the system.

Shift One: Let go of the "power of position"

In this, the first shift, you exchange power for connection and trust. Two circumstances illustrate how power can show up and how it can dampen connection and erode trust: 1) when someone is newly promoted into a leadership position, and 2) when people bring their ideas, proposals, and recommendations to a boss or a governance board or committee. These aren't the only places you will find examples, but they illustrate some of the dynamics that must change.

In the first circumstance, I can recall my own experience when a new leader came on board to lead our group. Ivan had come from another part of the business and he was extremely excited to have "won" the role. At first, he was inclusive and actively sought to build relationships with the new team. But slowly, he began to assert his power in the new position. He became, as we called it, "drunk with power." All decisions needed to be run by him for approval. He began telling us what to do and when to do it. He smiled—as if with a certain kind of self-satisfied glee—during those times he asserted the newfound power of his position. And increasingly, he told us *how* to go about achieving results. He hoarded access to leaders across the organization and set up new rules for how we could engage with partners, clients, and customers. He even went so far as to ask us to raise our hands in response to his questions.

Ivan got caught up in the power that came from his role. He claimed all the rights afforded him by that position (as set forth through decades of our collective buy-in) without thinking about the duties associated with it. Even viewed in the old model he was behaving badly, but not one of his peers or management called him out on it. Although we on the team complained among ourselves, neither I nor anyone else had the courage to confront Ivan directly or go to his manager. We were all too invested in keeping our jobs to risk standing up with courage and speaking about our experience.

As you can imagine, there was no way to co-create in this environment. The team responded by retreating into more entrenched Soloist behaviors—spending more and more time out of the team and with other partners. We lost connection with each other. People stopped coming to team meetings—something Ivan had originally demanded as non-negotiable. Having a leader who was drunk with power pushed us away—from him and from each other—and ultimately cost our team the opportunity to create something new and unique together. The promise of it was there at the start, but the power of position got in the way.

The second circumstance where the power of position can rear its ugly head is in the interaction between managers, governance committees, and decision-making boards and the people who come before them to pitch ideas or make recommendations. You may have had this experience, where you need to present your ideas or progress for review and approval. Typically, a group of senior leaders sit on a team or committee that approves which projects get funded and which don't.

In their leadership roles, they have become increasingly separated from the actual work and the innovations, nuances, and new ideas emerging in the field or domain. Yet they sit on committees that make decisions about what goes forward and what gets killed. They have the power of position, which affords them the right to make the decision, but they do not have the deepest connection to the actual work.

For the "guests," the experience can be brutal and rife with bad leadership behavior. Presenters are often treated in demeaning ways, disempowered, disrespected, and even disregarded. In the name of "truth-seeking," the criticism can turn harsh and personal. I remember one occasion where a few of us were presenting progress on a project to our leadership team. We had invested months working on the project and hours preparing for the conversation, agonizing about what to include and what to leave out. On this day, the leadership team were in a particularly contentious mood. Without reviewing any of the materials we had prepared and sent in advance, they asked questions about why we were even working on this project. This can happen when leadership teams divvy up the sponsorship of projects. They forget that they are collectively accountable.

Other members questioned our recommendations. Though we had been told we were empowered to draw conclusions from our data and findings, the leadership team members challenged our conclusions and demanded to see the raw data—to see if they would reach the same conclusions. It set the project back weeks. More importantly, it was a striking blow to trust. The exercise of the power of position undermined collective trust and all but ensured that we would be even more deferential and compliant in our future interactions.

It's a myth that anyone can "empower" someone else. That's because empowering automatically establishes and entrenches the very power dynamic I am describing. Someone in a position of authority grants some measure of that authority and permission to another. But in most cases, the granter still retains the right to pull that authority and permission back. Usually, they are still the "approver" or "evaluator" of the outcomes that come from those who are "empowered." Do you see how this just replicates and reinforces the power of position and who's in charge? To promote co-creation and sharing leadership as our primary mode for inventing inside social systems, empowerment must come from inside of ourselves and from a shared sense of trust and commitment to radical accountability.

Imagine a world without the kind of circumstances that enable an individual or a governing body to become drunk with power. What might be different? What would that mean for you, in your current role? How might that shift build trust and connection—instead of compliance? What would you have to start doing, stop doing, or continue doing—but maybe in a new way? I don't know if the formal role of "leader" will go away anytime soon. But maybe it won't be so fixed, so formal. Maybe it will begin to shift according to the circumstances and needs that are presenting. And maybe some of the rights and powers that have been associated with the role will begin to melt away.

Shift Two: Let go of "command and control"

The second shift required for sharing leadership involves releasing yourself from the trappings of "command and control." In fact, command and control has been under fire for a long time now. Several emerging frameworks and methodologies are helping to break the hold it has had on management styles for far too long. "Agile" is among these—and management consulting group McKinsey & Company has gone far in articulating the shifts needed to move from hierarchical organizational structures, processes, and systems to more networked, agile models. Frederic Laloux's book *Reinventing Organizations*[8] also offers a compelling framework for the evolution of organizational structures over decades. Using a color-coded schematic, Laloux describes how progressive organizations can evolve to be more of what he calls "Teal." Being Teal means bringing a greater sense of wholeness, grace, and wisdom to organizational and management practices.

If we are going to move into the fuller expression of our creative and leadership potentials, we will each need to scour through our mindset and behaviors to weed out the remnants of command and control. We need to pay careful attention. For people like Ivan, who deeply connect leadership with power and their sense of ego identity, this will take more work. Just catching themselves in the act will be a huge step forward. For most of us, whose primary Creative Style is Soloist, Rebel, or Entrepreneur, it will also mean paying close attention to anything that looks like we are telling, enforcing, approving, or granting "permission." For Regina and other Collaborators already attuned to the subtleties of co-creating, the shifts required might be more finely tuned. We will all need to call out any activities that get in the way of sharing leadership fluidly in a process of co-creation.

A while back, Regina introduced me to a colleague of hers in the midst of this kind of shift. Josh had recently left a role as a senior leader and had taken a new job in another part of the business. While the new role afforded him many opportunities, it also came with some challenges. "I didn't know I wasn't going to have my own team," Josh exclaimed with a mix of frustration and fear. In fact, the group that Josh moved to was experimenting with some of the newer models of leadership and structure. Managers would still have direct reports, but those reports would be people who *selected* the manager based on capabilities they wanted to learn and develop—not because their manager would oversee their work.

Notice that people got to choose their manager, instead of being assigned. This was already a step toward a different kind of interaction between "leaders" and "staff"—leaders were meant to be coaches more than resource managers. But this new experiment—and the way it played out for Josh—also meant that he would not have his own team of people to execute the work that he was accountable for. Josh was confronted directly with his own need for control as a habitual method for delivering results.

In this new role, without a formal team to assign tasks, how could he get people aligned and working toward a new vision? How would he get them to change habits and behaviors without authority over their compensation? Without control, how could he get people lined up and working on the projects he wanted to move forward? These were the questions in Josh's mind when we started to work together.

Like many of us moving into a new mindset and model of shared leadership, Josh was at a crossroads—in the Bump Zone at the very edge of learning on his leadership journey. Through the course of our conversations, it came clear that to succeed in his new role, he would have to shift his mindset and his behaviors. At that moment, Josh heard the call this new role afforded—a call into a new way of leading and sharing leadership. He committed to the inner and outer work it would take to let go of command and control and develop capabilities that would draw people to his vision, instead of achieving results through enforcing and complying. He came to see it as his own hero's journey of discovery—stepping into the unknown to explore a new way of being. He would have to let go of thinking that, as a leader, he was entitled to have things "his way." He would also need to let go of the idea of "owning" people and resources. And he would need a new frame for what it meant to be accountable for results.

As you can see, this shift, like the shift away from power of position, requires a big dose of letting go to build a new kind of trust and connection. Not the kind that can be manufactured by deference to structure and hierarchy, but one that blossoms through shared principles, shared vision and purpose, and a deep faith that everyone is creative, resourceful, and whole.[9] These are essential ingredients for co-creation, shared accountability, and shared leadership.

Shift Three: Balance task achievement with strengthening relationship

A third shift is necessary as you bring the gift of your creative potential forward, adapt your Creative Style, and awaken your potential to lead and share leadership. This shift involves balancing a focus on task achievement with one that builds communion through relationship. Here, the Leadership Circle Profile,[10] developed by Bob Anderson and supported by the Full Circle Group,[11] provides a valuable model to help understand what's involved and required for this shift. The model (which I encourage you to explore) helps illuminate where you might gravitate more naturally: toward driving for results or toward nurturing and building relationships. As we adapt our dominant style and bring more of the Collaborator forward, each of us will need to bring greater balance between these two ways of being.

This is where I found Isabela when we first started working together. Isabela had been with the firm for almost twenty-five years when she found herself in a leadership role in the same department as Josh. Over the course of that time, she'd bounced back and forth between holding formal leadership roles (with people management responsibilities) and being an individual contributor. While most people aim for a career trajectory that ascends the ladder of increasingly broader leadership roles, with greater scope and control, Isabela found her purpose in the work. She moved into new roles based on her evaluation of the impact she could have—and not on the position or level of the role. When I first met her, my best guess was that Isabela's primary Creative Style was a dead heat between Soloist and Entrepreneur, with a dash of Rebel and Collaborator.

Like Josh, Isabela was struggling with the new structure in the group. But her learning journey was about a different shift. Command and control were not her challenge—in fact she was viewed as "too hands-off" for some of the people she worked with (although others specifically chose to report to her because of the level of autonomy she offered). What was up for Isabela was this third shift—toward a greater balance between driving for results and investing in relationships.

For Isabela, it was all about the work—the results—and she demonstrated all the best qualities that come from being a task-focused leader. She had incredible power of will. On her best days, she showed up as decisive and as a systems thinker who was driven by strategy and purpose. She knew how to get things done. On her worst days, she was particularly rough on herself. It wasn't personal ambition she was after, or a drive for status or even perfection. She suffered when things stalled, when other people stalled progress, and when she didn't move things forward.

From her Entrepreneur style, Isabela was already skilled at building and strengthening partnerships—in service to achieving her own goals and the company mission. But now, Isabela was in a new kind of leadership role—one that would require her to achieve results through others and through networks, instead of by her own drive or by individual heroic acts. In her new role, she would need to lift herself out of the day-to-day work and build her capabilities as a Collaborator.

For Isabela, the shift was about developing the relationship side of the equation. That would mean connecting with people more from the heart than from the head. This wasn't easy because she valued progress, competence, mastery, and achievement. "I don't have time for all this people stuff," she once told me. "To tell you the truth, I don't even think about it. It's not on my radar. If people want feedback, why don't they ask for it? Why do they need me to recognize them?"

The shift from problem-solver to coach was a stretch for her. The idea that people are naturally creative, resourceful, and whole wasn't completely foreign, but her identity was so wrapped up in having the answers, giving advice, and solving the problem that she hadn't yet found value in considering how to grow and develop others. Isabela realized this is where she needed to focus to step into the promise of her new role and serve those who had chosen to report to her.

Isabela's practice involved opening up her heart, letting people in, and giving herself to others in a new, vulnerable, and personally courageous way. She was learning to trust others and to let go into that trust. For you, these shifts might also resonate. Conversely, to bring more balance, your shift might involve building out competencies associated with task achievement, like enterprise thinking and systems awareness, decisiveness, and a more strategic focus. Whichever is your learning edge, it is the interplay between relationship and task—and your fluidity in leveraging both—that will help activate shared leadership in service to co-creation.

IN SHARING leadership (as well as in co-creation), there is no place for hierarchical control, the power of position, or giving up our power to others. You—and everyone around you—become part of the web of support, guidance, care, and co-development that sparks innovation and brings your shared dreams and goals to life. Let the landscape of your life and the needs of your work shape when you step up or let go. And let your circumstances guide how you lead, support, and develop yourself and each other.

ASK YOURSELF...

Now, at the end of this chapter, take time to pause and reflect on the following questions.

- From your perspective, what function do leaders fulfill within a social system? Where do you fit in?

- How would you describe the leadership dynamic in your company, institution, or community organization, your broader network, and even your family?

- How might you change the way you interact to enhance that dynamic?

Unbuckling

- What would it mean to unbuckle yourself from what you believe about leadership?

- What is restraining you? What purpose do these restraints serve?

- What would "freedom from restraint" feel like? What would others notice in your behavior?

Embracing a New Story of Leadership

- What do you believe about your own "leadership potential"? How is that serving you?

- What shifts might help you bring your leadership potential forward and blend it with the style of the Collaborator?

- How could you build a greater shared sense of trust? What might you need to value more of or less of to make the shift?

Leading Co-creation from Any Seat

· · · · ·

EOPLE IN formal leadership roles can have a profound impact on how creativity shows up in response to challenges, constraints, and emerging opportunities. But in the fluid process of co-creation and shared leadership, one person's viewpoint has less power and influence. Anyone can lead from any seat. Potential arises, depending on what's needed on the journey, in relationship to the team or group's shared purpose.

Think about a project or effort you are involved in right now. Imagine for a moment that you are working together with colleagues and partners in a process of co-creation and shared leadership. What might be different for you? What would it be like if anyone could lead—if no one had to be appointed or anointed as the leader? What kind of trust would have to be deeply felt by all members in the effort? Let's explore four actions that will help you and your allies realize the promise and possibility of shared leadership—from any seat—in co-creation: 1) dancing between *me* and *we*, 2) creating your alliances, 3) acting as catalysts for each other, and 4) becoming mentors and coaches for each other.

Dancing Between *Me* and *We*

• • •

One of the most important, yet vexing, challenges you will encounter as you adapt your Creative Style toward the Collaborator, engage in co-creation, and share leadership is how you navigate the dance between *me* and *we*—between being an individual and being part of a group. That's because activating your creative potential starts within. It gets activated at the intersection of purpose, possibility, and constraint and is expressed in tandem with your Superpowers. For you to engage, you must be called to a purpose that is meaningful *to you*—and you must answer that call. You bring your unique perspectives and talents to move ideas forward. You're gifted with creative potential, and so it's not unusual to feel a sense of pride and to connect the expression of your creativity to your identity and sense of self-worth. Especially when you care.

But in a process of co-creation, you are also part of a *we*. This *we* is different than you, and different from any of the other individuals involved in the process. The *we* I am talking about has its own characteristics and needs. It's not just the aggregate of all the individuals—there's a collective *we* that takes on a life of its own. This shared *we* needs attention and care. It's not just the product of your ideas—made better by the involvement of others. The collective energy formed in the process of co-creation has its own consciousness. As you practice giving yourself to the process of co-creation, you will become increasingly attuned to what wants to emerge beyond the limits of your individual view. That means in co-creation, each of us needs to dance in the space between *me* and *we*—to concurrently bring forward our individual gifts and to give up our individuality.

This "dance"—and the skill of moving between *me* and *we*—has a different impact at different stages of the innovation process. A lot depends on how deeply you venture into the unknown at various points along the way. Vicky and I talked about this dynamic over the course of a few calls. As we worked through her reflections and learnings from leading the team that developed the Leadership Framework, we talked about the dance. In the early stages, where exploration and discovery involved less direction, more exploration, and more false starts, it was easier for Vicky to dance in the space between her individuality and the needs of the collective.

"We didn't know what we were doing or where we were going," she said. "We needed everyone to be scouts out there on their own and team players at the same time. There was a real sense of shared investment and, frankly, shared discomfort." Vicky didn't even think about the dance at this point. But as the team's understanding of the possibilities and constraints came into focus, the tension between *me* and *we* started to influence how the team worked together. In the ideation phase, things got harder. "I started to be way more directive," she reflected. "And when our prototype was rejected, I took over." Vicky's *me* blotted out the needs and the potential of the *we*.

Like Vicky, me, and countless others I have worked with over the years, people can find it challenging to move beyond habitual behaviors—especially if our Creative Style has less of the Collaborator in the mix. We might unknowingly dominate in the process of co-creation. What does that look like for me? First, I can fall in love with my own ideas (notice how "ownership" shows up). I tend to push them forward into the shared space. That means, as I build collective ideas and solutions, I might get stuck on my idea and keep trying to work it into new and emerging ideas. It can be hard to let go of. Or I might evaluate what's emerging and decide my idea is better—and shoot down other ideas early, without allowing them to blossom.

Second, as I envision a new possibility that meets our purpose, my visions tend to be more fully formed than those of some of my colleagues. That makes my viewpoint powerfully influential in the process—especially if we are on a tight timeline, or if there are members of the group who are more deferential or reluctant to share fragments of ideas that seem "half-baked." Finally, I readily volunteer to take some of the next steps that come up as we move projects forward. If I'm being honest, behind my generosity to take on these next actions, I am often ensuring that the products of our work will retain my stamp on them. All told, I tend to be more assertive in a process of co-creation. To share leadership, I need to hang back more often, with sensitivity to how my ideas and approach are influencing and shaping the process.

There is another side of the coin. I work with colleagues who need to come forward more in the process of co-creation. For them, sharing leadership in co-creation means being more vocal and bringing themselves forward more powerfully with their perspectives and ideas. Here, I'm thinking of one of my colleagues, Imani, who has amazing contributions and insights but is more passive in a process of co-creating. I've talked with Imani about this often; for her, the challenge is with confidence in her ideas. In the fray of the flow of ideas and possibilities, she will often hang back—either second-guessing the quality of her ideas and perspectives or not wanting to bring up an important constraint, worrying that it will dampen the process of ideation.

Imani self-selects out of the process because she is listening to her Inner Critic, who is feeding her messages about how her ideas are not good enough, formed enough, or well-timed enough to share with the group. Or maybe her ideas will be rejected—and Imani believes a rejection of her ideas signals a rejection of her. For Imani, navigating the dance between *me* and *we* would mean unbuckling her ideas from her identity, honoring her voice in the collective, leaning in, and participating to share her perspectives with greater confidence.

Whichever side of the coin you might be on, navigating the dance starts with you honoring your unique perspective, the gift of your creative potential, and your leadership potential. Then you can bring these gifts forward into the context of collective needs, as you all create something bigger than each of you individually.

Four practices can help you keep your balance and strength in the dance.

Practice One: Stay connected to how shared purpose inspires you personally

In the dance between *me* and *we*, this is your first and most important inner practice. Your connection to shared purpose is akin to your body's core strength: it provides stability and will keep you grounded and flexible in the ebbs and flows of letting go and leaning in. Your personal connection to shared purpose will ensure that in your participation, there is alignment and integrity between your contributions, intentions, decisions, actions, and movements. Hold tightly to your connection to the purpose and to your shared criteria for quality—but hold loosely to a particular idea path or avenue to get there.

Invest time to reflect and build a habit of asking yourself: "What is important to me about being here?" "Who am I becoming in this process?" and "What is my role and unique contribution?" Then let others know why being a part of the process is important to you. If your commitment wanes or other priorities arise, have the courage to renegotiate your commitment and connection—or bow out.

Practice Two: Manage your tolerance for ambiguity

Over my years of coaching groups involved in co-creation, I've seen people struggle with their tolerance for ambiguity—making it especially hard to stay in exploration mode when that's what is needed. "Not knowing," it seems, is one of our biggest collective fears. In the dance between *me* and *we*, your tolerance for this kind of ambiguity is a critical factor in how you share leadership. When stress creeps in— be it from time pressure, changing demands from stakeholders, new obstacles, or any other number of stressors that might show up—tolerance for not knowing typically declines sharply. Then what's good for *me* can get in the way of what's good for the collective.

In co-creation, the person with the lowest tolerance for ambiguity will set the bar for how much exploration is possible—especially if that person is in a formal leadership role. Without even realizing it, they will take the lead and influence how much space there is for discovery. In the discomfort, you may find the team reverts to a few of what Matthew May calls the Seven Sins of Solutions,[12] like shutting down further ideation with the first idea that "satisfices," or downgrading quality criteria. Pay attention to how your discomfort with uncertainty might be diminishing shared leadership. I encourage you to be vigilant—and to openly discuss whose discomfort with uncertainty is running the show.

Practice Three: Be genuinely and generously interested in others

This third practice is about the bridge between you and the others with whom you are co-creating. Your curiosity about and care for others will go a long way in generating one of the most important conditions for creative collaboration: "psychological safety."[13] This is the level of safety you and your collaborators feel is present to take risks, challenge the status quo, and allow for the inevitable dip in competence that comes from learning something new.

To help foster a sense of safety for exploration, get curious about other people's motivations and their personal commitment and connection to shared purpose. Why did they answer the call to co-create? What are they hoping to learn as a partner in the process? What brought them to this space and time?

Bring forward your Superpower of Seeing Beyond to look past your own interests and agendas and become attuned to those of others. Ask questions to discover why this effort is important to your colleagues, and practice being in service to their passions, mission, and learning and development. Your genuine interest and a mindset of service will act as an important guide. And it will convey that this is a safe place for people to open up, share, screw up, learn, let go, and lean in.

Practice Four: Keep attuned to what wants to emerge

The best result might be different from your own vision or your team's original vision. In a way, attuning to what wants to emerge is the culmination of all the other practices. As you navigate the dance between *me* and *we* in the space of what is emerging, trust yourself and your intuition. But be mindful that your confidence—as it might mix with ego—does not slide into asserting your will into the collective space. Be watchful for times when you believe you are "right." When you declare your perspective as "the truth," you can lose sight of how this impacts energy, a collective sense of safety, and engagement. Asserting your individual will into the collective space can easily blot out what is emerging and diminish collective accountability.

Develop awareness of what is percolating and stirring individually and collectively—both at the level of ideas and at the level of interpersonal dynamics. When you are open to what is emerging, you can follow ideas and let them reveal themselves to you. New ideas will continue to emerge as you test and implement them. Rather than executing to plan, follow what is emerging from these experiments and let the outcomes guide your next steps. Iterate. Allow yourself to get lost. Even seek to fail through bold and risky experiments.

At the same time, pay attention to interpersonal dynamics, like the shifting nature of shared leadership. Sometimes you will need to step back so others can step up and step forward. Other times you will need to step forward yourself. Notice how the processes of decision-making, direction-setting, communication, and evaluation of progress are shared within your group or team. Ultimately, these arenas are where the most challenging aspects of the dance between *me* and *we* take place in both our inner and the outer world.

Creating Your Alliances

• • •

The second action for leading co-creation from any seat focuses on the networks and the interconnected web of alliances you have with internal and external partners. Remember: in co-creation, it's vital that you leverage your network and stand together. The same is true for sharing leadership. Your networks and alliances are critical for elevating your impact beyond specific projects or endeavors. When your alliances are broad and diverse, they become like a neural net that generates resilience, strength, and sustainability.

Not long ago, I was talking with Alan, an intern, about his career. He had just recently graduated with his master's degree. I asked, "What does job security mean to you?" Without skipping a beat, he answered, "My network." In a way, this was a wake-up call for me and a sign of things to come. For Alan, security and strength came from the web of alliances and contacts he had to help him sense opportunities across multiple systems at the same time. When there is a sense of mutuality and generosity across the network, and a sense of shared purpose, these kinds of interconnected ecosystems of alliances are powerful forces for co-creation.

This kind of security from your network can only be generated when there is durable, shared accountability. But it doesn't just happen on its own. You will need to invest in crafting principles and agreements for collectively owning and sharing the value that comes from ideas, progress, and outcomes. It may sound funny, but these agreements are quite sacred vows—and they deserve to be treated with reverence. They become the container for you to stay aligned, work toward the same vision, and strengthen trust that's deeply felt by all members in your effort.

Some of your agreements will be implicit—like with Alan's network of friends and contacts that help share connections, job openings, referrals, and support. But in a process of conscious co-creation and shared leadership, it can be helpful to make these agreements more explicit, so that they contribute even more energy to your process, guide you when you are deep in the unknown, and help form a bond of trust that lives beyond a specific project or moment in time. Unfortunately, many people don't invest the time to create their alliances consciously and explicitly. Or they treat them too lightly and as without consequence—despite their critical role.

When any group comes together—whether for a day, a few days, or a longer-term endeavor—we need shared agreements for how people will share accountability, exchange and honor ideas, and learn together. Without these agreements, interactions can devolve into bad behavior like petty arguments, posturing, and checking out. And it's easier for the Inner Critic to show up and take a seat in the front row.

When we're in more familiar territory, such as in execution mode planning, scoping, and developing metrics, it might not matter as much. Typically, we know how to do "execution" together through years of practice. The principles for behavior in familiar territory are understood to some degree without the need for conscious articulation.

But when we venture into uncharted territory in a process of co-creation—with aspirations of sharing leadership—the agreements and alliances we craft together are even more important as an anchor. As I've incorporated this learning into my practice, there are a few key agreements I include in any process of shared leadership and co-creation. It's not just about identifying them at the beginning. After we craft our initial alliance, we need to honor these principles and agreements, hold each other accountable, revisit them frequently, and correct course when necessary. Here are some of my favorites.

No bystanders. This agreement means that no one gets to check out of being an owner of the process or to stand by silently while something is happening that does not match shared agreements. Everyone needs to be fully engaged for movement and forward progress. Everyone is responsible for reframing resistance—both personal and collective resistance—into commitment and accountability. When decisions are made, we all stand by them and actively participate in moving decisions into action.

Speak up and challenge. It's vital that people feel safe to speak up and challenge, play devil's advocate, and debate ideas—especially when those in leadership roles with the power of position are involved. But speaking up is a two-sided coin; you can speak up more or less effectively, and you can be the receiver of someone speaking up—and respond more or less effectively.

SPEAKING UP FRAMEWORK: A 2-SIDED COIN

Receiving Information

Sharing Information

Receiving information from someone who is speaking up requires that you *invite* input through an attitude of appreciation and graciousness. Acknowledge that people are taking a risk and acting with courage when they speak up. Then it's critical to *inquire* to understand what is being shared. Demonstrate curiosity, listen for the intention behind the content of the message, and ask open-ended questions. Finally, it's important to *explore* how to move forward with the information being shared. Consider who else needs to be involved and follow through on commitments.

Speaking up effectively is the other side of the coin. Here, self-awareness is at the heart of challenging the status quo. First, *reflect* to understand your intention for speaking up. Are your motives in the best interest of the collective? What are your assumptions? Are you aware of what's at stake for speaking up and how it might impact forward progress? Next, *prepare* your communication in a way that honors others by considering timing, venue, and the values of people with whom you are sharing. Finally, *share* authentically: talk straight and demonstrate integrity and ownership of your message. Show others that you are open to learning and to exploring alternative points of view.

Trust each other. Do you focus more on being trusted or on trusting others? I've seen so many people make this fundamental error in perspective on the topic of trust. Of course, we all want to be trusted—and it's important that you take steps to engender the trust of others. But in a process of co-creation, it's even more important that you demonstrate that you trust others.

Done is done—for now. Develop shared criteria for success, for quality, and for what "good enough" and "done" look like. The earlier you do this in your process the better. Remember that the criteria for determining if something is good enough ("fit for purpose," as many say) can only be known in relationship to your context—the landscape of your journey. Some aspects of fit for purpose will stay constant and some will change as the landscape and context changes around you. Continue to revisit standards to ensure they still serve what is emerging.

Fail fast and learn. This is one of my favorite agreements, because it links directly to your Superpowers and to the tests you will face. Failing fast means that together you design purposeful experiments that can test assumptions, options, and ideas in short cycles. Action and learning from action—with shorter timeframes—yields more immediate feedback and can help you learn from mistakes and failures with lower risk. I also find that the fail fast and learn principle helps teams find constraints and quickly rout out options that won't work. Combined with agility, you're able to build on what emerges with flexibility and speed.

Talk with others, not about them. "Triangulation," as it is called in psychology, happens when you talk about interpersonal challenges with anyone other than the person you are having difficulty with. You're on the Drama Triangle—likely playing the victim in search of a rescuer—and stuck in an unhealthy pattern that doesn't help to improve your situation. Have the courage to talk directly with people when you need to clear the air. Assume positive intent and state your commitment to resolve conflicts that arise. Activate your Superpowers: use Questions to practice curiosity and leverage Learning to better understand yourself and others.

Acting as Catalysts for Each Other

• • •

The third action for leading co-creation from any seat is inspiring and catalyzing each other. At a conference I attended a few years back, one of the participants—an aerospace engineer—was explaining how his colleagues use "gravity assistance" to accelerate a spacecraft on its journey. The basic idea is to make use of the gravitational force of planets or moons along the way to bend the path and fling the spacecraft into a new direction. If you're curious about how it works, I encourage you to look it up. As I listened to him explain it, I could only imagine the complicated foresight and planning (not to mention the math) that must be involved in plotting a spacecraft's course so that it approaches—in sequence—different celestial bodies that act as catalysts to give just the right boost and send it on its new course.

HOW GRAVITY ASSISTANCE WORKS

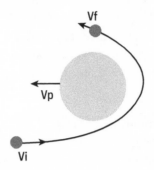

Luckily, it's not as complicated to act as catalysts for each other when we are co-creating and sharing leadership. But like the boost each planet or moon in turn provides, you can accelerate progress and bend the path on the journey from idea to implementation. This requires that you bring forward the Collaborator—along with a trusting, generous mindset, a learning orientation, and your genuine interest in the success and fulfillment of others. Together, you generate enthusiasm and energy to navigate likely tests and spark new ideas. In addition, as catalysts for each other, two Superpowers come into play: Questions and Seeing Beyond. (To explore these Superpowers further, consider reviewing chapter 4 in Adventure One.)

- **Questions** helps you facilitate and shape ideas and solutions. The key to *facilitating* is asking questions that grow others' capability rather than solving their problem for them. When you facilitate, instead of giving advice, you generate the conditions for people to come to their own conclusions. Through your questions, you ease people toward generating better outcomes for themselves. When you catalyze through *shaping*, on the other hand, you more directly influence the direction of co-creative efforts. It's an act of sculpting where your own perspective, ideas, advice, and recommendations alter the path and accelerate progress. The key to acting as a catalyst while shaping is bringing a curious mindset, watching out for the Inner Critic, and being clear who the ultimate decision-maker is when suggestions are offered.

- **Seeing Beyond** helps you illuminate possibilities and constraints that others might not see, by paying attention to opportunities and filling in the gaps. When you catalyze by identifying *opportunities*, you listen for new value embedded in how people talk about purpose, possibilities, and constraints. You might help to organize people's thinking, so the pieces fit together more coherently. When you share your observations, it's critical to do so with a mind that is open and at the same time prepared. When you catalyze by *filling in the gaps*, you pay attention to what is missing from people's view. Maybe they are overly focused on the near term. Or untested assumptions are floating around that might not be true. As you identify what's missing, bring a spirit of generosity and positive intent and a focus on moving toward shared goals. Otherwise, your insights may be interpreted as an attempt to block or inhibit progress.

Becoming Mentors and Coaches for Each Other

• • •

The fourth action for leading co-creation from any seat focuses on how we support each other's growth and development. Regina, for example, gets a lot of requests from people to be their mentor. It's understandable. She's successful at balancing task and relationship, she shares leadership and demonstrates followership publicly, she's vulnerable and courageous, and she is highly inclusive. She coaches her direct reports instead of telling them what to do. Regina is an active, senior leader sponsor of one of the company's employee resource groups, and she regularly speaks at her peers' department meetings. She maintains a public presence and advocates for the company on external panels and at conferences. And she builds strong coalitions both internally and externally—based on trust and partnership.

While she demonstrates many of the qualities people look to in a mentor, Regina believes we have work to do. "I'd like to see more people mentoring each other rather than looking up to a particular person," she said the last time we spoke about it. "Why does a mentor have to be someone who's made it into a formal leadership role?" She told me on multiple occasions how she believes we all need to become mentors and coaches for each other, based on our values, expertise, and experience rather than on our positions. Why is this prospect so challenging? One reason is our tendency to look up into the hierarchy for examples of people who are demonstrating the qualities we'd like to emulate and develop.

We already look up for direction and permission before we act. "Up" is where a select group makes decisions about people, their compensation, and their potential for future roles. Up is beguiling because—in most of our worlds—it still contains the power of position, the broader view, and the wider opportunity to influence. Up is often where the enterprise action is. Someone who's "made it" and has qualities we admire is attractive as a mentor or coach.

But mentors and coaches can come from anywhere. Wisdom is not correlated to hierarchy. While those who've made it will have certain valuable information and expertise to share, we must let go of the idea that leadership is attached to a role or to a level. That's the trap of "up." When we truly view leadership as coming from any seat, we can find mentors and coaches all around us.

What if we also looked to ourselves with greater confidence for answers within? What if we started with our own inner resources—our creativity and leadership potentials, our Superpowers, and all our gifts—and learned to access them in service to self-mentoring and self-coaching? How might the act of bringing a more conscious awareness of our inner mentor and coach improve co-creation? I'm not suggesting we don't still need guidance, direction, and the wisdom that comes from others who have gone before us and who can provide their learnings and different perspectives. We do—especially on hero's journeys into the unknown. But I'm not sure we leverage our intuition, for ourselves, as often as we could.

What if becoming mentors and coaches for each other starts within us instead of "out there"? What would be different in how you access and trust your intuition? What bridges might you have to cross and what forests might you have to traverse to deepen this relationship with yourself? These were some of the questions I confronted during my years enrolled at the University of Santa Monica as a student in their program of Spiritual Psychology. I started in the program when I was twenty-one years old—a deeply impactful point in my life where I had the opportunity to look inside at the man I was and ask, "Who do I want to become now and how can I develop a deep faith in accessing my own inner resources to guide me?"

What I've learned over the course of my life (building on this early work) is that it is a choice—day by day—to live from this place of inner resourcefulness. What's happening in the external world is alluring. And I can see, looking back, how very distracted I became as I sought success out in the world. I lost some of that deep connection to the mentor and coach within. I got caught up in looking externally for answers. Occasionally there would be a bolt of insight from inside, and I got good at accessing my inner resourcefulness to serve others. But I did—for many years—forget to engage in the conscious process of accessing my inner mentor and coach for myself.

Maybe you are already on a journey to build and deepen access to your own inner resources. Maybe you're just starting out. Maybe you're thinking to yourself as you read this, "This guy is whacked." Regardless, I have learned that once you build a strong foundation— as a mentor and coach *to yourself*—you will bring that inner strength to the experience of being a mentor and coach for others. It might also make it easier to receive the gifts that come from allies, mentors, and sponsors all around you.

There's a generosity of spirit in this exchange. There's humility and gratitude and grace. There is communion and achievement. There is trust, connection, and a new kind of honest, respectful, creative abrasion within the exchange of ideas, perspectives, and experiences.

There is emotion and deep meaningfulness that can be expressed and shared. There is disagreement, resolution, and compromise. These are the gifts that come from an open exchange as we step more fully into becoming mentors and coaches for ourselves and for each other.

WE NEED to get better at co-creating and sharing leadership as we face a world that's changing right before our eyes. In the new world of work, going it alone won't work any longer. Creating together is how we will thrive in our increasingly complex, interconnected, and inter-dependent world. It's how we will learn faster than we make mistakes. And it's an ongoing, lifelong hero's journey—to change our minds, collectively, about how creativity, innovation, and leadership happen most effectively in social systems. Practice moving the Collaborator onto the stage in the theater of your life. Commit to your own learning path while, together, we change and transform each other and our collective circumstances.

I can't promise it will be easy or comfortable. You will face new kinds of tests and places where you won't be sure how to move forward. There will be Swamps to navigate on this next phase of your journey—even when you're living with deep trust in your creative potential. That's because the systems that you work and live in look after their own survival. They resist change and seek certainty, alignment, replication, and predictability. They tend to stamp out ambiguity, uniqueness, and unknowing. But you are different now: you want a different way of living in the world—a way that honors who you are as a creative being with the potential to share leadership. This is what you will take forward into the next unknowns ahead.

ASK YOURSELF...

Now, at the end of this chapter, take time to pause and reflect on the following questions.

- What beliefs and assumptions might need to shift to foster an environment where people can lead from any seat?

- Who is best to include in conversations about these shifts?

Dancing Between Me and We

- What challenges do you face, personally, as you dance in the space between *me* and *we*? Do you need to bring yourself forward or step back a bit to better serve the process of co-creation?

- What practices might help you honor yourself, even while you are sharing leadership?

Creating Your Alliances

- As you consciously craft your partnerships and alliances, which key agreements are most important for you to strengthen trust?

Acting as Catalysts for Each Other

- As you co-create, what clues might help you decide whether to facilitate (draw out answers from others) or shape (make recommendations and advocate)?

- How might you point out possibilities or constraints that others may have missed—without unintentionally dampening enthusiasm and momentum?

Becoming Mentors and Coaches for Each Other

- Who are some of the people in your work and life who act as mentors and coaches for you? Are these relationships formal? informal? Who else might you include if you were to think about it more expansively?

- What experiments could help you become better mentors and coaches for each other? What might you do to become a better coach to yourself?

6

Crossing the Swamp

• • • • •

I N CHAPTER 5 of Adventure One, we explored a test I call the inner Swamp. That's where—in your thoughts, feelings, and awareness— it feels like you're stuck in dense fog, mud, and quicksand. The villains of fear and self-judgment abound (often mixed with guilt, shame, and self-doubt). It's hard to move forward. Your thinking can be murky, and without clear signposts it's hard to find a way out.

Inner Swamps are a formidable challenge on any creative quest. But they don't happen in isolation—they arise in response to outer conditions. All kinds of hurdles, roadblocks, constraints, and challenges may test us out in the world, especially as we invent and disrupt the status quo. These outer Swamps are treacherous, tangled-up places you and your allies will need to cross as you venture on journeys of discovery. The good news is you won't be alone.

Given what you are working to co-create, some Swamps may seem harmless. Others will be downright nightmarish. And while we could dig deeper into many kinds of outer Swamps, I'd like to focus on those that come from co-creating inside companies, organizations, and social systems.

When you impinge on a social system with your creativity— whether you are bringing forward simple improvements, broader adaptations, new inventions, or significant disruptions—you will be asking people to change. And typically, people within any given system tend to protect the status quo—even when they understand the value change will bring. That's because they depend on the system, knowingly and unknowingly perpetuate it, and in some cases "manage" it. Three Swamps that you and your allies will encounter as you put pressure on the system are most treacherous: 1) resistance and protecting, 2) organizational sludge, and 3) bad actors.

Swamp One: Resistance and Protecting

• • •

After our seminar where Andrew, Lily, Mark, Regina, and others came together, I was in Boston working with clients. Out of the blue, Andrew called. He had come out from Oregon to visit his father, Doug, up in Vermont. They'd gotten to talking about creativity and the challenges that can come from bringing innovations forward in big, bureaucratic organizations. "You've got to come up," Andrew said on the phone. "Doug has amazing stories, and the scars to go with them. He wants to meet you." Intrigued, I flew up to meet them over the weekend.

Resistance

For over thirty years, Doug had worked as a chemical engineer for a global oil and gas company. Doug was an inventor—a true intrapreneur who spent his entire career inside the system. His Creative Style mix led strongly with Soloist and Entrepreneur, but he also had a fair measure of the Rebel. "I got that Rebel part from you," Andrew said, smiling, to his father as we had breakfast together out on the porch.

Over the years, Doug accumulated numerous valuable patents and developed a reputation for turning ideas into products with commercial value. He and his team built a brand for solving tough problems and developing inventions that saved significant time, cost, and waste in the manufacturing process. Together, they weren't afraid to challenge the status quo. And Doug wasn't afraid to challenge others when he knew he was on to something important.

While Doug, Andrew, and I took a walk in the woods, we got talking about resistance to new ideas. Even with a great reputation, supportive managers, and resources to experiment, Doug had encountered painful resistance as he moved ideas into implementation. "People's entire careers are built on the very things you're going to change," he said. "New technologies are threatening. You might have good arguments for what you want to do and why your idea might work, but you won't have the proof for why it will be better than what already exists." There's a lot at stake when you're coming forward with a new approach that challenges the current model. "The burden of proof is on you," Doug said. "And you can bet there are a whole host of skeptical people who likely agree with each other that they are right, and you are wasting your time."

He turned to his son. "Andrew, did I ever tell you about the time the big boss called all the leaders in our group together?" Back in the 1970s, Doug had proposed an idea that would fundamentally alter the manufacturing process for an entire class of plastics. The change would require millions of dollars to develop. The vice president responsible for making the decision called the Research and Development (R&D) leaders together to hear Doug's idea. After listening to his presentation, the VP asked, "Who thinks this *won't* work?" Everyone in the room except Doug and one other person raised their hand.

It seemed somehow fitting to be talking with Doug and Andrew deep in the forest. In an ancient grove of trees, I could see clearly how, when a new seedling takes root and starts to push its way up to the light, the surrounding trees don't just bend out of the way. Some stand their ground, blocking out the light. Others have developed strategies to actively thwart new growth, poisoning the ground to any foreign intruder. A bear might happen by and trample it, or a deer could strip all its leaves in one meal. A hard freeze might kill it before it has a chance take root. Just like that new sapling that must find its foothold and its place in the canopy, you and your partners will need to navigate both benign and toxic forms of resistance.

In Doug's case, there was a lot going on in the room that day the VP asked what people thought. On the one hand, many colleagues had sound scientific arguments against his idea. As challenging as it was to face a room of colleagues voting down his idea, Doug knew that some of the resistance sprang from healthy skepticism. "They weren't ill-meaning," he said. "Science isn't black and white." The key, Doug explained, is to reframe this kind of resistance—and the people who bring it forward—as allies. Use it to hone your ideas and challenge yourself. Leverage skepticism to make your ideas stronger and better. "If you get a good result every now and then, don't just accept it," Doug said. "Ask what your staunchest critics might say about that result. Did you leave any loopholes? Is the logic sound? Have you tested your most challenging assumptions—or just the safe ones?"

Doug was talking about people who resist based on questions of validity, merit, and value. But you'll also encounter people who are afraid to risk supporting you in an unproven venture—even though they may see potential merit in your idea. As frustrating as their risk aversion may be, you'll benefit by staving off judgment and keeping these folks as allies-in-waiting until you have more certain evidence of value.

As your idea grows and begins to take up space and light, other colleagues will resist because they are assessing the impact to their own projects. If resources are limited, your search for supporters will inevitably be seen as competition. The green light for your idea may mean that other projects will be sidelined, paused, or stopped completely to make room for investment in yours. To convert these kinds of resisters into allies, use your Superpower of Seeing Beyond to look past your own remit. Bring forward the strategies and practices of the Collaborator. "Get out in front of it," Doug said. Avoiding people's concerns—or publicly calling out their fear or self-orientation—won't help build goodwill.

The most toxic kind of resistance occurs when people harbor resentment and jealousy for your new idea. Your venture will likely threaten existing technologies, processes, and approaches. Promotions and careers have been built upon these prior achievements. Your success, and the light that emanates from creative ventures, may tarnish what once was their shiny latest and greatest.

New ideas tend to stand out in a sea of execution and implementation. In any large organization, a substantial number of folks haven't claimed the gift of their creativity and haven't answered the call to bring it out into the system: they are just biding time, staying within the lines, keeping their heads down, working for a paycheck, and giving the boss what's been asked for. Your advances and the passion and commitment that come along with it can highlight the complacency of others.

You may be wondering what happened in the meeting, back in the early 1970s, when all of Doug's colleagues except one voted to shut down his proposal. As it turned out, the one vote for moving forward came from Doug's former boss, Stan. He had watched the way Doug worked in the past and knew that when he was on to something, it usually panned out. The VP knew Stan wouldn't raise his hand against a roomful of others if he didn't have confidence in Doug. As we continued our walk through the woods, Doug said, "I think that VP knew all the reasons behind those raised hands. This guy understood resistance. He'd probably seen it in all of its forms in one way or another." In the end, he funded Doug's project.

Protecting

Another Swamp you and your allies are likely to encounter is protecting. This can come from possessiveness, if you—or others—believe that the ideas and output of your inventing are "yours" instead of part of a shared co-creation with others in the ecosystem. We've explored how Soloists, Rebels, and Entrepreneurs are more susceptible to this kind of ownership and may be prone to protect (even hoard) knowledge, ideas, and data. "My idea," "my accomplishment," "my spreadsheet," "my data," "my budget," "my access to customers" can all become a kind of territory people claim.

Protecting can also arise from a mindset of scarcity: the belief that there are limited resources, limited possibilities, and limited space for new ideas to take root and flourish. This is a mindset of constriction, where you are locked in competition with others or fearful your idea will be cut if it comes to light. Maybe you've seen this in your world.

People have pet projects they are reluctant to share. Or managers hoard budget even though they may not need it—while new ventures starting up in other parts of the organization could benefit from an infusion of capital. Departments hoard and protect people too. I can't tell you how often I've heard a leadership team say, "Don't give up that head count. We'll never get it back if we need it down the road."

People also hoard knowledge: "I can't share the decisions made in last week's meeting because we're still working out the details." Just last week I heard someone say, "I can't share my presentation with you because it hasn't been approved by the leaders yet." This constriction of knowledge, ideas, and resources dampens collective creative potential among the network of teams in your organization. It limits forward progress, diminishes agility, and slows the creation of new value.

Other factors can also contribute to the depth and expanse of this Swamp. Consider the unintended consequences of financial, legal, and human resources controls that direct and restrict the flow of investment, resources, and talent—and the availability of all three for new ventures. Right now, you might be thinking, "But everyone can't just go around doing whatever they want, can they?" Of course not. And I'm not suggesting that we bash Finance, Legal, and HR functions—the people I know working in these departments have tough jobs and care deeply for the missions and success of the institutions and companies for which they work. I'm also not suggesting we blame managers for directing resources to the priorities they're accountable for—or Legal departments for protecting patents and the value they afford. In and of themselves, these control mechanisms inside organizations have their place.

But it's easy to see how a mindset of scarcity and the protection of what's "mine" can infect these mechanisms and restrict the flow of resources, diminish shared purpose, limit transparency, and strengthen control. Years ago, I learned of a team that was trying to improve the experience of new employees joining the company. One of the biggest complaints new folks had was that it took anywhere from three to five days to get them a computer. "What if we simply had one budget center for all computers for new employees?"

someone asked. "Then we could have them ready to go on day one, when employees come to orientation."

What a tangle of controls, restrictions, and false ownership emerged as the team dug into this challenge! Departments didn't want to give up control of the ordering and presenting of the equipment to new employees. They also wanted the equipment to belong to them and believed that down the road they would lose control. Eventually, this simple solution had to have the approval of the CFO (four levels above in the hierarchy) before it could be implemented. This one example illustrates how the misuse of structural control mechanisms can awaken the dark side of protecting in even the simplest of improvements.

It doesn't have to be this way. Doug told Andrew and me about a time in his career when he thought he could help another department. Doug's R&D group was in New Jersey. Normally, they wouldn't have gotten involved in solving challenges outside their remit. But Doug heard about a big problem in the French manufacturing plant. Some of the equipment was corroding and rotting away, and despite numerous attempts, no solution had been found. Doug had an idea he thought just might work.

Back then, if his proposal was to be considered, he would need to fly over to France to deliver it in person. If they accepted his idea, they'd have to find money in the budget and engineers who weren't already allocated to projects to implement it. "I'd really like to go and make my presentation," Doug told his boss. "What will you do if they accept it?" his boss asked. "There's no money. Its mid-year." They both stopped talking for a moment. Then, unexpectedly, his boss said, "You go present. If they accept, I'll find the money."

Budget and concerns about sharing talent across boundaries could have easily been a bottleneck in this situation. Doug's boss had to dip into the already allocated budget for unplanned travel expenses. And then there was Doug's time. What about all the other work on Doug's plate that would have to get distributed or put on hold if the proposal was accepted? Doug and his boss were committed to solving these challenges as they moved forward—and not letting fear and control stop what they believed was the right thing to do. Though Doug's experience happened many years ago, I still find we need more of this kind of enterprise thinking in our workplaces today.

Another manifestation of protecting can happen in response to mistakes or failures. Mistakes, failures, dead ends, missed deadlines, and costly accidents are a part of any true venture into the unknown in search of new value. Even with a sound idea and strong data to suggest an initial proof of concept, a string of early failures can stop a new venture in its tracks. Management might resort to blame, protecting, and distancing themselves from further investment. Teams can be shut down too quickly. And the learning from mistakes and failures is lost—even though it could have made future iterations smarter.

Any new foray into uncharted territory is in jeopardy when there are early mistakes or failures, especially if the stakes are high and the project has the attention—but not the longer-term commitment— of leadership. Some common ways protecting can show up include blaming, scapegoating, and over-rotation on delivering short-term value. These behaviors will dampen the passion for going out on a limb to explore new possibilities. Other individuals and teams are likely to take a cue from watching how things unfold, and vow not to risk experimentation and failure. Still others, in a misguided attempt to prevent such failures in the future, might install overcomplicated controls, processes, and procedures. Without clear outcomes, without clarity of your convictions and a strong connection to your purpose, and without a network of support, it's easy to get lost and give up.

The reason this all matters is that protecting stifles the processes of co-creation and sharing leadership. If protecting can stymie a harmless idea to get computers to employees on day one, imagine how it can stifle innovation when the stakes are higher. That's why it's vital you become aware of the shape, size, and depth of this Swamp. First, ask yourself, "Am I engaged in any measure of protecting? Am I hoarding knowledge, assets, data, or ideas? Am I restricting others' access to partners and stakeholders? How might any measure of a 'yes' answer to these questions be limiting collective creative potential?" Then scan the dynamic in the environment. Ask the partners with whom you're co-creating, "Is protecting active here—influencing how we set priorities, share resources and knowledge, define risks, draw boundaries, decide who to communicate with and involve, or how we test ideas and solutions?"

Occasionally, some measure of protecting can be fit for purpose, given the needs and priorities of your environment. But often we create this Swamp out of habit, traditional thinking, and unquestioned assumptions. New ways of working are emerging that require networked co-creation, sharing leadership, and the value that will be drawn from access to data across technologies and systems. Protecting will have an increasingly detrimental impact on solving tough issues that cross disciplines, domains, and industries. Anyone who works and creates inside of larger institutions or corporations knows that the unintended consequences of protecting (control, constriction, and separation from others who might otherwise become allies) must give way to more open, transparent, and generous sharing.

Swamp Two: Organizational Sludge

• • •

Resistance and protecting—and the fallout they can trigger—are challenging enough. But there are other Swamps you're likely to face "out there" as you venture on journeys of discovery inside the system. One of the most challenging comes from the very way the system is set up—the processes, policies, governance structures, cultural norms, incentive frameworks, and all the other trappings of bureaucracy and hierarchy. In *Humanocracy*,[14] Gary Hamel and Michele Zanini reveal how layers of supporting mechanisms work to ensure consistency, reliability, standardization, and compliance. Challenging the system can feel like the fight of your life, like wading through sludge and being sucked into quicksand all at the same time.

Over the years, I have experienced countless examples of the Swamps you may cross when creating into the morass of bureaucratic norms and procedures. I've also witnessed the inner Swamps of frustration, anger, despair, and disillusionment this morass can engender.

One example, however, stands out and illuminates several of the different hurdles that can form organizational sludge.

Not long after attending the seminar with Andrew, Mark, Lily, and others, Regina introduced me to Mei, a senior leader who had been recruited to create an entirely new department. Regina believed this new group would help revolutionize the business, but she knew that critical challenges lay ahead that would make or break their success. As part of her master plan to "kick some ass" and help activate creativity across the company, Regina connected me with Mei.

"In the automobile industry, we've been at a crossroads for decades," Mei explained as I got up to speed on some of the pressures facing her new department. "Since I joined, we've been building our capabilities and some of the foundational platforms, but now we're at a critical inflection point. We have to demonstrate tangible value." She explained there was mounting evidence her boss might be preparing to scale back what was already a multi-million-dollar investment to invent new technologies.

Mei's function sat nested among a mix of other research and development groups that also built or bought new technologies. There were complicated interfaces to manage with the global manufacturing and sales functions as well as alliances between government, academic, and private industry partners. Mei's challenge—stated by the head of her division when she was recruited—was to completely reimagine foundational components of the product development process.

"When we started building our tech platforms—that's when things got messy," she said during one of our coaching sessions. By architecting the foundation, the team was claiming the spaces and places where their group would drive new value. They put pressure on the system and exposed a host of problems: a general unclarity of purpose and overlapping remits; conflicts between different departments for recognition and credit; long-held resentments from fights over resources and budget; and fundamental disagreements about who was responsible for innovation, how new ideas would be developed, and which ideas would be funded. This was the epitome of a Swamp mired in organizational sludge.

But there was still another treacherous stretch of the Swamp ahead. A well-established system has an insatiable drive for the demonstration of tangible value. It's called "deliverables." Exploration without deliverables or the promise of deliverables (products, services, commercial value, and so on) is virtually impossible in a large, interconnected system that prizes task achievement, return on investment, and shareholder value. The tolerance for exploration and for venturing into the unknown to see what you might find is short-lived—even if you're fortunate enough to be sanctioned, sponsored, and well-funded.

The part of the machine that measures progress in any bureaucracy is formidable. It will test you and your allies. The system is hungry for evidence, for progress that can be commercialized and productized, and for the generation of short-term results. You will be asked to prove value and explain your plans. But metrics, key performance indicators (KPIs), goals, milestones, and project plans are not the preferred tools of exploration. They are tools of *execution*—not of mystery, adventure, and discovery. Used inappropriately, they can work against creative ventures into the unknown.

Understanding and navigating the dynamic between exploration and action, and between discovery and tangible value creation, is part of your job. In co-creation, you and your partners will need to learn how to preserve and negotiate for time, exploit unforeseen events and unintended consequences, and create alliances. You'll need to recontract when people ask for deliverables too early in exploration. And together, you'll need to learn when to cut exploration short and start producing tangible results. These are critical lessons as you create together inside the system.

Working with Mei and the team, we explored some of their most challenging hurdles in the face of mounting pressure to perform and to prove value. "In a way, you have to become curious about how the system works," one team member shared. "I've never thought of myself as a psychologist or an anthropologist," another said, "but once we got serious about making real investments, we had to become students of how to change people's minds to change the system." "I just wanted to focus on our work," another said with a chuckle. "Then I realized: dealing with the sludge is how our creativity turns into innovations."

As we talked over lunch that day, four organizational hurdles stood out. Depending on the size and scale of what you're working on, you may run deep into Swamps like these, or you may just skirt the edges. But when you're inventing inside, you are sure to encounter some measure of these four.

Hurdle One: Overcomplicated processes

In the industry that Mei and her team operated, clarity and standard-ization of processes are critical. Not surprisingly, numerous processes for workflows, interfaces, decision-making, and quality compliance had built up over time. Each time there was a failure or mistake, another item was added to the checklist and another step added to the process. As these processes evolved, they became fixed and unchangeable in people's minds. "It's like the hull of a boat," one team member said. "Over the years, barnacle after barnacle has been added until the hull has become completely encrusted." Many of the most defended barnacles had been there so long, no one could even recall why they were part of the process to begin with.

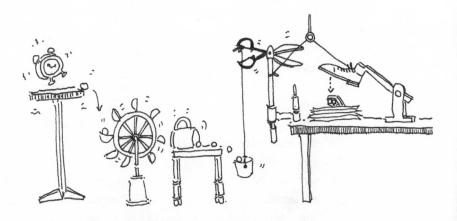

Are you inventing amid overcomplicated processes? Scan the eco-system in which you are co-creating. Which arenas might suffer from overcomplicated processes that generate organizational sludge? How is that making it difficult to move forward?

To overcome these hurdles, bring together partners and collabo-rators from across your value network in an open, transparent, and trusting dialogue. Talk about scraping the hull clean. Seek opportuni-ties to renegotiate and redesign long-standing processes. Talk about what is truly non-negotiable, what could be changed, and what could be deleted. Explore new technologies that could simplify things. And finally, identify unnecessary complexity at key interfaces and hand-offs where viscosity is stifling forward momentum. The key is to simplify together in a process of co-creation.

Hurdle Two: Incentives reinforce the way things are done

People tend to do more of what they are rewarded for. I'm not just talking about monetary rewards (though these are powerful levers for influencing what gets done). I'm also talking about incentives that build up self-esteem (like recognition and praise for a job well done), raise visibility (for example, exposure with senior leadership), or offer the promise of new experiences that develop expertise.

There are a host of arenas where incentives do not match up with behaviors that support discovery, co-creation, and innovation. Mei and Regina shared openly about how incentive structures in their organization reinforced what they called "siloed thinking." That's when people are rewarded for delivering only what serves their imme-diate goals or remit. It's the opposite of "enterprise thinking."

When teams think only of what will serve their immediate project or just the department they work in, the landscape becomes littered with disconnected solutions: like IT platforms and systems, train-ings, frameworks, and processes that may have met the goal at hand but that don't speak to each other. Also, we don't incentivize the development of emerging talent. We don't reward a generous and transparent approach to sharing resources. We tell stories about indi-vidual heroics and we reward behavior that protects the status quo.

Unconsciously, we bookmark the kinds of behaviors and competencies that are valued.

Are you inventing amid incentives that stifle creativity and innovation? If so, get "in the sandbox" together with your partners, customers, and even your competitors. Find common principles for knowledge sharing, capture, storage, access, and retrievability. Identify specific incentives for ways of working together that promote new, desired behaviors like collaboration, transparency, co-ownership, and alignment. Identify priority arenas to focus on that would have the greatest impact given your project and stage in the journey. Find early adopters and begin to collect examples of new behaviors and the value that's been created. And remember to explore how incentives are linked to cultural norms, which live below the surface. These links are harder to break and will require more attention and investment to alter.

Hurdle Three: Elaborate layers of governance
A while back, Regina brought me in to work with her leadership team. She hoped to simplify the layers of oversight, approvals, and reviews that took place as decisions were made in the procurement process. Many groups across her company were forming new partnerships, investing in new technologies, and practicing new behaviors that enabled agility, iteration, and fast decision-making. Often, her group was named as a key blocker to innovation.

Together, we took a good, hard look at three conditions that generated unnecessary bottlenecks for people across the organization. First, in many cases the leadership team didn't even know how decisions got made, who the decision-maker was, and how the effectiveness of decisions was evaluated. Second, there was a lack of alignment among the leadership team. "Just when I think we're all in agreement about who makes the decision, a new situation arises, and we come up with different answers." Third, they realized they were sending mixed signals to their staff. They were asking people to "be empowered," but in fact they were throwing people into the lion's den—without support—and seeing if they made it out alive.

Are you inventing amid elaborate layers of governance? Are you *contributing* **to this kind of organizational sludge?** The first step is to get honest about what is going on. Use your Superpower of Seeing Beyond to practice looking clear—combined with radical candor—to identify behaviors that muddy the waters of decision-making. Test out different decision-making frameworks to expose deeper assumptions, beliefs, and values that get in the way of trust and empowerment. Collect evidence to help managers and senior leaders understand how swampy decision-making slows things down. Next, provide coaching and support to help people learn from decisions that didn't yield anticipated results. Demonstrate you "have people's back" even while setting them free to make important decisions about investing in— and inventing—new approaches. Finally, evaluate your collective risk tolerance and find places where you can take Creative License without asking for permission.

Hurdle Four: Competing priorities among key partners

In any large organization, different divisions and functions are going to have competing priorities. These can give rise to some of the trickiest Swamps to cross as you bring a new idea or venture forward. Everything we've talked about up till now can come into play: active resistance, fear of taking risks, politics, people's sense of identity, competition for budget, organizational boundaries that divide people, fights for resources, and layers of review and approvals. You name it and it's going to be a part of this Swamp. That's because competing priorities expose all the other Swamps lurking around.

Within a few months of our meeting, Mei's team had plummeted directly into this Swamp. One of their most promising, yet potentially disruptive, technologies crashed directly into the timeline for building a new manufacturing facility. As a capital investment, the new plant had been planned some years back and construction had just begun. However, it was designed to manufacture on the old platform. If the team's technology worked, it would make the plant obsolete— but the technology wasn't yet proven or fully developed. Ultimately, management decided the new technology was too risky and built the plant as originally specified. That meant years of lost benefit and advantage, not to mention learning from trial and error. It was a tough blow for the team. "People quit because of it," Mei told me on a call some months later.

You're likely to encounter many other types of competing priorities. The conflict might be within layers above you—as it was for Mei—or it might be closer to home within your own group of allies. Some might have a priority on speed at any expense while others value cost savings and efficiencies. Or a drive for speed might conflict with a priority to incorporate new technologies that could slow things down. Some might aim for the highest possible quality and come into conflict with people who are aiming for iterations of minimum viable products. There are potential conflicts between short-term value and long-term sustainability, value for us versus value for all, and doing what's urgent today versus investing in mechanisms for renewal.

Are you inventing amid competing priorities? Working at cross-purposes will be one of the most insidious Swamps you are likely to face. That's partly because you likely won't realize you're in this Swamp until you're already deep within it—where turning back is a tough pill to swallow. Also, it can be difficult to change the value structures that underlie what makes something a priority to one person or another. They're tied up with values, identity, ego, and people's sense of safety, security, and control. To work through this hurdle, start by clarifying your own priorities—and how these priorities link to your values, principles, and sense of identity. Knowing what shapes your priorities will help you explore potential conflicts and seek common ground. Talk about priorities right from the start—as you contract and craft alliances with key stakeholders. And remember to revisit priorities frequently as you conduct retrospectives to assess your progress.

Swamp Three: Bad Actors

• • •

Mark recently told me a story that illuminates a different kind of outer Swamp you are likely to encounter. José, a teacher from Mark's school, went to work on the cleanup that ensued after the BP oil spill back in 2010. José had a background in waste reclamation and thought he could help capture as much of the oil as possible before it came ashore. Everything was in place: the equipment, boats, booms, and other resources had been mobilized out in the water along a stretch of coast.

The crews were just about to deploy when they got a call to stop everything. To José's dismay, the call was from the mayor of the very town that was threatened, located on one of the beautiful gulf coast beaches. Turns out, the mayor was expecting a TV crew to film the horror and devastation as the oil lapped up on shore. The crew was running late and had phoned ahead to see if the cleanup could be delayed until they got there. For the mayor and the crew, filming the devastation was more important than preventing it. "These guys were bad actors," Mark told me.

The story of José's experience got me thinking. There are bad actors all around us, in every walk of life. These are the monsters in our Swamps—and the devastation and destruction they create can take years to clean up. But I want to narrow the focus to those bad actors that act as toxins and inhibitors to co-creation and shared leadership. The ensemble cast of characters you're likely to encounter has the potential to kill your creative spirit.

There's Albert, the director who yells, calls people names, and badmouths people in the room under his breath. Do you know someone like Albert? He's a bully who might say things like, "You'll try that idea out over my dead body," or "He's such an idiot," or "You're fired." Because he has the power of position, Albert's Swamp reeks of fear and intimidation—the kind that can strip the shine off your enthusiasm in a New York minute.

Then there's Deborah, the ambitious mid-level manager who steals other people's ideas for her own gain. Do you know someone like Deborah? She'll brazenly present your idea as hers. Because she's a level or two above you in the hierarchy, she's often in meetings you are not invited to. Later, you might hear about a great vision she had or an idea she came up with that really caught people's attention. But you know that it came from a conversation where you and your colleagues shared some of your latest thinking. Only you can't prove it. The Deborahs in this world ensnare you in a web of fear. Her Swamp erodes the kind of trust that lubricates co-creation and constricts the free flow of ideas and fragments of ideas that are so vital to a vibrant creative process.

Colin is ambitious too, but in a slimy, self-promoting way. You're likely to find him cutting rivals down, stepping over people, and blaming others for his mistakes. Most of the Colins of the world talk a lot and promote themselves, even though they haven't accomplished much for a long time. Doug had a few Colins in his work life. When Doug won the global most valuable patent award two years in a row, any number of Colins bad-mouthed him, claimed the award review process was unfair, and eventually got the company to eliminate the award altogether. Colin will complain when you go above and beyond—because it makes him look bad. He's jealous, he's a backstabber, and he will undermine you behind the scenes. Do you know a Colin?

Don't forget Josef, our lead on the Creative Leadership project, with his own special brand of narcissism, arrogance, and righteousness that stomped out exploration and healthy risk-taking. And there's Kristina, the "absentee landlord." With her apathy and lack of involvement, she undermines people's faith that it's safe to take risks and experiment in ways that might lead to failure. Kristina will say, "I've got your back," but then she's not there if you falter. If you pay attention, you'll realize she's already used the same excuse for not showing up multiple times. What about Vikram, the taskmaster, stifling innovation with micromanagement, fear of anything that can't be proven, and his overwhelming orientation toward execution. And we've already talked about Ivan, drunk with power, and spraying his command and control all over your creative pursuits like weedkiller.

These bad actors—and many others I am sure you know—can roam the Swamp openly, or they can hide in the shadows, behind the scenes. You may see them coming, or they might surprise you. It's tempting to view them as villains and step into the quicksand of the Drama Triangle with them. But the trick is to treat them as you would any other obstacle in your way: don't let them undermine your resolve, your connection to your purpose, and your faith in your gift of creativity. Easier said than done, right? It can be downright maddening to turn your creative energies away from your goals and dreams to deal with bad actors. As opposed to resisters, who you may want to invest in, build connection with, and enroll in your mission, bad actors rarely turn into constructive allies.

Instead, experiment with ways to make them irrelevant to your purpose. Sometimes it's easier; you can stay where you are and find a workaround that eliminates the need for their involvement. You can cut them out of the picture. Other times, you may have to extract yourself, leaving behind progress you've made, relationships you've built, and investments you've set in motion.

It's a tough choice to leave. Andrew faced this choice when he left the county treasurer's office in search of a new opportunity to bring his whole self and his creative gifts to his work. I've faced this choice multiple times through the twists and turns of my career. Every time I've left a situation where I was challenged by a bad actor, I was rewarded by an immediate sense of freedom and possibility, a newfound optimism, and renewed creative inspiration.

It's also possible to learn from bad actors. I'll never forget my surprise when a colleague told me how—after taking his kids to see an action-hero movie like *Batman*, *Thor*, or *The Avengers*—he talked with them about the creativity demonstrated by the villains in the film. What a fascinating and novel idea. Just like everyone else, villains are creative. Get curious about what they create with their gift. Notice their tactics and methods and what motivates them. Watch your reactions and learn about what you value, what you can and won't stand for, and what triggers you. And look inward to recognize when you might be—in certain small ways, times, and places—seen as a bad actor to others. Call on your Superpower of Learning to deepen your self-awareness and gain familiarity with the Swamps bad actors inhabit—so you can identify them early and develop a workaround, or know with greater faith when it's time to leave.

BECAUSE THE Swamps of resistance and protecting, organizational sludge, and bad actors can come in so many different forms, it's impossible to plan for and prevent them all. Learning from them, and taking creative accountability while you traverse these Swamps, becomes one of your most important practice fields. All the likely tests will show up: the Blank Canvas, Mistakes and Failure, challenges with Time and Timing, any number of Obstacles, and of course, inner Swamps. As you navigate the inner Swamps that arise in response to outer circumstances, you will become attuned to your secret places of pain and fear, of longing and disappointment, and of striving and separation.

Swamps will challenge who you know yourself to be and who you think you are becoming. They will challenge your resolve and connection to purpose. Through the Swamps you cross with others—in a process of co-creation and sharing leadership—you will hone and refine the ways you create together.

And you will be different. The landscape you interact with will look different and you will see things you might not have noticed before. Your Superpowers will have a new quality of depth and impact. Different kinds of adventures might appeal to you than the ones you embarked on in the past. You may notice that the strength of your conviction brings more energy to meaningful, collective pursuits. And you will surely know more about who you are as a creator and how to co-create more effectively.

ASK YOURSELF...

Now, at the end of this chapter, take time to pause and reflect on the following questions.

- What are some of the most challenging Swamps you have faced in your work and life? How did your creativity play a role in helping you cross through them?

- How did you leverage your Superpowers to navigate through?

- How do people's inner Swamps impact collective progress? What practices might you use to help each other?

Resistance and Protecting

- What forms of resistance have you experienced as you brought new ideas to light?

- Which strategies help you leverage resistance to generate opportunity? What have you tried that doesn't work?

- In which arenas might you be protecting—even ever so slightly? How is that serving (or not) the purpose of your quest?

- When you encounter protecting, what can you do to promote more open, transparent, and generous sharing?

Organizational Sludge

- What have you learned about challenging the status quo inside social systems?

- Who in your experience effectively manages the trappings of hierarchy, bureaucracy, politics, and control? What can you learn from their example?

- How can you bring creative accountability to help navigate through organizational sludge?

Bad Actors

* Think of a bad actor from your past. What did you learn about yourself from your experience with them? How did they help to shape who you are and who you are becoming?

7

Coming Together Anew

• ◦ • ◦ •

HEN I first started writing this book, I thought it would be about changing the structures, policies, and processes "out there"—the hurdles that get in people's way and dampen and numb creative expression. I thought I would write a book about changing our bureaucratic, hierarchical systems and shaping organizational cultures to foster creative accountability. But I realized that the answer to unlocking creative potential in everyone lies less in focusing out there—on the system—and more in awakening a movement of people who are bringing forward a way of being—what I have been calling conscious creativity—to collective opportunities.

That means bringing a new level of self-awareness to creative action and making different choices—like spending more time together in discovery and adventure and learning how it works across different contexts. Pay attention to what you're learning about yourself as you practice the strategies and behaviors of the Collaborator. Notice what you learn as you join with others, cross new thresholds into the unknown, and share leadership in a fit-for-purpose manner. And use every Swamp to deepen your relationship with yourself and others.

A deep and enduring faith comes from being attuned to this learning process. Gratefulness and graciousness come from enjoying this new way of being—marked by inclusion, kinship, and community.

When more of us are consciously awake to our process and practice, we become a beacon of light for each other in the darkness—to help unleash each other's potential. By vulnerably and courageously being our truest, most conscious creative selves, we will illuminate new futures for the companies, organizations, and causes whose missions we share.

Elevate Your Impact

• • •

Lily ended up losing her job after all. Remember Lily? She worked as a biostatistician in one of the life sciences firms in northern California. When I first met her, Lily had already lost a few close friends at work in waves of job cuts and restructuring. To demonstrate her value and hopefully avoid a similar fate, she was working hard, taking initiative on projects that created more accessible and reusable data platforms. But that dreaded day finally came and she was let go in yet another wave of restructuring.

It turns out that for Lily, the uncertainty about losing her job was nothing compared to the intense inner Swamp she had to cross in the months that followed. There was anger, bitterness, judgment of self and others, and a deep feeling of helplessness in this new Swamp. There was loneliness as Lily turned inward instead of reaching out. She got sick and struggled to find the energy to look for a new job. It was more difficult than ever to take care of her children, and her relationship with her husband began to suffer. During this morass, a friend invited her to a gala benefit for one of the leading Breast Cancer Foundations.

"I almost didn't go," she told me when we met for a catch-up a few months later. "I wasn't in the mood for a party. But at the dinner, it's like a lightbulb went off." Lily shared how moved she was by the stories of courage she heard that evening. She was struck by the contrast between the challenges she faced finding a new job and what the brave women she heard from that evening were enduring. In the days and weeks that followed, she felt inspired to be of service.

Volunteering brought new energy and new connections—and ultimately a new job opportunity as a data science program manager for the Bay Area affiliate of the foundation. Lily had found her way through one of her most challenging Swamps.

Not long after she and I met, Lily joined Mark, Regina, Andrew, and others in a "reunion retreat" I led for graduates of my seminars. Those who knew Lily from before noticed profound changes in the way she put her ideas forward, shared insightful feedback, and advocated for others. The timid, reserved Lily was gone; in her place was a relaxed, confident, collaborative, and highly attuned woman. We experienced someone who had come into a deeper faith in herself as a creative Collaborator.

"It's like the gates opened up and I ran out into an open field full of flowers," Lily told the group. "I'd been so isolated and steeped in emotion and focused on avoiding and 'againstness' that everything was muddled. All I could see were constraints." But when she came forward with curiosity, opportunity revealed itself to her. She saw it, seized it, and shaped it into a new "practice field" where she could elevate her impact and bring her whole creative self to work.

It is profound to witness someone coming forward to stand in the fullness of faith that creative potential is *always there* no matter what. That ultimately, there is no way to lose it. That we are not alone in seeking to make a difference in our work and our world, and that the futures we seek are also seeking us. That day, the room lit up with energy. Lily inspired us with her passion and the stories of how her work was making a difference in the lives of women and their families. Others shared how their creative practice was strengthening because of the collective play and courageous vulnerability they experienced within their networks and communities. We saw how each of us can elevate our impact by combining conscious creativity with attention, care, and concern for the well-being of others.

What about you? Energy, new ideas, and opportunities to elevate your impact *want* to come through you. When you are consciously engaged in moving *toward* what you want, an inexhaustible wellspring of creativity becomes available. Can you feel the pull of a bigger, broader adventure drawing you forward? What is the future that's calling you to enter and join in? What urgent imperatives have caught your attention and interest? Where could you be a catalyst—to spark innovation that addresses some of the most pressing challenges of our times? These are critical questions about potentially new focus areas for your creative attention.

As you seek opportunities to elevate your impact, remember to use every experience to learn. Explore the rhythm and the pace of your dance with creativity. Trust the forces around you that converge in support when you claim new, meaningful purposes with accountability. Show up and do the work, pay attention, follow your intuition and curiosity, and take steps forward even if you're not sure they are the right ones. Join with others and invite them into your creative process. These are the kinds of practices that help translate your deep and enduring faith in your creativity into collective value and impact. Making a difference in the world, together with others, may be one of the most important and meaningful journeys of discovery you will experience in your life.

Enjoy the Ride

• • •

A few months before our graduate retreat, I touched base with Andrew. He had signed up to join us and we set up a video hangout to check in. As he shared his journey since we last spoke, I was caught off guard. Coming out of the Swamps he navigated as he left the county treasurer's office, Andrew had battled a deep sense of injustice, unfairness, and a measure of righteousness that made sense given his Rebel style. Back then, I remember wondering if the wounds he experienced from those Swamps would linger and get in the way of moving toward what wanted to emerge next.

I laughed out loud in surprise and delight when he told me how he had run for—and won—a four-year term on the Board of County Commissioners. "I've got my eye on the Oregon House," he said with excitement in his voice. "And then, maybe the US House." What a change from the Andrew I had known previously. He'd found a path forward, transformed by the foment he had experienced. He had started "enjoying the ride," as he put it.

It turns out that the roller-coaster of ups and downs that vexed him in the past now spurred him on to deeper levels of commitment and passion. "It's not about fixing problems anymore," he told us at the graduate retreat. "I'm building coalitions to grab opportunities. It's all about working *with* people. I've become an opportunist," he exclaimed, with a big grin that stretched from ear to ear.

We learned a lot from Andrew, and I for one am grateful. Enjoying the ride is not something I can claim as a strength; I regularly get caught up in the stress of hurdles that show up in my path. I tend to focus on what needs to get done, and I can get thrown off and frustrated when obstacles get in the way of accomplishing it. Andrew's example was inspiring. He found joy in connecting with people— really communing with them, listening to their concerns, following his heart, and working together to shape challenges into collective opportunities. He found a way to fall in love with people: to have fun with them, laugh together, take time to learn about people's lives and fears and passions, and to work with them to invent solutions that lift everyone up.

Regina also attended the retreat and shared how moved and inspired she was by Andrew's story. His transformation resonated with her deeply held belief that relationship is our most important work together. "The shift from focusing on tasks to focusing on people first isn't easy," she told Andrew. "I don't often see people who are successful at it." But Regina found more than just confirmation of her beliefs that day. Andrew's insights into enjoying the ride sparked something in Regina that she had been struggling with for some time. For Regina, the demands of her role as a senior leader meant frequent travel, calls with colleagues in different time zones, 24/7 access to technology, and a barrage of emails every day. The trappings of her leadership role had started to take their toll. "It's not a job," she told the group. "It's a lifestyle."

While Regina and her team were successful in reducing much of the burdensome governance that created organizational sludge, it seemed as if she had even less time than before. "I'm being pulled in so many different directions," she said. "It's exhausting." Regina longed for more opportunities to spend time strategizing about the future, acting as a catalyst for change, and developing others—all of which were vital to her sense of duty as a leader in the organization. "I don't feel like I'm enjoying the ride," Regina said solemnly. "And I don't think many others in my department are either. How can we reinvent ourselves, take better care of ourselves, *and* have more fun?"

For Regina and her team, sparking innovation was at the root of their desire to reshape work practices. But instead of simplifying things, they had replaced burdensome governance with "collaborative overload."[15] That's when people stop making conscious choices about what and who they say yes to, and when we allow our networks to become bloated beyond the purpose they are meant to serve. For Regina—already naturally attuned to the skills of co-creation and shared leadership—these new ways of working were like collaboration on steroids.

Across her organization, a sense of burnout was taking its toll on people's well-being. The push for accelerated productivity was overtaking space for new ideas to take root. Everyone was talking about prioritizing work, but all around her Regina saw people building new initiatives, getting overly involved, and duplicating efforts. "Invention isn't just about starting new things," she told us. "Sometimes you have to stop starting."

We didn't resolve Regina's challenge there at our retreat. How could we? It would take practice over time, and the engagement of many others in her organization, to make the kinds of changes she envisioned. But one thing we all realized from working with Regina and Andrew was that enjoying the ride is mostly a state of mind. It comes when we are making progress on meaningful work with a deep sense of purpose, truly letting go and sharing leadership across our network, and exercising the discipline to stop things, say no, and simplify. It arises when we come together around a collective vision and shared principles while freeing each other to figure out the *how*. And it happens when we connect deeply with people, opening to communion and community with vulnerability and courage. Add in a sense of mischievousness, experimentation, playfulness, and Creative License while you collaborate and you're almost there!

The last part of the equation, as Regina was learning, comes when achievement is balanced with a conscious focus on well-being and self-care. JOMO (the joy of missing out) replaces FOMO (the fear of missing out) as each of us learns to let go, reduce collaborative overload, and clean up the kind of clutter that can come from too much starting and not enough stopping.

For Andrew, enjoying the ride meant finding opportunity in both the swell and the slack times and connecting with others in a way that nourishes him through and through. For Regina, it meant creating more space for self-care, reflection, strategic visioning, and supporting others. For me, enjoying the ride means connecting with myself and others in a wellspring of gratefulness and graciousness. When I am attuned with thankfulness for the gifts all around me, instead of focused on the problems and obstacles, I'm free to consciously move toward what wants to emerge in any given moment.

What does "enjoying the ride" mean for you? It's likely connected to the shared, creative realization of what you value most.

Unleash Each Other's Potential

• • •

As you bring your fullest creative self into the world, you will unleash the creative potential of others. By your example, you will support them as they connect with their creativity, engage their Superpowers, and learn from the Swamps they cross. And others will do the same for you. It will happen simply when you and the people around you bring your authentic, creative, whole selves to work. Your humble demonstration, and the energy you bring forward as you create into the unknown (despite the challenges and risks of doing so within the confines of the system), will inspire others.

You don't need to make a big splash about it as you walk through the world in this way. A dear friend of mine once asked me to imagine I was at a wedding. Just as the bride starts down the aisle, the dressmaker jumps up and shouts, "I made the dress! I made the dress!" Everyone turns, and suddenly, no one is focused on the bride anymore. It's all about the dressmaker. That day, she helped me see that you can contribute and inspire others without bringing the focus to yourself. Helping others unleash their potential can be a quiet practice. It is connected to becoming a servant leader and your aspiration to have a positive impact in the world around you.

While this will happen as a matter of course—whether it is explicitly stated or not—there may be times when you intentionally seek to unleash each other's creative and leadership potential as you work together. In this case, I encourage you to declare it openly, as a shared, explicit intention. This was the experience Mark shared when he joined our graduate retreat. His story highlights the impact we can have when we consciously focus on unleashing creative potential.

If you recall, Mark had a vision for a new approach to teaching science within the LA Unified School District. His idea was to bring science to life for students by linking it with the cultural and lived experience of communities and including other disciplines like math, social studies, and storytelling. Mark envisioned teachers across the district coming together to co-create lesson plans and materials, which could be shared and adapted locally.

Back then, he chose to protect his vision from the corrupting influence of others (a common reaction for Entrepreneurs). But as his idea garnered attention, Mark started to lose control and things evolved away from his initial vision. He became frustrated and disinterested—and finally detached himself from further involvement.

After almost a year, however, the initiative wasn't getting the traction officials had hoped for. The director of Secondary Science Curriculum sought out Mark and asked if he would consider rejoining and leading the team. Mark reached out to me for some guidance.

I suggested that if he decided to rejoin, he should make a conscious choice to show up differently—in his head and in his heart—and practice new behaviors. We talked about setting things up as a conscious practice field for co-creation and sharing leadership, and making this an explicit goal.

We also talked about letting go of control. What if Mark took more of a coaching role—rather than a traditional directing role—to open opportunity for others instead of being the star? We talked about what elements of his Entrepreneur style might have to recede for the Collaborator to come forward. I could feel Mark's trepidation. He knew his patterns and triggers well and wasn't sure if he'd be successful. After our conversation, I wasn't sure what he would do.

Later, at the graduate retreat, Mark shared how important it was for him to take up the challenge and how much he had learned. He had decided to experiment, to see what would happen if he stated his intention to the team: to make this experience one where team members work together to unleash each other's creative potential. He shared his aspiration to be more inclusive of different views, instead of being the decision-maker with all the ideas.

For Mark, this journey became a study in the practice of empowerment and accountability. At first, it was hard to let go and not take control. "I kept reverting back to making it about my agenda, gate-keeping, and telling people what to do." But slowly, with feedback from the team, introspection, and attention to his mindset, intentions, and assumptions, Mark opened to a new way of operating in his role as team lead.

"People think if you're empowered, it means you get to do it your way. That's not what it's about—just shifting control to another person. True empowerment means you have even more responsibility to seek out different perspectives and get input from others. You get feedback early and often. And you have to thank people and let them know how their contribution made a difference." All of us benefited as Mark shared some of his most valuable lessons. "It's really an art to listen to others without trying to solve their problem," he said. "I got so much better at asking questions—ones that really helped people come to their *own* answers." In fact, the entire team of teachers became measurably more effective at coaching each other, giving feedback without solving or fixing, and supporting each other in creative exploration.

Mark continued with more of his insights. "People really want to know that you're going to have their back if they're going to take more risks and make decisions without having someone else approve everything. You need to stay involved and interested, as a coach and not someone who has all the answers." It had to be safe for the team to come to Mark when they faced unforeseen challenges or when they weren't sure how to move forward. He shared how vital clear agreements were to unleash each other's creativity. Making sure everyone is clear who the decision-maker is, sticking to that, and then standing behind decisions that have been made by others (whether or not the decision was the one you would have made) is a key ingredient for delegating and for empowerment.

"The hardest part is when people's decisions go badly—and I've let go of control," Mark said with a grimace. "That's when empowerment and accountability can really get mixed up. Who's accountable when people are empowered? Who has responsibility if things go wrong?" Mark shared how the team had decided to set up "incubator labs" as a key part of their strategy for engaging teachers across the district. In these labs, teachers would co-create lesson plans, design materials, and curate resources on different topics in the curriculum. On one occasion, a conflict erupted, and the facilitator didn't know how to handle the situation. Things escalated, and news of the conflict spread quickly across the district.

"When I first heard about it, I didn't know what to do," Mark told us at the retreat. "My inclination was to step in and take over. Like the situation was somehow a reflection on me, personally, as the team lead. It was really hard not to lay blame or point the finger." But Mark was able to stay objective and help the team work together to sort things out. It was critical he demonstrate support for taking risks and experimenting without letting the outcomes bias him against any individual. It was also critical that he help the team avoid jumping to the conclusion that the idea was bad because of how things played out. "That's what I find most often," Mark said. "If something goes awry, or people get a result that they weren't expecting that they interpret as negative, they quit. They decide it didn't work."

Instead, Mark talked with the team about what they'd learned and what they might do differently next time. They weighed the pros and cons of continuing to experiment along these lines. Instead of using the experience to stop them, they used it to refine and iterate their approach. As we talked together at the retreat, Mark shared two of the most valuable lessons from his experience—about the importance of trust and the value of purposeful experimentation. As you dig into these lessons, consider what actions you and your allies can take to unleash each other's potential.

Lesson One: Trust is the foundation for unleashing each other's potential

For Mark and within his initiative, each team member had to let go of control. They had to trust the choices and decisions of their fellow teammates—as well as their "customers" (the teachers, in this case). And—even more critical and potentially challenging for Soloists, Rebels, and Entrepreneurs—they had to endorse and commit to supporting decisions they hadn't made and may not have fully agreed with.

Does this sound like something you and your colleagues aspire to? As you reflect on the lessons from Mark's experience, talk with your allies and partners about the conditions that are necessary for trust to flourish:

- **You believe each other to be reliable.** You show up when people need you, and your words and actions match up. You are dependable, you're clear about priorities, you follow through with commitments, and you stand behind decisions together. When you make a commitment or promise, you keep your word.

- **Together, you are credible.** Over time, people see that you know what you're talking about. You seek the truth and speak the truth from your experience and wisdom—regardless of circumstances—and consistently remain true to your core values. You can say, "I don't know." As you traverse the unknown, true credibility comes from demonstrating self-awareness, humility, an open mind, and an orientation toward learning.

- **Everyone has each other's interests at heart.** People invest in knowing and understanding each other and look beyond their own self-interests to ensure everyone benefits. You show that you care about each other as whole people—both within the workplace and in life outside of work.

If you were to compile a Trust Balance Sheet (see the QR code at the end of the chapter), where would you and your allies net out? Would you have a surplus of trust or a deficit? Take time to invest in building trust—it is the cornerstone of empowerment and accountability.

Lesson Two: Purposeful experiments yield valuable learning

Mark and his team practiced designing and conducting experiments, which might fail or succeed. In fact, they came to see most everything they did as some form of experiment. Viewing things in this way relieves so much of the pressure we can put on ourselves to make the right decision, succeed, and "get it right the first time." But to experiment within systems oriented toward control, certainty, and success, everyone must confront their fear of the unknown and relax into the process of iteration—making decisions and then adjusting things along the way.

"We used to call these experiments 'smart risks,'" Mark said to us at the retreat, "because they had data and a sound logic to suggest a high likelihood that they would work out. But over time, we agreed that 'purposeful experiments' allowed for more play in the space between success and failure." There, in that space, is the key to the generation of new value and the experience of indelible learning.

In these experiments, the clarity and strength of your shared purpose is critical. Together, talk about your assumptions and hypotheses.

Clarify which ones, specifically, you will test—and don't shy away from testing assumptions that might "kill" your idea. Co-create the design of your experiment and identify any potential mismatches in your shared criteria for evaluating outcomes. And open the door for mystery and surprise. While smart risks may strive toward a particular outcome, purposeful experiments allow for 360-degree learning, including a greater chance for unexpected results, failures, successes, and happy accidents.

That day at the retreat, based on what we learned from Mark, we crafted two commitments to support purposeful experimentation: *We will use unexpected results to generate new opportunities*, and *We will trust each other to create and adjust along the way.*

People talk a lot about being "change-ready." Among my colleagues and clients, this often means first accepting that change has become a constant state in our lives. And it means getting better at coping with change and adapting to new information, shifting directions, changing requirements, and shifting expectations. In a way, this is the essence of the "agile" movement: you get better at adapting and adjusting nimbly without slowing down.

But there's something even more powerful—and more opportunistic—than adapting and adjusting. When things go wrong or in an unexpected direction, we can use the circumstances as leverage to invent and even to disrupt. "I learned never to pass up an opportunity to be bold when things go sideways," Mark said at our retreat. "There's even more play in the system than when things are going along the way people expect them to."

Regina chimed in to share about what she calls "strategic stealth." She described how she carries around a few "someday maybe" ideas in her back pocket that she knows would add value when the timing is right. Like Mark, Regina learned that unpleasant results could generate a kind of openness to new ideas and possibilities. "I wait for these moments," she said. "And then, I pull out one of these ideas and help people understand why something like this would make a difference."

These examples helped us all understand the power of using unexpected results to spark innovation and generate new value. But that doesn't mean it will be easy or even fun. The kind of learning that comes from conscious, purposeful experimentation can be unpleasant, embarrassing, and downright painful at times. If you're really challenging yourself and your colleagues to learn from stretching into the unknown, you will fail often—in more and less visible ways. You must be able to manage the Inner Critic that shows up in your head— as well as the critics that show up "out there" in your environment. When you see people starting to engage in blame, be vigilant to name it. Rather than striving to celebrate failure, celebrate the learning that failure yields. That's how purposeful experimentation becomes an asset on the path toward generating bold, opportunistic outcomes.

We must also trust each other to create and adjust along the way. Together, as we bring our creativity forward in purposeful experimentation, we become practiced in "building the plane while we fly it." As you move forward through the landscape, new constraints will show up, and new possibilities and opportunities will come into view. Mysteries will unfold and confusion will clear. You will have breakthroughs, but new paradoxes and problems and puzzles will emerge to vex you. Whether you succeed or fail, derive unexpected results, run into dead ends, or enter the Swamp, you will keep moving forward. There are times to pause and look around, and times to plow forward along the course you've set. There are times when it will feel like you're out on the open ocean with no markers or signposts to signal you're moving in the right direction. And every step forward involves choice.

When these choices are taken as a group, within the context of co-creation, the complexity increases exponentially. How in the world can you keep everyone aligned so that these micro and macro choices are in harmony with your collective purpose? Who's in charge of deciding what is and isn't in alignment with your direction? Does someone have veto power over a decision to go left or go right? If so, why do they have this authority?

The path forward will require that you create and adjust along the way. This is where the investment you've made in building trust will pay off. Each of you must trust that you are connected to a common purpose. Use this trust—and your shared purpose—to guide your

choices, to ask and answer tough questions, and to talk about conflicts that arise. Some decisions about creating and adjusting will be
made together, but many will not. If things go in a different direction
than you would like, it is not a personal rejection of anyone's inherent
gifts or wisdom.

Start Unlearning

• • •

As we discussed these commitments in our small group at the graduate retreat, Lily shared some insights from her new perspective. For
years, Lily had worked in a corporate environment before moving into
her new role at the Breast Cancer Foundation. "I had to unlearn some
habits and patterns I'd gotten used to in my old world," she told us.
"It's really different where I am now. Not that we don't have our own
patterns that get in the way... but changing roles highlighted some
behaviors that don't support purposeful experimentation."

Over the years working with teams, I have come to find many of
the same patterns and behaviors that Lily discovered, operating just
under the surface of a group or team's creative efforts. Breaking these
habits is more challenging because each of them will need to be broken individually—by you—as well as collectively in the dynamic of
interaction that you all participate within. Here are some of the recur-
ring patterns Lily, the group, and I uncovered.

There is an expectation of perfection on the first try. If, in your world,
people strive for between 80 and 100 percent "done" or "right" before
you bring your ideas, solutions, and inventions out into the system,
you can be sure you are not living the commitment of creating and
adjusting along the way. Don't wait until things are perfect before
engaging the broader system of people who will implement, use, and
benefit from your efforts. You lose time and the learning potential
that comes from seeing early iterations of your idea in action. Instead,
aim for a minimum viable version of your idea at the start, and then
iterate and build on that as you observe the results of your experiment.

People are afraid of making a decision. When your organization stigmatizes people for making decisions that don't work out, this habit can be particularly difficult to break. That's because decisions are viewed as some kind of "end." The word *deciding*, in its literal roots, means killing other options by choosing one. But when you are engaged in purposeful experimentation, no decision is final; every decision is just a step along the way. Instead of delaying decisions, build the shared expectation that decisions will evolve with the landscape. See what one choice reveals about new possible directions, investments, or experiments. Be prepared to adapt along the way to align with new and emerging information and constraints.

People defer to the loudest voices. Some people are more forward in expressing their ideas and in advocating for their perspectives. Others are quieter and may need to be drawn out. Make sure you hear *all* the voices and share the opportunity to see everyone's ideas and perspectives play out in creative action. Instead of jumping forward with the first idea that will work from folks who speak often, think of your collective more like a jazz ensemble where everyone is involved, everyone has a unique contribution of expertise and perspective, and everyone gets to play. Then move forward together.

We avoid getting input from diverse sources. When your idea is in its infancy, it can be challenging (even distracting) to receive input about which direction to go, what will and won't work, and what to watch out for. That's because each bit of input and feedback needs to be considered in some way. Some will inspire new thinking and others will be discarded or set aside for later. Some may feel like a block but contain useful information. As the project progresses, it can be even more challenging to hear about new constraints and obstacles, given the investments you've already made in a particular path. Instead of waiting, get feedback early and often. Listen to the input and feedback with an open mind and an open heart, with an attitude of gratitude. Accept it all, understanding that you are the ones who will take that feedback and use it to improve ideas and solutions.

These are a few of the vexing patterns of behavior that you will need to watch out for—and work together to break—as you engage in purposeful experiments. Talk with people about the kinds of experiments you can conduct in your work context. Strategize about what might get in your way, what capabilities you'd like to collectively work on, and what each of you wants to improve as you explore and discover together. Identify shared commitments—like the ones our small group made at our retreat. And cut yourself and each other some slack along the way.

GETTING CREATIVE together is fast becoming the best way to generate value that is scalable and sustainable in the new world of work. It's also one of the most powerful forces for change and transformation. That's because we learn about ourselves, about others, and about the world around us. Take a moment now and reflect on the way your inner experience is shaping the way you participate out in the world where co-creation happens. And consider how your adventures out in the world are shaping who you are becoming as a creator. There is a dynamic interplay. Through co-creation, we become anew, together.

Keep all that you have learned about the power of your creative presence in the forefront of your mind and in your heart as you walk through your world. Wherever you can, seek to inspire, support, and develop others. Let yourself fall in love with the people you work with. Take it as a daily intention to see them flourish and lean into their potential. Catch them when they begin to falter. Share your ideas generously and with respect. Trust others to make decisions even if the path they choose looks different than the one you might take. Coach each other from a place of wisdom and help people engage their Superpowers. And even as you focus outward, always remember to return back to yourself—to your own growth and learning—on your path toward a fuller expression of your creative potential.

ASK YOURSELF...

Now, at the end of this chapter and our second adventure, take time to pause and reflect on the following questions.

- What are your deepest insights from exploring Adventure Two: Getting Creative Together?

- What has shifted in both your inner experience as well as your behaviors out in the world?

- Of all that we've explored, what has challenged you the most?

- How might your own journey become a beacon of light for others as they bring their creativity forward in their work and life?

Elevate Your Impact

- In what ways are you demonstrating a deeper faith in your creative potential?

- What big dreams and urgent imperatives might benefit from your creative participation?

- Who can you join with to make bold changes that make a difference?

Enjoy the Ride

- What does "enjoying the ride" mean to you? Who exemplifies this way of being? What can you learn from their example?

- How could your Superpowers show up more prominently to help you relax and enjoy what is emerging for you?

Unleash Each Other's Potential

- What, specifically, can you do to strengthen empowerment, trust, and accountability within your circle of allies? across your organization more broadly?

- What are you working on right now that might benefit from a more "experimental" approach? How might that change how you drive for results?

Start Unlearning

- What habits might you need to break to get better at purposeful experimentation? What, specifically, will you practice?

Keep Going!

• • •

How do you shape cultures to foster creative accountability? Scan this QR code or go to **creativetogetherresources.com** for my in-depth article on the topic:

Use the Trust Balance Sheet to calculate your team's net capability to work together in ways that build trust. Scan this QR code or go to **creativetogetherresources.com:**

ADVENTURE THREE

LEAPING FORWARD

"I want to recommend a seminar that takes very little extra time and no extra money. It is highly interactive and has incredible 3-D graphics. This seminar is your everyday life. You've been enrolled in it since you were born."

W. TIM GALLWEY, in *The Inner Game of Work*

N ADVENTURE One, we started the inner work to overcome CDD—by *strengthening your relationship with your creativity*. As we saw, creativity is different than most people believe. It's not an ability. It's a potential that's always available. It's activated when a meaningful purpose meets both possibility and constraint. Creativity is the spark that drives innovative results. That's where new ideas are born—and new value comes to life.

Claiming your gift is the foundation for igniting a fuller expression of your creative potential when you greet the unknown, navigate change, and invent your future. It's an essential step on the path to more effective co-creation. We explored how to flex your Superpowers and use them in the tests you're likely to face on creative quests—to move beyond thinking that life is happening "to you" and step into a new story of who you are as a creator. In this new story, you have *creative choice and agency* in every moment. You may still forget your gift or lose your way in a murky inner Swamp. You might fall into old habits and make unconscious choices. But you can *never not know* that you have the power to create new value for yourself, together with others, and for the beneficiaries of your life-force energies.

As you claimed your gift, we embarked on our second adventure: taking your gift out into the world to *co-create more effectively within social systems*. Remember: your creativity is meant to be shared. We explored the strategies of your Creative Style, which emerged as you grew into who you are today. While your natural style might have served you in the past, we all can adapt our style to become more collaborative, conscious, and connected. Co-creating and sharing leadership are the keys to generating new value in the new world of work. Together, they strengthen your odds of success and help you cross through the inevitable Swamps that are part of creating inside social systems.

Now it's time to embark on your third adventure. This adventure starts the moment you close this book. It's about standing at the threshold of whatever lies ahead—together with your colleagues, allies, and partners—and stepping into the intersection of purpose, possibility, and constraint. It's about practicing the GIFTED methodology every day: Greeting the unknown with passion; Igniting your creative potential; Flexing your Superpowers; Thriving in co-creation; Experimenting in the Swamp; and Daring to dream big.

Activating your potential and returning to dance in the center of the intersection is an ongoing practice. It's not so much about what you *do* together when you're in this powerful place where ideas come alive. That will unfold while you are there—and it will be different for every one of you. This adventure is about continuing to learn who you *are* in this centered, conscious, and creative place, and how to return there if you find yourself outside of it.

Your next adventure marks an important shift *from awakening to becoming.* At your core, you are a creative being on a shared journey of discovering your life. Become a conscious, self-aware student on that journey. *Get creative together.* Lean into the collective strength that emerges when you move past the familiar routines of execution to spark innovation. Adventure together on journeys of discovery into the unknown. Claim your gift: creativity with no limits. Keep reclaiming it every day. It's a lifelong quest without a fixed destination.

You won't know what futures lie ahead. And I won't be there with you day to day as you venture forth. But hopefully, through our work together in these pages, you may hear my voice along the way—urging you to press forward, believe in yourself, stand together with others, and claim the power of your creative potential. Together, we can generate a movement—a network and community of people who, wherever we are and whatever we're doing, bring our full potential to our work and to our lives.

Imagine what's possible when more and more of us co-create, share leadership, and light the way for others. Imagine the promise of bringing all that we've learned together to discover and adventure in the new world of work. Together, we will fulfill both individual and collective purposes and passions. Together, we will architect new places in which to live and work. We'll focus our creativity on paradigm shifts that bring forward new solutions to the most complex challenges we face. Together, we can change our world in ways that benefit the planet and generations to come.

Now it's up to you.

Keep Going!

• • •

Join our growing movement of people like you—learning to thrive in co-creation, elevating our impact, and daring to dream big. Scan this QR code or go to **creativetogetherbook.com** to join in:

Check out my tips for returning to the center of the intersection of purpose, possibility, and constraint as an ongoing practice every day. Go to **creativetogetherresources.com** or scan this QR code:

And finally, take some time to pause and reflect on how your journey through this book has transformed the story of who you are as a creator and how you create together with others. Go to **creativetogetherresources.com** or scan this QR code:

ACKNOWLEDGMENTS

• • • • •

THIS BOOK is the gift arising from all that I have learned as I continue to seek answers to the question, "How can each of us reclaim our gift of creativity, and create together more effectively inside social structures and systems?"

In my quest, I've learned from many guides, teachers, and colleagues. Psychologists like Carl Rogers and Rollo May and educators like Michael Ray, Craig and Patricia Neal, Ron and Mary Hulnick, Gregory Cajete, David Allen, and Carl Weinberg have enlightened me. Authors and researchers including Gary Hamel, Teresa Amabile, Gary Pisano, and Clayton Christenson have influenced my understanding of how creativity and innovation play out in the world of business. Sages like Joseph Campbell have brought a deeper understanding of the forces that drive us to cross the threshold into the unknown, illuminating what happens when we do venture forward and are fundamentally transformed. Participants in my doctoral research along with thousands of clients, colleagues, and friends—represented in the pages of this book as fictional, composite characters—have offered insight into the practical realities of creating inside complex organizations.

Finally, this journey into the unknown we call "writing a book" was made possible with the support of Melanie Bates, the crew at Page Two Publishing, and the love and unwavering encouragement from family, friends, and from my partner George. Together, we danced in the center of purpose, possibility, and constraint.

NOTES

* * * * *

Adventure One

* * *

1. Carl Weinberg, "The Existential View of Creativity," *UCLA Educator* (1976).
2. Matthew May, "Mind of the Innovator: Taming the Traps of Traditional Thinking," 2007, Creative Commons Attribution-NonCommercial-NoDerivs License, available on porchlightbooks.com.
3. Barry Schwartz, *The Paradox of Choice: Why More Is Less* (Harper Perennial, 2004).
4. Rollo May, *The Courage to Create* (W. W. Norton & Company, 1975).
5. LinkedIn Talent Solutions, "2019 Global Talent Trends," linkedin.com.
6. Irving Wladawsky-Berger, "Automation and the Changing Demand for Workforce Skills," *Wall Street Journal*, October 12, 2018.
7. Joseph Campbell, *The Hero with a Thousand Faces* (New World Library, 1949).
8. Gregory Cajete, *Look to the Mountain: An Ecology of Indigenous Education* (Kivaki Press, 1994).
9. David Wagoner, "Lost," from *Traveling Light: Collected and New Poems* (University of Illinois Press, 1999).
10. Nils Parker, "The Angel in the Marble: Modern Life Lessons from History's Greatest Sculptor," blog post, July 9, 2013, nilsaparker.medium.com.
11. Tom Kelley, from a speech "In Conversation" at Genentech, Inc., April 2016.
12. Nann Kyra, "A Treatise on Noticing" (doctoral dissertation in Theological Studies, Peace Theological Seminary, 2002).
13. Kyra, "A Treatise on Noticing."
14. Steve Donahue, *Shifting Sands: A Guidebook for Crossing the Deserts of Change* (Berrett-Kohler Publishers, 2004).

15. L.S. Vygotsky, *Mind in Society: Development of Higher Psychological Processes* (Harvard University Press, 1978).
16. Amy Edmondson, "Strategies for Learning from Failure," *Harvard Business Review* (April 2011).
17. Michael Ray and Rochelle Myers, *Creativity in Business* (Broadway Books, 1986).
18. Diane Scanlon and Greg Smith, "Time Is a Healer," sung by Eva Cassidy on *Songbird* (1998).
19. Ray and Myers, *Creativity in Business*.
20. K. Gutierrez, "How Talk, Context, and Script Shape Contexts for Learning: A Cross-Case Comparison of Journal Sharing," *Linguistics and Education* 5 (1994): 335–65.

Adventure Two

• • •

1. Steven Kowalski, "Teachers' Beliefs About Creativity" (doctoral dissertation, UCLA, 1997).
2. Francesca Gino, *Rebel Talent* (HarperCollins, 2018).
3. Gifford Pinchot III and Elizabeth S. Pinchot, "Intra-Corporate Entrepreneurship: Some Thoughts Stirred Up by Attending Robert Schwartz's School for Entrepreneurs," Fall 1978.
4. Gifford Pinchot III, *Intrapreneuring: Why You Don't Have to Leave the Corporation to Become an Entrepreneur* (Harper & Row, 1985).
5. Marc Lesser, *Know Yourself, Forget Yourself* (New World Library, 2013).
6. Stephen Karpman, "Fairy Tales and Script Drama Analysis," *Transactional Analysis Bulletin* 7, no 26 (1968): 39–43.
7. Frederic Laloux, *Reinventing Organizations* (Nelson Parker, 2016).
8. Laloux, *Reinventing Organizations*.
9. Co-active Coaching, coactive.com.
10. Robert Anderson and William Adams, *Mastering Leadership* (Wiley, 2016).
11. Leadership Circle, leadershipcircle.com.
12. May, "Mind of the Innovator."
13. Amy Edmondson, *The Fearless Organization* (Wiley, 2019).
14. Gary Hamel and Michele Zanini, *Humanocracy: Creating Organizations as Amazing as the People Inside Them* (Harvard University Press, 2020).
15. Rob Cross, Reb Rebele, and Adam Grant, "Collaborative Overload," *Harvard Business Review* (January-February 2016): 74–79.

INDEX

· · · · ·

Note: Page references for figures are in *italic*.

ABOUT THE AUTHOR

. . . . .

STEVEN KOWALSKI, PhD, is a leading voice in the global movement for conscious creativity. He has more than twenty-five years of experience as an organizational development expert facilitating the creativity of scientists, engineers, business leaders, and professionals across industries to blaze new trails, catalyze creative potential, and deliver real-world innovation. He brings curiosity, passion, and perspective to shape organizational cultures and reinvigorate how teams co-create new value. Throughout his career, Steven has worked both inside companies and externally as a coach, speaker, and consultant-partner focused on organizational creativity and transformation. This "inside-outside" perspective gives him deep insight into the structural, interpersonal, and process dynamics that inhibit the realization of change. Building on these insights, he delivers bold solutions that are scalable and sustainable through his firm, Creative License™ Consulting Services.

Steven holds a PhD in adult learning and organizational creativity from UCLA and is the author of over one hundred workplace learning programs. When he's relaxing, you might find him taking photos at the beach, traveling to experience new cultures, gardening, discovering new ways to cook old favorites, and connecting with friends and loved ones.